THE HUAWEI *MODEL*

THE GEOPOLITICS OF INFORMATION

Edited by Dan Schiller, Amanda Ciafone, and Yuezhi Zhao

A list of books in the series appears at the end of this book.

THE HUAWEI MODEL

The Rise of China's Technology Giant

Yun Wen

UNIVERSITY OF
ILLINOIS PRESS
Urbana, Chicago, and Springfield

© 2020 by the Board of Trustees
of the University of Illinois
All rights reserved
Manufactured in the United States of America
1 2 3 4 5 C P 5 4 3 2 1
♾ This book is printed on acid-free paper.

Library of Congress Control Number: 2020946414
ISBN 978-0-252-04343-7 (hardcover)
ISBN 978-0-252-08533-8 (paperback)
ISBN 978-0-252-05231-6 (e-book)

Contents

List of Illustrations   vii

Abbreviations   ix

Acknowledgments   xi

Introduction   1

1 Huawei's Domestic Accumulation: A Path Intertwining with China's ICT Development   19

2 Going Global: Outward Expansion into the Global South   54

3 March into the Global North: Opportunity or Peril?   90

4 From Path-Dependent to Pathbreaking? Huawei's Technological Capability Development   115

5 Ownership, Management, and Labor Discipline   143

Conclusion   177

Notes   201

Index   229

Illustrations

Figure 1.1. Huawei's Annual Sales Revenues, 1992–2000 (RMB billion) 38

Figure 1.2. China Telecom's CDMA Equipment Market Share, 2007 46

Figure 1.3. China Telecom's CDMA Equipment Market Share, 2008 46

Figure 1.4. Huawei's Revenue by the Business Segment from 2012 to 2017 (RMB billion) 51

Figure 2.1. China's Inflow/Outflow FDI (US$ billion) 60

Figure 2.2. China Exim Bank Concessional Loan Cycle 76

Figure 2.3. The Global Submarine Cable Map 84

Figure 2.4. Huawei Marine Submarine Cable Projects 84

Figure 5.1. Huawei Labor Composition 159

Abbreviations

3GPP	The 3rd Generation Partnership Project
BRI	Belt and Road Initiative
CADF	China-Africa Development Fund
CDB	China Development Bank
CDMA	code division multiple access
FCC	Federal Communications Commission, US
FDI	foreign direct investment
FIE	foreign-invested enterprise
FOCAC	Forum on China Africa Cooperation
FYP	Five-Year Plan
GSM	Global System for Mobile Communications
IC	integrated circuit
ICT	information and communications technology
IPR	intellectual property right
ITT	International Telephone and Telegraph
JV	joint venture
M&A	mergers and acquisitions
MEI	Ministry of Electronics Industry
MIC2025	Made in China 2025
MII	Ministry of Information Industry
MIIT	Ministry of Industry and Information Technology

MOC	Ministry of Commerce
MOF	Ministry of Finance
MOFTEC	Ministry of Foreign Trade and Economic Cooperation
MPT	Ministry of Post and Telecommunications
NGN	Next Generation Networks
NSA	National Security Agency
NWICO	New World Information and Communication Order
OEM	original equipment manufacturer/manufacturing
OFDI	outward foreign direct investment
PBX	private branch exchanges
PLA	People's Liberation Army
PTB	Post and Telecommunications Bureau
SOE	state-owned enterprise
SEZ	special economic zone
TCC	transnational capitalist class
TD-LTE	time division long-term evolution
TD-SCDMA	time division synchronous code division multiple access
TNC	transnational corporation
TRIPS	Trade-Related Aspects of Intellectual Property Rights
TVE	township and village enterprise
WCDMA	wideband code division multiple access
WFOE	wholly foreign owned enterprise
WIPO	World Intellectual Property Organization
WTO	World Trade Organization

Acknowledgments

I owe a great debt of gratitude to many people in finishing this book. My utmost gratitude goes to Yuezhi Zhao, my senior supervisor in the School of Communication at Simon Fraser University. Zhao's intellectual and moral commitments have always been a source of inspiration for my research. She not only helped me develop my original ideas in this book but also provided truly helpful suggestions and feedback throughout the different phases of my research and writing. I must thank Dan Schiller for his generous support and encouragement. Dan read and commented on an earlier draft of this manuscript. I have benefited enormously from him for helping me define my theoretical framework and clarify some ideas in the book. Thanks are also given to Enda Brophy, Katherine Reilly, Jing Li, and Jack Linchuan Qiu for their insightful feedback and constructive suggestions. I would also like to thank the anonymous reviewers who provided well-reasoned criticism and comments, helping me to sharpen my writing with more refined arguments and empirical evidence. Responsibilities for lingering problems, of course, remain mine.

I owe my profound gratitude to individuals who provided their generous support for my fieldwork research. I am also grateful to Daniel Nasset, acquisitions editor at the University of Illinois Press, for his help in the making of this book.

Last, but not least, my eternal love and gratitude goes to my family. They are sources of never-ending love, encouragement, and motivation.

Introduction

On December 1, 2018, Meng Wanzhou, the top executive of China's foremost technology champion, Huawei Technologies Co. Ltd., and daughter of the founder, Ren Zhengfei, was arrested in Vancouver by Canadian authorities executing an extradition request from the United States. Following the arrest, the US war on Huawei escalated amid US-China trade disputes. In May 2019 the Trump administration added Huawei to a trade blacklist, curtailing the company's access to critical US suppliers. Already the prime target of the United States' "new technology cold war" against China, Huawei was dragged into the spotlight again. The questions concerning what Huawei is and why it matters have grabbed worldwide attention. *The Huawei Model: The Rise of China's Technology Giant* investigates the story of Huawei as a microcosm of China's evolving digital economy to explore the ramifications of the global rise of that country's corporate power. It explicates why Huawei matters by placing the company's story in the broader context of China's information and communications technology (ICT) development and the country's reintegration into global digital capitalism.

Debate regarding China's rise has been evolving along with the structural reconfiguration of transnational capitalism in recent decades. As critical communication scholar Dan Schiller argues, the rapid development of ICTs and China's economic growth have constituted the "two poles of growth."[1] This book examines the dynamic intersections of these two poles—that is, China's linkages to transnationalized digital capitalism—with a focus on the Huawei case. Huawei's story illustrates how China's most competitive ICT firm was born and developed, how it forged connections with the Chinese state and intertwined with the trajectory of China's ICT development, and how it responded to the various forces of "the globalization of corporate China."[2] As an expression of larger historical and political economic changes, this story aims to explore the relationships among transnational capitals, state interests, and class transformation underlying the rise of China's ICT giant.

Since the 1970s, the development of the global economy has been characterized by the transition toward transnationalized digital capitalism, within which information and communications technologies have increasingly played a pivotal role in restructuring the global capitalist system. The mushrooming of these technologies not only underpinned capitalism's network connectivity and facilitated transnational corporate powers' global expansion, but the ICT sector also became a leading growth engine and a lucrative site of capital accumulation.[3] Although the sector was projected as a strategic impulse to drag the capitalist system out of a long-standing depression, the unsustainable development of digital capitalism still paradoxically contributed to "a resurgence of the very economic crisis."[4]

As an integral part of the ongoing transformation of the global capitalist system and an indicator of the rise of emerging market economies, China has increasingly become a geopolitical and geoeconomic heavyweight capable of shaping the course of the global system. The country not only possesses the largest numbers of internet, telephone, and mobile phone users in the world, but it also has become a leading provider of ICT infrastructure and services with its growing ICT manufacturing capabilities. In 2003 China overtook Japan and the European Union and in 2004 replaced the United States to become the largest exporter of ICT products in the world. In 2006 China became the world's second-largest ICT manufacturer, accounting for over 15 percent of the international trade of ICT products.[5] At the same time, China strove to make a leap from a "world factory" to an advanced technology "superstate."[6] This effort is exemplified by the rise of a number of Chinese ICT enterprises that are approaching transnational stages and obtaining outstanding presence in global high-tech markets.

The globalization of Chinese ICT enterprises has become the next frontier in the economic battlefield for global leadership. Chinese corporate players' high-profile cross-border investment, their thirst for external worldwide markets, and the strong alliance of business and government, all characterize

China's new initiative of corporate globalization. Among these rising China-based ICT multinationals, Huawei has been established as one of the most celebrated cases to represent the powerful force of "globalizing China" and China's endeavor of climbing up the global value chain in the strategic telecommunications sector. The trajectory of Huawei's development, especially its course of internationalization, not only provides firm- and sector-specific information with regard to China's corporate globalization, but it also sheds light on the political-economic dynamics and tensions underlying the intersections of the two poles of growth.

Global Digital Infrastructure and the Multinational-Led Communications Order

For some, the rise of China's ICT corporations and their challenge to US economic and technological power possesses some similarities to the hegemonic rivalry between Great Britain and the United States during the geopolitical transition from the end of the nineteenth century into the twentieth. To better shed light on the role played by China's ICT multinationals in reconfiguring global digital capitalism, this study begins with a close scrutiny of the historical evolution of the international communications order.

The birth of corporations finds its historical roots in the process of capitalist expansion. Emerging in the sixteenth century, the earliest forms of capitalist corporations often acted as important instruments of settlement and colonization through overseas trading activities, serving the "territorialist logic of power accumulation" for their respective governments.[7] At the same time, joint-stock companies were formed as a key model of corporate organization, providing the fundamental principle for modern enterprises' business operations. The advent of industrial capitalism in the nineteenth century then saw the beginning of the internationalization of productive capital and the origin of modern transnationals.[8] The expansion of an international communications infrastructure prepared the stage for the creation of a more integrated international economy and a newly unified world market. From the mid-nineteenth century onward, Western countries underwent a network-building boom to spread information infrastructure networks across national frontiers in order to "wire the world," giving rise to a number of leading telegraph and cable companies that rapidly moved into monopolized positions of power.[9] Britain's Eastern Telegraph Company, for instance, dominated almost half of the world's cable networks during this period.[10]

The expansion of submarine telegraph cable and transatlantic ocean links played key roles in reinforcing the British empire. After the launch of the first transatlantic submarine cables in the mid-1890s, British telegraph companies made the effort to extend the reach of their networks, attempting to link Europe to the Middle East, India, and beyond. These companies' expansionary initiatives in building international communication grids not only coincided with the British government's imperial scramble for markets, natural resources, investment sites, and labor but were also in concert with peripheral countries' "modernization" initiatives.[11] Functioning as part of "cooperative imperialism,"[12] British cable companies chose to cooperate with local elites to extend network connections from colonies to many other peripheral countries.

By the late nineteenth century, growing inter-imperialist rivalry had extended to the domains of international communications, with digital infrastructure becoming a strategic resource for struggle. Control over the strategic communications network reflected the dominant economic, political, and military power structure of the era.[13] From the late nineteenth century into World War I, the United States emerged as Britain's leading rival among great powers in control of the international communications system. Along with British companies' expansion, some US telegraph companies, such as American Telegraph Company and Western Union, established their own cartel, rapidly acquiring unified control over independent networks in the US domestic market.

During World War I, the initiatives of reconstructing a US-centered information infrastructure were incorporated into US economic, diplomatic, and military planning, with a desire to realign the international communications order by minimizing Britain's predominant position and to expand American power throughout the Pacific and the Caribbean.[14] This geostrategy was achieved through the creation of radio communication networks, a new technology originally controlled and managed by the US Navy. The initiative to build out the US-centered extraterritorial telecommunications network also gave rise to several large American electronic communications corporations, such as the Radio Corporation of America (RCA) and International Telephone and Telegraph (ITT), which represented a new wave of concentration in the nascent North American electronic communications market. In collaboration with US political and military forces, these companies expanded quickly and crafted more ambitious regional and global strategies. For instance, starting in the late 1920s, ITT made a vigorous entry into South America and Europe to internationalize its manufacturing and sales subsidiaries, making it the "paragon of multinational telecommunications enterprises."[15]

After World War II, the United States emerged as the strongest single power in the world system. The rise of the new "American Empire" was marked by the growing predominance of American corporations on the global scale.[16] More important, the rise of American corporate power involved not only the increase in American transnational firms but also the widespread emulation of the American corporate model, which signified the advent of corporate capitalism in the global capitalist system. However, within the context of the Cold War, "corporate America" confronted greater challenges due to escalating geopolitical conflicts. The militarized technological development strategy became an investment priority for the United States to deal with these challenges during this period, luring American information companies into war-related commodity chains.[17] This military-driven strategy spun off a large number of technological innovations in different ICT domains, such as microelectronics, digital computing, data processing, networking computing, and operating software. The combination of the national interest to safeguard national security and commercial imperatives contributed to massive growth of US-based transnational ICT corporations on the threshold of the era of global digital capitalism.

Another vector of change in communications technology in this period was the development of satellite technology, which laid the ground for the most efficient and expansive means of international communications.[18] However, what was less noticed was that the rapid development of new communications technologies effectively precipitated new alliances of a few electronics giants and gave birth to new transnational conglomerates.[19] The formation of Comsat (Communication Satellite Corporation) in 1962, with funding from the US government and large American telecommunications companies like ATT, ITT, RCA, and General Telephone and Electronic Corporation (GTE), represented such a trend of alliance. In 1964 the United States proposed to Western countries the establishment of an international consortium called Intelsat (International Telecommunications Satellite), with Comsat acting as an administrator. Functioning as more than an international corporate consortium, Intelsat also served as an instrument to increase the United States' political leverage in international governance and to contain the power of the socialist camp during the Cold War. The way Intelsat operated actually exemplified what Armand Mattelart referred to as the "hypermodern corporation," characterized by the spectacular extension of corporate power from the economic sphere into the political and ideological spheres.[20]

Although the issues of corporate control over global information and communications had been taken up by the movement of the New World Information and Communication Order (NWICO) during the 1970s, structural inequality underlying renewed corporate imperialism continued to plague third world countries, bringing even greater systematic imbalance. Since the 1980s, the policy shift to neoliberalism, along with the development of modern information and communication technologies, has further accelerated the process of corporate capitalism, in which business power became a dominant expression in the global system. Despite global unevenness in such a transition, a trend of "privatization, trade liberalization, liberalization of capital flows, deregulation of national financial systems, the collapse of communism, and the advent of information technology" largely contributed to "the epoch of unprecedented concentration of global business power."[21] Technological developments in computers, microelectronics, and telecommunications especially had a dramatic impact on the global economic system, freeing capital to escape national restrictions and to build a new transnationalized economy. This gave rise to a massive surge in expenditure on ICT products and services needed to support large-scale intracorporate and intercorporate communications. These systematic changes in digital capitalism, in concert with China's integration into the global capitalist system, have provided a historical backdrop for the rapid development of China's ICT sector since the late 1980s.

The neoliberal reform in the realm of information and communications industries unleashed forces of transnational capital that sought marketplace dominance on the global scale. US media and telecommunications industries particularly underwent a surge of consolidation after the Telecommunications Act of 1996. The 1997 World Trade Organization's (WTO) Basic Telecommunications Agreement further institutionalized neoliberal telecommunications reform on a global scale and empowered transnational corporations (TNCs) with "extraterritorial corporate charters" to expand abroad.[22] In the aftermath of the burst of the internet bubble in the early 2000s, another powerful wave of consolidation in media and information industries emerged, with a few communication and media conglomerates standing at the apex of convergence and concentration.[23] Since 2008, high-tech companies have become the key catalyst for changes in the global economy. In rankings of the world's largest companies, American technology giants, including Apple, Google, Microsoft, Amazon, and Facebook, dominated the top five on a list that previously had been occupied by long-established companies in the energy and finance sectors. Meanwhile, there has been an important trend in US technology giants extending their control over physical infrastructure by turning themselves into infrastructure backbone providers. They are fundamentally reshaping the evolution of the internet infrastructure by joining with incumbent telecommunications carriers to build and operate international submarine cable systems.[24]

Regardless of the US domination in international communications, a continuing rise of competitors from the rest of the world has both changed global political-economic dynamics and tended to destabilize the US-led international communications order. As an integral part of China's reintegration strategy, the Chinese state has made a consistent effort to construct globally powerful high-tech companies that can compete on the "global level playing field."[25] For instance, Chinese telecommunication equipment manufacturers Huawei and Zhongxing Telecommunication Equipment Corporation (ZTE) are ranked as the world's top companies in the network sector. Among the top ten internet companies worldwide, four are from China—namely, Alibaba Group, Tencent Holdings, Baidu Inc., and JD.com.[26] The rise of Chinese ICT corporations represents the forces of corporate China that hold considerable power within national, regional, and international contexts.

The historical account of the evolution of a multinational-led communications system is vitally important to understand what made corporate power reach such prominence in international communications and what featured the hegemonic transition in the field's ever changing order. But history requires theory to make sense of the nature of capitalist transformation and the interaction of transnational corporations with the capitalist system as a whole. What is in question is not only the modalities of the transnational corporation but also how capitalist social relations have been shaped by the dynamics of capitalist accumulation. In expanding on this line of inquiry, some questions remain crucial: Has the rise of transnational corporate power undermined or transcended state authorities? What are the relationships between capitalist corporations and their hosting nation-states? How have the changes of transnational capital accumulation affected the relations between capital and labor? And what is the impact of the unprecedented concentration of global corporate power in the global political-economic order? These crucial questions are framed to capture the nexus of capital, state, and class, which can be seen as essential elements in analyzing the Huawei case.

The Nexus of Capital, State, and Class: A Theoretical Framework

The rise of Chinese multinationals has raised particular attention in the field of international business in recent years, with the focus on the firm-specific advantage perspective.[27] Under this approach, the current literature on

Huawei has focused mainly on the firm's international marketing strategies, business management, leadership skills, and technological entrepreneurship.[28] These studies have been not only limited to descriptive analyses of Huawei's business activities but also grounded in celebratory accounts of the expansion of Chinese capital in international markets. Such accounts have lacked critical insights into the nature of capitalist accumulation and have been abstracted away from the structural analysis such as evolving social relationships that are embedded in corporate power.

Another group of studies took the institutional approach to the globalization of Chinese firms,[29] focusing on the effects of China's institutional change on a firm's strategy and performance. However, this institution-based view was built on an assumption of the static relationship between the state and the firm, which premised either the state as an agent of Chinese corporate power or the Chinese firm as a passive recipient of the state's institutional changes. Such a dichotomous state-capital framing neglected the dynamic processes that shaped not only China's integration into global capitalism but the complicated interrelations between the state and capital as well.[30]

This book, in contrast, rejects the reified idea that views the transnational corporation as a static institutional unit. It argues that the formation and restructuring of the transnational corporation should be seen as a historical process, replete with contradictory elements and complex historical consequences. At the core of these central tensions is the mutual constitution of capital, state, and class, which is embodied in the transnational corporation's activity and its interaction with the political-economic system. This book locates the analysis of Chinese ICT corporation in the international political-economic framework, offering an approach to capturing the dynamics of power structure and social relations underlying the globalization of corporate China. It not only delineates internal contradictions of Huawei's development at the firm level, but it also shows its complex interactions with other political economic forces.

Debate over the relationship between capital and the state in the globalization era has been taken up in various critical studies. On one side of the debate was the structuralist view of globalization, which situated the internationalization of capital within an institutional system that centered on the nation-state. Among diverse critical paradigms, the world system theory provided an eloquent explanation of the exploitative relationship within the system of capitalism.[31] However, this perspective implied a nation-state-centric approach and regarded the nation-state as a concrete territorial and institutional unit. In a similar vein, communication scholars working within the world system paradigm also laid emphasis on inter-state competition for the control over communications among superpowers, with corporations mainly serving as tools of the state.[32] Such structural functionalism saw that power is anchored in states and that the capitalist interest is an external relation to state power.

At the other extreme, the post-structuralist perspective deconstructed the nation-state power by emphasizing the borderless logic of capital accumulation. It claimed that the unbridled flow of transnational capital, which is primarily embodied in transnational corporations' cross-border activities, actually transcends the traditional sovereignty of nation-states and gives rise to a new capitalist logic.[33] Although this perspective foregrounded a new logic of global capital accumulation, the argument was still a problematic one for characterizing the current stage of capitalism. It both overestimated the "smoothness" of transnationalized capital accumulation and downplayed the role of state power in the production of capitalist social relations.

The debate from both sides highlighted the tension between the nation-state and capital. But it should be noted that neither state-centrist nor post-structuralist thinking grasped a full picture of the dynamics of capitalist globalization. In contrast, this book's theoretical framework postulates that global capitalism is constituted by the interplay of the territorial logic and the capitalist logic, or two forms of competition: geopolitical and economic.[34] The territorial logic ensures the political, diplomatic, economic, and military strategies that are used to sustain the sovereign power and exert external influence over other states. In the context of international relations, the competing territorial logic of power is reflected in the form of geopolitics or geopolitical competition—that is, inter-state conflict for control over territory, resources, and important geographical positions.[35] In the contemporary era, geopolitical rivalry over communications and information has also remained a primary form of competition in reconstituting power distribution in the global communications order.[36] This directs our attention toward the inter-state system through which state power remains a constituent unit of transnational capitalism. On the other hand, capitalist logic is driven by the imperative of endless capital accumulation across spaces and borders, which has already led to concentration of capital power in only a few TNCs' hands.[37]

David Harvey has further argued that "new imperialism" is a result of the assertion of the capitalist logic and territorial logic through which imperialist powers strive to realize the universal logic of capitalism and to sustain the legitimacy of the neoliberal regime on the global scale.[38] Under these intertwined logics of global capitalism, other emerging centers of capital accumulation are involved in the global capitalist system. This further drives these newly emerging states to look for geographical expansion for surplus capital outlets, resource extraction, market penetration, and profit maximization in order to sustain their rate of growth and resolve the potential crisis of overaccumulation. Harvey referred to such a tendency as "sub-imperialism."[39] This perspective is useful to understand the pattern of capitalist accumulation and political power accumulation by emerging powers.

The dialectic framework between territorial logic and capitalist logic is important to overcome the dualism between the state and capital. However, it is important to note that neither capital nor state is a "thing"; rather, they are both constitutive of capitalist social relations. As noted by William Robinson, globalization is a class project, marked by the formation of the transnational capitalist class (TCC) in the process.[40] The making of the TCC was intrinsically bound up with globalizing corporate power.[41] Recently some scholars have paid particular attention to the organizational forms of the TCC through the wide-ranging analyses of corporate power networks and the hierarchical structure of corporate organizations. This perspective provides an approach to understanding how Huawei's corporate power is structured and how particular interests are represented at the institutional level.

At the same time, scholars have carried out expanded studies of the TCC in specific countries in order to discuss the integration of the national bourgeoisie into the bloc of the TCC. Jerry Harris has studied the "statist fractions" of the TCC in the process of China's reintegration into the global economy.[42] He argues that Chinese "national champions" have been used to incubate and promote this dominant class's interest in global economic integration. Other scholars have paid particular attention to the sectoral factions of the TCC that emerged out of some transnationally oriented economic sectors. For example, Carol Upadhya studied the Indian TCC rooted in Indian software outsourcing companies.[43] In short, these studies shed light on the interactions of various power blocs and factions of the TCC in specific political-economic conditions. Following these studies' research focus, this book also looks into how the Huawei case displays the formation and characters of the Chinese TCC in the country's reintegration into global digital capitalism.

The TCC has received the lion's share of attention in international political-economic research. In contrast, transnational, or "global proletariat," labor remained "under-explained and under-theorized."[44] In more recent years, the studies on the transformation of labor in digital capitalism have increasingly received greater attention from writers in the political economy of communication.[45] However, the labor implications in relation to the rise of Chinese transnational corporations has been largely absent in the extant literature. This calls for a new research agenda to examine the restructuring of global labor forces, the nature of the labor process, and capital-labor relations along with the transnationalization of Chinese capital. The Huawei case offers a typical perspective to reassess transnational class relations in its process of transnationalization.

In short, this book is premised on interrelated, dialectic relationships between state, capital, and class. It sheds light on the constitutive role of the state that contends and colludes with transnational capital on one hand and applies class analysis to examine class reconfiguration and class relations in the transformation of global capitalism on the other.

National/Transnational Articulation: Huawei in the "Chinese Model"

Huawei's growth is deeply intertwined with China's political-economic transformation, indicating the "dialectic interplay" between global capitalism and national conditions.[46] Conventional approaches to China studies often place the world as the reference point and China as the subject in order to reflect global realities.[47] Rather than simply applying established theories to explain Chinese experience, this study intends to develop more productive, decentered ways of knowledge production. In this framework, China and the world become "dynamic, interentangled processes instead of static entities in isolation."[48] By articulating the Huawei story with China's political-economic configuration, this book contributes to our understanding of the unique model of China's ICT development and offers new perspectives based on multipolar globalization.

China's impressive development over the last thirty years has evoked wide-ranging debate with regard to the nature of the Chinese model and the global impacts of China's rise. Some scholars emphasized the "peculiar path" of China's post-Mao transformation toward "neoliberalism with Chinese characteristics" or "full-fledged capitalist restoration."[49] While some writers acknowledged the social legacy and industrial foundation laid in the Maoist period, they also asserted that there is no unique Chinese model existing in China's trajectory of modern development.[50] For these authors, China's rise in the post-Mao era merely represents "a major, competitive capitalist power" in the world market, which is no different from other capitalist powers.[51]

Alternatively, some scholars argued that China has experienced a different pattern of development from prevailing neoliberal-oriented capitalism. By drawing on the experiences of the industrializing countries of East Asia such as the so-called Japanese model,[52] scholars of the "developmental state" school advocated for state intervention in fostering China's industrial policies. For them, the essence of the Chinese model lies in the Chinese state's strong capacity in defining developmental priorities and promoting strategic industrialization.

As political scientist Lin Chun claims, the weakness of mainstream arguments in most recent debates on the Chinese model is the absence of a critical appreciation of China's socialist commitment.[53] She then describes the "social-national-developmental" framework to explain the distinctiveness of the Chinese model. According to Lin, *socialism* stands for the Chinese state's commitment to equality and social justice; *developmentalism* implies the effort to overcome backwardness and to "catch up" with the West; and *nationalism* denotes nationalist ambition for national building and development. These three interconnected dimensions constitute the vital elements of China's socialist modernity and developmental trajectory. The tensions and dynamics underlying these three pillars provide an insight to examine the policy framework that shaped the contour of China's ICT firms' development.

This framework incorporated an analysis of China's engagement with particular social relations, policy struggles, and geopolitical interests. It also shed light on a critical research question related to China's ICT industry's development: Does China's ICT developmental trajectory represent an alternative model of technological and social development? This was also the fundamental question posed by critical communication scholar Dallas Smythe when he questioned China's choice for technological development and economic growth in his reflective piece "After Bicycle, What?"[54] Smythe argued that the distinct pattern of China's technological development was China's ability to reject the capitalist logic of development and its search for "proletariat politics." However, as Yuezhi Zhao put it, Smythe's binary analytical framework regarding the "socialist road" versus the "capitalist road" was inadequate to comprehend the geopolitical-economic conditions China had encountered and the complex path of China's post-Mao development strategy.[55]

Departing from Smythe's inquiry about the technological politics in China, Chinese communication scholar Hongzhe Wang provided a complement to Smythe's inquiry by incorporating more dialectic analyses on the country's geopolitical structure, socioeconomic factors, and class agency.[56] Wang's discussions illuminate the socialist legacy in China's technology-related policy struggle, the class character of technological development, and the relevance of a self-reliant technological development model to China's revolutionary modernity. His inquiry was helpful in clarifying the historical background in which Huawei was embedded.

Bearing the questions about China's "catching up" strategy in mind, Lutao Ning paid particular attention to the role of the state in the development of China's ICT industry with specific reference to the East Asian developmental model.[57] However, the developmental and institutional framework Ning used was committed to dualism between the state and market. It should be noted that the state is not a monolithic unity as suggested by the developmental state literature.[58] Instead of viewing the Chinese state as a centralized organizational structure, Adam Segal paid particular attention to the interaction between the central and various local governments involved in promoting Chinese high-technology enterprises.[59] Segal's framework avoided abstract generalizations of a country's developmental model and re-embedded local trajectories in specific institutional, political, and social configurations.

Although Segal's institutional analysis emphasized the role of locality in the national economy, it is important to note that China's ICT development must be situated in the transnational political-economic context. Following this inquiry, Schiller contextualized Chinese initiatives in his theoretical framework of "digital capitalism" and discussed the role of China as a new "pole of growth" in renewing the structure and function of transnational capitalism.[60] Although Schiller remained open to the discussion of the nature of China's development, he agreed that China has constituted "a pronounced exception to the post–World War II historical pattern."[61] For Schiller, the vital feature of such a pattern lies in the Chinese state's capacity to foster the import-substitution policy to reserve its own national market for homegrown ICT corporations. In the new epoch of digital capitalism, China's ICT sector exhibits what Schiller called the pattern of "growth amid depression," suggesting a trend of geopoliticization toward a new global communications order.[62] Drawing on Schiller's conceptualization of digital capitalism, Yu Hong's *Networking China: The Digital Transformation of the Chinese Economy* looked into the restructuring of China's digital economy as part of geopolitical struggle in the post-2008 era by focusing on the interplay of China's network-based economy and the transformation of global capitalism.[63] Her discussion on the relationship between the state, market forces, and class interests overcame the prevailing state-business dualism in the literature, providing a more dialectical framework to investigate the struggles underlying the unprecedented growth of China's digital economy.

By taking up Smythe's developmental questions and Lin's framework, Zhao engaged in a dialogue with Schiller by further re-embedding the analysis of the Chinese ICT-driven development path in a broader discussion of political, economic, social, and cultural contexts.[64] Zhao emphasized the impact of the Maoist socialist legacy on China's "digital revolution" and offered a profound critique on the unsustainability of China's entrenched developmental strategy. An examination of China's digital revolution, according to Zhao, should not be blind to various social forces' struggle for social justice.[65] In this sense, China's socialism is not only rhetoric from above, or a "name without substance"; it also encompasses a broader struggle from below and "a pursuable objective in reality."[66] Echoing Lin's conception of "alternative modernity," Zhao asserted that the legitimacy and outlook of socialism remains a defining element of China's future development.

In view of China's role as the "world factory" in the global ICT industry, some scholars paid particular attention to labor issues behind China's spectacular growth of the ICT sector.[67] Their work distinguished themselves from Western scholars' studies on "knowledge labor" or "immaterial labor."[68] They viewed the role of China's industrial workers as formative agents in the making of informationalized, transnationalized capitalism. These studies, starting from the Marxian conception of class, presented the transformative social relations between capital and labor and opened up the dimensions of class formation in transnational networks of ICT production.[69]

Extensive studies have been conducted to discuss China's manufacturing competitiveness in the global ICT production network, or what I refer to as the "Foxconn model."[70] These studies described China's development scenario from the inside, with particular focus on China's internal accumulation, or domestic development, in the ICT industry. China's most recent endeavor of climbing up the value chain has also generated emergent research interests in the country's restructuring strategies as well as its rising role in global digital capitalism.[71] However, Huawei's global expansion displays some new features of China's evolving digital economy, which is still under-explained in communications literature. Has the Huawei model provided a different pattern of internationalization from its Western counterparts? What are the political-economic implications regarding the growth and expansion of Chinese ICT corporations in global markets? Does the growing presence of Chinese capital outside China represent a neocolonial power or the redress against the US-dominated global order? These questions are highly relevant to understanding the evolving features of the Chinese model and China's self-repositioning in the current order of transnational capitalism. They are also situated at the heart of this book.

Why Huawei Matters

The Huawei model allows us to grasp deep understanding of the paradoxical nature of China's ICT development as well as the globalization of the country's corporate power. The rationales of choosing Huawei as the focal case are significant.

First and foremost, as Huawei's growth was deeply intertwined with the developmental trajectory of China's digital economy and policy struggle, the story of Huawei is representative of the rise of Chinese indigenous high-tech enterprises in the period of the country's transition from a state socialist economy to a market economy. Founded in 1987, Huawei has grown into a multinational Chinese ICT giant and a globally recognizable brand. Its Carrier Network core business has exceeded Sweden's Ericsson to become the largest global seller of network gear. Its smartphone brand, launched in 2010, replaced Apple in 2018 as the second-largest smartphone seller behind Samsung. Huawei's success provides a greater scope to address larger strategic efforts and concerns in restructuring China's digital economy. Meanwhile, this work tends to respond to the speculation on Huawei's links to the Chinese government and military, a prevailing claim premised on the state-business collusion in China. In fact, Huawei's non-state ownership status generated more complicated interactions with the Chinese state, transnational capital, and other state-owned domestic players.

Second, the potential impact of Huawei's rise reaches far beyond the domestic economy. Huawei, as one of the most successful Chinese ICT companies that has gone global, presents certain patterns of outward expansion among China-based enterprises. Its transnationalization has been closely entangled with the Chinese government's foreign policy interests, which attempt to extend China's control over transnational network infrastructures and to recast the country's role in the global political economy. Huawei's involvement in the Chinese state's geopolitical-economic strategies, especially in the most recent Belt and Road Initiative (BRI),[72] calls attention to the complex relationship between Chinese corporate players and the Chinese state in reshaping the global communications order. However, the state-business alliance that underlies Huawei's outward expansion also engenders a great deal of conflicts in different parts of world markets. The Huawei case, which was caught in the vortex of US-China technological rivalry, displays multifaceted inter-capitalist and inter-state tensions in reshaping the geopolitical-economic landscape.

Third, Huawei's strategic growth is closely related to its technological innovation. The Huawei case has broader implications for the future shaping of

China's technological development. The company's strategies of developing self-reliant research and development (R&D) and innovation provide practical experience for Chinese domestic high-tech firms in nurturing their technological and innovative capabilities, which may avoid the developmental predicament most domestic ICT firms—such as ZTE Corporation, another of China's technology giants—face by reducing their overdependence on foreign core technologies. Moreover, the company has not only served as a major driver of technological upgrading in the domestic market, but it has also developed a wide range of international ICT standards and intellectual property rights in international markets. The participation of non-Western actors in global technological governance challenges the power monopolized by Western countries and firms, suggesting a potential change toward a multipolar communications order.

Fourth, the case of Huawei also raises issues about capital-labor relations. The company's experiment with employee shareholding provides part of a vision of democratic management through the redistribution of power and control at the firm level. Its labor practice can also be seen as a contradictory mixture, comprising socialist residues and Western-style management. At the same time, Huawei's transnationalization gave rise to a transnationalized labor regime and the mechanism of transnational managerial technocracy. Having an analysis of the company's ownership structure and labor issues is necessary to unpack the relationship between power and control.

This empirical research not only aims to produce an empirically accurate account of the case but also contributes to the theoretical discussion of the Chinese model. In short, the Huawei case yields multifaceted observations and multiple readings to understand the complexity and uniqueness of China's ICT development. Moreover, this case does not necessarily lead to any closure in findings. Rather, we can expect both determinacy and indeterminacy by viewing the case as a continuous, dynamic process of constructing.

Chapter Outline

Moving beyond the firm-specific approach, this book combines ICT industry studies with a critical political-economic approach to explore the Huawei model at the macro, meso, and micro levels. It traces the trajectory of Huawei's growth in both domestic and global markets. Particular attention is paid to the company's innovation in its technology development strategy as well as its ownership structure and management. The study uses a triangular approach encompassing the methods of documentary research, semistructured interviews, and nonparticipant observation. It also combines "inside-out" and "outside-in" analytical perspectives to explore Huawei from different angles.

To explain how Huawei has grown to its current state in the domestic market, chapter 1 traces Huawei's history against the backdrop of China's ICT development. As historical and political economic context, it also unfolds China's transition from self-sufficient industrial development in the Mao era to industrialization dependent on foreign direct investment (FDI) in the post-Mao reform. By dividing Huawei's history into several critical stages, this chapter also focuses on how Huawei's developmental trajectory epitomizes the Chinese state's major policy shifts in forging an ICT-led national economy.

Chapters 2 and 3 shift the focus from Huawei's domestic growth to its exterritorial expansion by exploring its strategies of internationalization. Chapter 2 first looks at Huawei's expansion into the global South in terms of its motivations, practices, and implications. As an exemplar of China's "going-out" strategy and external economic engagement, the path of Huawei's internationalization is representative in analyzing the patterns of Chinese corporations' outward expansion and the relationship between states and corporate power. Huawei's increasing presence as a new source of investment and technological support in the global South exemplifies the growing influence of corporate China in these regions. But at the same time, the Chinese firm's globalized operations also generate a great deal of conflicts with local communities. The tensions between state-backed Chinese corporate capital and local societies are discussed in this chapter. The analysis also tends to respond to the critiques on China's threat with regard to the country's economic engagement in the global South.

Despite the growing presence of Huawei's products in developing countries, the company's entry into developed countries was marked by difficulties and obstacles. US action against Huawei demonstrates how Huawei was attacked as a prime target by the US government in order to contain China's economic and technological power. Chapter 3 examines Huawei's move to the global North, particularly to the high-end European and US markets. The differences in Huawei's practices in the global South and in the global North are manifest in terms of its entry modes, its marketing strategies, and its relationship with local vendors, governments, and labor. In the meantime, the global increase in protectionism has given rise to fierce inter-state and inter-capitalist competition, which directly changed the dynamics of capitalist accumulation by transnational corporations. Being at the center of the confrontation, Huawei has also faced huge setbacks in the global North.

The dilemma of Huawei's expansion in the North offers an illustration of the tensions between territorial and capitalist logics.

Chapters 4 and 5 shift the focus from Huawei's external expansion to its corporate power as well as its innovative capabilities internal to the corporate structure. Chapter 4 delineates Huawei's path to its cutting-edge technology and innovation leadership. Current analyses of China's technological innovation often focus on initiatives by the state or local government but rarely on the role played by firms. In contrast, Huawei offers a distinct look into the firm-driven initiatives of technological innovation aligning with the state's endeavor. This chapter also highlights the paradoxical dynamics between the techno-nationalist initiative and the logic of capitalist accumulation underlying Huawei's technological innovation.

Huawei's innovative capability is reflected not only in its technological progress but also in its distinct innovation of its ownership structure. From the perspective of the political economy of communications, corporate ownership structures provide one of the clearest expressions of power distribution and capital-labor relations. But different from a conventional political-economic analysis, Huawei's case presents some distinctive experience. The company's experiments in designing its employee-shareholding ownership structure can be viewed as a result of organizational innovation during China's market-oriented institutional transformation, particularly in the context of China's corporatization and ownership diversification reforms. Meanwhile, Huawei's transnational production regime has given rise to a wide web of transnational labor control in line with the emergence of transnational managerial technocracy. Chapter 5 attempts to examine Huawei's innovation of its ownership structure and to incorporate class analysis to examine the resulting capital-labor relations.

The book closes by discussing the implications of Huawei's developmental model in reshaping China's economic restructuring plan and the global communications order.

CHAPTER 1

Huawei's Domestic Accumulation
A Path Intertwining with China's ICT Development

Huawei's developmental trajectory was deeply rooted in the systematic restructuring of China's national economy and the state's reinsertion into transnational capitalism. China's market reforms in forging an ICT-led digital economy in the post-Mao era have shaped the company's strategies of production, research and development, and modes of accumulation, creating tensions between the state, domestic corporate players, and transnational capital. The reorganization of global corporate power in turn redefined the role of state in national policies. The interaction of local dynamics and transnational accumulation circuits constitutes what Jerry Harris calls "dialectics of globalization."[1] The rise of China's corporate power in global digital capitalism, thus, should be examined in such dialectics or, specifically, in the context of a national-transnational nexus. To better understand the making of the Chinese ICT giant, it is vitally important to first examine Huawei's development within the context of China's history of industrial development.

Before turning to an analysis of Huawei's growth in the Chinese domestic market, this chapter provides an overview of the country's ICT developmental trajectory in order to highlight the domestic roots in which Huawei has been embedded. The transition from the self-sufficient industrial development in the Mao era to export-oriented, FDI-dependent industrialization in the post-Mao reform is examined to provide the historical lessons and structural context that shaped the development of homegrown ICT firms. Against such a backdrop of the Chinese state's industrial restructuring and reforms, Huawei's growth followed a multistage path. This chapter then historicizes Huawei's three crucial stages of domestic accumulation, which to some extent have paralleled the evolution of China's ICT sector and major domestic policy shifts: (1) the initial stage of capital accumulation in the fixed-line sector from the 1980s to the mid-1990s, (2) the struggling developmental stage in the domestic mobile telecom market from the mid-1990s to the early 2000s, and (3) the stage of strategic reorientation since the mid-2000s.

A Historical Contour of China's ICT Development

Huawei was founded in the late 1980s, a period of China's epochal transition that synthesized historical continuities and contradictions. One who upholds neoliberal doctrines might attribute the success of Huawei to China's reform and opening policy. This assumption amounts to a dismissal of the industrial and technological achievements China made during the Mao period. In essence, the internal accumulation of the Mao era enabled the country to enter the reform era "on relatively favorable terms and with highly successful economic results,"[2] laying down the foundations for the rise of China's ICT industry. However, the policy shift of the post-Mao market reform completely changed the trajectory of China's ICT development as well as the nature of China's integration into the world system. The capitalist transition generated growing tensions and contradictions for Huawei's internal accumulation in the domestic market. Before unfolding Huawei's growth path, it is necessary to gain an insight into the contradictory development of China's ICT industry by taking a look at the holistic background that shaped Huawei's initial stage of development in the transition period.

SEARCH FOR AN ALTERNATIVE PATH OF ICT DEVELOPMENT IN THE MAO ERA

China's electronics and telecommunications industries started from "poverty and blankness" after the Communist revolution in 1949. The telecom infrastructure during this period was extremely poor and unequally distributed. There was no nationwide network across the country. Advanced telecom systems were concentrated in coastal cities, while the vast countryside had low penetration rates of telephone lines.[3] No domestic electronics or telecom firms enjoyed independent manufacturing capacities.[4]

Starting in 1953, the Chinese state accelerated the pace of socialist modernization and industrialization. The electronics industry was assigned as one of the priorities of the national economic development.[5] In the 1956 "Long-Range Plan for the Development of Science and Technology from 1956 to 1967," several electronics projects were granted national importance, including telecommunications and broadcasting systems, radio electronics, semiconductor technology, and computer and radio technology for national defense. Under the technical and financial assistance from the Soviet Union and East Germany, eleven national projects in the electronics and telecommunications industries were launched with the establishment of a number of pillar electronics enterprises across the country. By the end of the First Five-Year Plan (FYP; 1953–1957), China had been able to produce some key electronics components and products, including wireless communication equipment, automated telephone switches, broadcasting transmitters, and a few consumer products. From 1953 to 1957, the electronics industry grew at the average annual rate of 49.5 percent.[6] Especially in the field of telecom equipment manufacturing, a breakthrough was achieved by the Beijing Wire Communication Plant in 1957 when the enterprise produced the first automated central office telephone switches in China.[7] China's overall capacity of local office switches had improved rapidly, increasing from 320,900 ports in 1950 to 2.31 million in 1960.[8]

At the same time, the central government began to pay attention to the disparity of telecom infrastructure expansion between cities and the countryside. In 1956 the Ministry of Post and Telecommunications (MPT) established the goal of constructing telecom networks at the county and commune levels as one of the central tasks of rural development. Substantial efforts for telecom network construction were made via the nationwide campaign "telephone to every township" (*xiang xiang tong dianhua*). By 1960 the number of rural telephone subscribers had reached nearly 920,000, almost twenty times the 1951 number, which also greatly outnumbered urban telephone subscribers.[9] At the same time, 99.1 percent of people's communes and 86.9 percent of production bridges installed telephones.[10] The rate of telecom equipment installation increased severalfold.[11] The rapid growth of rural telephone lines laid a solid foundation for rural industrialization. For example, in 1960 the country launched a mass campaign to construct irrigation systems in the countryside. Along with this campaign, more than seventy thousand kilometers of telephone cables and thirty thousand telephones were installed at construction sites to facilitate the project.[12] In concordance with the expansion of telecom infrastructure, rural radio broadcasting networks developed rapidly. Since the mid-1950s, expanding telephone lines had been used for transmitting broadcasting signals to the vast countryside, fulfilling the country's effort of constructing national broadcasting networks and providing public service for rural demands. Under the initiative of rural telecom development, the gap between the rural and urban areas was significantly reduced.

However, the deterioration of international relations in the 1960s, especially the Sino-Soviet split, not only undermined developmental conditions inside China but also confronted the country with external military threats. In 1960 the Soviet Union withdrew all technical assistance and terminated provisions of key electronics components and equipment. In response to the risky international environment, Mao placed greater attention to "basic" industry and focused more on industrial construction in inland areas than in coastal cities. In addition, the Maoists also called for China to develop an independent and indigenous technology that combined "old considerations of national pride and new economic considerations."[13] In line with this tenet of self-reliant industrial development, the prime task of electronics and telecommunications enterprises was readjusted to facilitate military-related development such as nuclear, missile defense, and aviation technologies.

To carry out this strategy, from the mid-1960s to 1970s China implemented a massive development program, "The Third Front Plan," to reconfigure China's industrialization. Increased investment was directed to the southwestern remote region and Western China to construct an alternative industrial base. A large number of existing factories and research institutions were relocated from coastal cities to the mountainous hinterland. The Third Front Plan actually dominated China's industrialization efforts in the late Mao era. Investment in this plan accounted for 52.7 and 41.1 percent, respectively, of total national investment in the Third and Fourth FYPs.[14] As one of its construction priorities, the electronics industry obtained substantial policy support and played an important role in this military-driven industrialization. From 1960 to 1970, the total number of electronic factories increased from 460 to 2,500.[15] The value of industrial output increased from 2.33 to 10.6 billion yuan, with the average growth rate at 31.4 percent during the Third FYP. From 1966 to 1976, more than eighty national projects were initiated.[16] In the provinces of Sichuan, Guizhou, and Shanxi, large-scale electronics industry bases were established, which were turned into local backbone enterprises under the policy of the "Small Third Front Plan." These Third Front enterprises played significant roles in restructuring China's ICT industry and rebuilding the country's manufacturing capacities in the reform era.

During the period of Maoist industrialization, China made substantial technological breakthroughs in a few strategic sectors such as satellite, telecom equipment, and computer technologies. In 1964 the first Chinese-developed digital computer was launched.[17] In the same year, China's telecommunications technologies also achieved a major breakthrough with the launch of independently developed symmetrical cable carrier telephone systems and microwave cables. And in 1966 the first Chinese-made integrated circuit was invented, marking a significant progress in electronics technologies.[18] Since then China enjoyed large-scale production of integrated circuits and wide application to other electronics products. These technological advances were noteworthy, indicating the country's dynamic technological and innovative capabilities under the self-reliant mode of development.

China's industrial development in the Mao era was not merely a response to external forces but a project of exploring an "alternative modernity."[19] The country's self-reliant development, first and foremost, rested on the Chinese state's rejection of the blind importation of Western technologies as well as "capitalist consumption relations."[20] Apart from military and national defense functions, the construction of China's electronics and telecommunications industries also included the aims of meeting basic social needs and building the socialist goal of egalitarianism. These social functions were manifest in China's industrial policies.

In addition, China's industrialization during the Mao era highly relied on the accumulation of labor resources, the Communist Party's capability of social mobilization, and the promotion of socialist subjectivity. Because the scarcity of capital input in China's internal accumulation required labor as a complement of productive resources, massive investment in labor resources was made during the Mao era, which led to the formation of a generally educated, healthy, and disciplined workforce for China's industrialization and modernization.[21] The unique Chinese experience of industrialization and modernization also depended on the approach of mass mobilization that fully integrated people's professional expertise with mass-based production. The Third Front Plan, for instance, was conceived as a mass movement that had mobilized nearly 4 million Chinese people, including workers, technicians, and engineers, to transfer from coastal cities to inland industrial bases. Moreover, it is important to note that the realization of self-reliance was largely built upon the emancipation of Chinese people's subjectivity, which constituted "the motive force and the end of development."[22]

As Maurice Meisner points out, the masses—who were capable of engaging in "the course of everyday productive work, learning the necessary skills and expertise in the course of doing, studying while working, and applying their newly-acquired knowledge to immediate productive needs, and in ways appropriate to suit local conditions"—were believed to create and master modern technology.[23] From Maoist rural modernization to urban industrialization, this "mass line" approach of technical development was exemplified in numerous practices and mass movements, such as the emergence of "barefoot electronics engineers" (*chijiaodiangong*), the campaign of developing "people's computer technology," and the progress of automation technology achieved at the factory shop floor.[24] In contrast to the linear process of theoretical research and laboratory experiments, the result-oriented "learning-by-doing" model emphasized extracting experience directly from production and applying it to local conditions. In terms of organizational structure, the system of expert rotation, which required cadres and technical experts' participation in production practices to generate insight into various local conditions, was prioritized over the elite-led R&D process.[25] Taking the innovation of China's first integrated circuit, for instance, technicians and engineers who were sent to the shop floor of Shanghai Electronics' components factory accumulated experience and made breakthroughs in numerous experiments during the course of their production work. This unique approach was essential for bringing collective wisdom and workers' subjectivity into productive practice. Simply put, these practices amounted to a unique Chinese experience in the country's self-reliant development, which exerted significant influence on the post-Mao development.

RELINKING TO WORLD MARKETS IN THE 1970S

With the dramatic transformation of the world system structure and international relations in the 1970s, China underwent deep changes in its strategic options in the late Mao period by seeking linkages to world markets. These changes were first marked by China's regaining a seat in the UN Security Council and its normalizing relations with the United States, Japan, and a few former foes, such as some Western European countries, in the early 1970s. The repositioning of China's role in the world's geopolitical landscape in turn geared the country toward reorienting its national economy. Specifically, the domestic development strategy was gradually shifted away from the autarkic, military-dominated strategy and toward the civilian economy.

Meanwhile, a number of top Communist Party leaders, including Zhou Enlai, Chen Yun, and Li Xiannian, proposed to rebuild the country's foreign trade system and to strengthen economic relations with Western countries. In the early 1970s the Chinese government launched the "Four Three Plan," investing $4.3 billion in technological transfer and machinery importation from Western industrialized countries. This plan was seen as the People's Republic of China's (PRC's) second "opening-up" policy after the Soviet-assisted "156 national projects" in the 1950s as well as a prelude to China's outward-looking market reform after 1978.[26] The investment mainly concentrated in productive material industries such as the chemical fiber, fertilizer, and petroleum industries, aiming to revive the Four Modernizations developmental strategy, which had been superseded by the Third Front Plan, and to balance the light and heavy industries in the national economic system. The electronics and telecommunications sectors were also involved in this wave of "opening-up." In 1972 Canadian telecom giant Nortel Networks became the first Western telecommunications company to sell transmission equipment in China,[27] which was later used in televising the historic meeting of Mao and Richard Nixon by Chinese broadcast media.[28] Moreover, in the domestic market, production lines of consumer communication goods, such as color televisions, were established based on technological transfer and imports of key electronics components from Western countries. At the same time, China started to reestablish its network connectivity with the outside world, especially with the West. In 1971 China restored direct telephone and telegraph lines to the United Kingdom and the United States.[29] In the following year, the first data transmission circuit connecting Beijing, Shanghai, San Francisco, and Toronto was launched.[30] In the same year, the International Telecommunication Union restored China's seat, which strengthened China's presence and power in the governance of global telecommunications.

These moves can be seen as China's initial effort to relink with the capitalist system in the late Mao era, which also paralleled concurrent transformations in the world system. To some extent, China's opening-up strategy in the early 1970s was more a triumph for capitalist countries than for China, because the hope of saving capitalism out of the systematic crisis largely hinged on China during this period. As noted by Dan Schiller, the age of Nixon was marked by great changes of capitalist development along with restructuring the global political-economic order, which led to great transformations in the geopolitics of information in the following decades.[31] To overcome the crisis of the 1970s, principal industrialized countries sought to explore alternative markets to export surplus products and capital in order to sustain profitable growth around digital networks. The communications industry, especially the newly emerging ICT sector, undertook a special role in responding to this crisis by creating new territories of profit.[32] China was conceived as one of these new centers of capital accumulation. With its "selective linkage" to world markets, the intersections of the "two poles of growth"—China's integration into transnational digital capitalism—were taking place, which constituted unique political-economic conditions for the rise of Chinese ICT enterprises in the post-reform era. Meanwhile, starting in the 1970s, capitalist restructuring around digital networks has accentuated international competition for leadership of the global communications order.[33]

POST-MAO REFORMS

China's post-Mao reforms underwent epochal changes, with a transition period marked by dramatic policy reversals, industrial restructuring, and market-oriented enterprise reforms.[34] It essentially departed from the developmental ideology of the Mao era and embraced economic growth as a legitimate part of the "socialist market reform." As a key part of the initial structural adjustment during the transition period, the national economic structure was shifted away from military-oriented heavy industry to consumer, labor-intensive light industry and consumer goods production. In this process of policy shift, electronics and telecommunications industries were given greater weight in the national economy. In 1977, after the meeting of the National Electronics Industry Conference, the *People's Daily* published an editorial on the electronics industry, declaring, "All branches of the national economy must be equipped with the technology of electronics before they can advance at high speed.... The electronics industry, as an important material and technological basis for the four modernizations, should be the first to be modernized."[35] Later, in 1979, Deng Xiaoping further noted that telecommunications should be placed as one of the most vital areas of public investment, along with other strategic sectors such as energy and transportation, in order to lay the foundation for infrastructure construction.[36] In 1982 "the acceleration of telecommunication development" was enshrined in the report of the Twelfth National Congress for the first time. The minister of Post and Telecommunications at the time, Wen Minsheng, even declared that this goal should be achieved through the expansion of telecommunications networks in the urban areas,[37] a suggestion that dramatically contradicted Mao's egalitarian policy of electronics and telecommunications development. Moreover, the post-Mao Chinese technocratic elite's thirst for reintegration into the global capitalist system converged with the Western vision of the "informational" or "postindustrial" paradigm that viewed the "information society" as a fetish of social development as well as an inevitable path toward modernization. This tendency was exemplified in the popularization of Alvin Toffler's book *The Third Wave* in China in the 1980s, which further prompted the Chinese reformist elite to articulate the idea of "information revolution" with China's modernization drive.[38] However, as noted by Zhao, underlying the dominant ideology of "information revolution" or "the Third Wave" was the overriding logic of commodification and capitalist accumulation.[39] China's imperative of building an ICT-led mode of economic development was actually integrated as an essential part of the world's capitalist restructuring, which was later translated into specific domestic policy initiatives at different levels.

First, at the central decision-making level, a Leading Group for the Revitalization of the Electronics Industry was formed within the State Council with Vice Premier Li Peng as its head. In November 1984 this group put forth a "Report on the Development Strategy for Our Country's Electronics and Information Industry," calling for the priority of applying ICTs in various social and economic spheres, with a special focus on the development of telecommunications equipment and computer technologies.[40] During the Seventh Five-Year period (1986–1990), twelve principal ICT application projects, mainly concentrated in national public service spheres, including banking, transportation, public security, and military services, were launched to restructure traditional industries with modern technologies.

Second, measures of industrial restructuring were implemented in the ICT sector according to the market logic. The first step involved large-scale defense conversion projects. The central government cut down the investment budget for military-related projects and diverted resources toward the civilian sector. The share of military spending in central government spending fell dramatically from 25 percent during the height of the Third Front Plan in the 1960s to around 8 percent by the mid-1980s.[41] As the market logic gradually gained legitimacy in industrial reforms, the primary organizing principle of ICT production was no longer established to meet the demand of militarization or public service but to create new sites of commodification for consumer markets and to pursue the imperative of profit accumulation. Paradoxically, if the uniqueness of Mao's industrialization and ICT development lay in China's rejection of capitalist consumption relations, the post-Mao industrial reforms not only turned the country into a key supplier in the global consumer goods chain to serve global capitalist markets but also unleashed "rampant consumerism" as a universal ideology.[42] The market-oriented industrial drive became the pivotal factor shaping the direction of China's ICT developmental trajectory.

Third, China's ICT enterprises underwent dramatic transformations in many respects. Because of declining financial support as well as shrinking military-related demands, a large number of Third Front electronics enterprises were closed down. In 1985 a rectification plan was implemented to restructure and relocate Third Front enterprises. A number of traditional electronics enterprises were forced to relocate to coastal cities and to engage in export-oriented manufacturing activities. For example, the Zhenhua Electronics Corporation, which was one of the backbone electronics enterprises in the Third Front Plan, was reorganized by the Ministry of Electronics Industry (MEI) to establish more than ten business and production facilities in Shenzhen. The restructured enterprises primarily engaged in the production of printed circuits for export and color televisions for the domestic consumer market. By mid-1987 over one thousand Third Front electronics enterprises had been restructured.[43] These enterprises played significant roles in post-Mao industrial reforms, contributing large shares of the country's consumer goods production during the transition period. More important, their research and development capacity as well as their manufacturing know-how, which had been accumulated during Maoist industrialization, was absorbed by other homegrown ICT enterprises like Huawei. There is no doubt that the legacy of China's industrialization laid a solid foundation for the country to nurture indigenous technology and to build competitive domestic players.

Accompanying market-oriented industrial restructuring, China's ICT sector also witnessed liberalized institutional reforms. In the early 1980s, an initial state-owned enterprise (SOE) reform was launched in the ICT industry as part of wider market reforms. The primary goal of this reform was to separate centrally controlled administration from enterprise management by allowing SOEs to act independently in product planning, marketing, R&D, and profit retention. In 1982 the State Council implemented a rectification plan covering 1,606 state-owned electronics enterprises, accounting for about 56 percent of the total number of enterprises in the ICT industry.[44] With the policy of decentralization, provincial telecom enterprises obtained relative autonomy from the centralized government. In the mid-1990s, the Chinese SOE sector underwent a second wave of radical enterprise reform along with the country's neoliberal reform, which further accelerated the pace of China's liberalization in the corporate ownership control and management system.

Apart from the SOE reform, the non-state sector grew rapidly with the lift of ownership control. To escalate the scale and scope of China's "digital revolution," the state encouraged massive entries of non-state-owned enterprises into the ICT manufacturing industry. Although the SOE sector still dominated high-tech production within the industry, growing collectively owned enterprises played a significant role in organizing labor- and process-intensive ICT production throughout the 1980s.[45] Beginning in the mid-1980s, a number of ICT companies, including Huawei, ZTE, TCL, Lenovo, and Haier, all of which had originally registered as collectively owned enterprises, sprang up and grew rapidly. Moreover, hundreds of thousands of township and village enterprises (TVEs) in peri-urban areas primarily took the subcontracting role by cooperating with urban SOEs.[46] Such a cooperative production relation not only recovered the urban-rural linkage in the early period of reform, but it also strengthened the self-sustaining mode of development in China's domestic market. According to statistical records for this period, the number of TVEs increased to 12,002 in the field of electronic goods production and 4,536 in telecommunications equipment, with shares of 37 percent and 13.9 percent, respectively, of total electronics output.[47] Before the Chinese state shifted the ICT policy toward the export sector and initiated the privatization of rural collective enterprises in the mid-1990s, China's burgeoning TVEs primarily served as the engine of rural takeoff and laid a solid foundation for the Chinese ICT manufacturing economy.

The ICT sector not only served as a forerunner of domestic market reforms but has also been closely bound up with the Chinese state's opening-up initiative. In 1977 the Chinese government had already expressed interest in cooperating with Western companies to build infrastructure for modern communication networks.[48] During the initial stage of economic reforms, demand for advanced communication services, especially from transnational business, exploded. China's underdeveloped domestic ICT products and technologies, however, were unable to match the ever increasing market growth. To leapfrog into the market-driven digital revolution, the principle of self-reliance gradually gave way to an outward-looking mode of ICT development. The acquisition of Western technology and foreign capital was used as the most efficient means to jump-start the domestic ICT capital accumulation and capacity buildup. In 1983 the Chinese state relaxed the restrictions of foreign direct investment in joint ventures and allowed wholly foreign-owned enterprises in the country. Then in 1986 the government further liberalized FDI through a series of preferential policies, which included lowering taxes and removing administrative restriction, allowing foreign firms more freedom in their operations, and easing restrictions on the acquisition of foreign exchange.[49] The field of ICTs became one of the most popular sectors for the inflow of FDI. According to the earliest available data from the Ministry of Electronics Industry, the output value of foreign-invested enterprises production increased twelvefold from ¥0.23 billion in 1983 to ¥2.9 billion in 1987.[50] Throughout the 1990s, inflow FDI soared at astonishingly high rates, which made China the world's number one destination for foreign direct investment.

The Chinese emergent technocratic elites' enthusiasm for global capitalist markets also aligned with multinationals' interests that intended to "assign China a niche position" in the systematic restructuring of global ICT production.[51] Since the 1970s, East Asian countries have risen as outsourcing centers for transnational ICT corporations due to these countries' strategic status in the global geopolitical-economic context and their low cost of labor. Yet rising production costs as well as labor shortages in these countries forced transnational capital to flow toward Mainland China, with China functioning as an assembly hub for ICT final products in global fragmented production networks.[52] Encouraged by the Chinese state's export-oriented, "attracting-in" policy in the late 1980s, the total export value of electronics products in China increased more than ten times from $0.68 billion in 1986 to $8.11 billion in 1993, with foreign-invested enterprises accounting for 54.6 percent of total exports.[53] By the end of 1991, more than 2,600 foreign-invested ICT enterprises had been established in the country.[54] Despite the unprecedented growth of China's ICT industries in the past several decades, this uneven developmental path—one that was especially marked by the domination of transnational corporations—posed formidable challenges to the development of indigenous firms, a trend of which the Huawei story is illustrative.

As mentioned above, the development of Huawei was contingent on Chinese development strategies at both the general and ICT-specific levels. A historical review of China's ICT development from Mao's era to the initial stage of post-Mao reforms, which reveals a process of socialist construction, industrial restructuring, and tendency of capitalist transition, provides a necessary prehistory to understand the political-economic background in which Huawei developed. The following section moves to the analysis of Huawei's history. It can further shed light on the interaction between Chinese corporate power, the Chinese state, and transnational capital.

Huawei's Developmental Trajectory in the Domestic Market

THE FIRST STAGE: "CIRCULATING CITIES FROM THE COUNTRYSIDE"

In December 1987, Huawei was founded in Shenzhen—one of the first four special economic zones (SEZs) designated in 1979—with only six employees and ¥24,000 registered capital. Prior to the mid-1990s, the Chinese national government did not see Huawei as a favored champion. The company's phenomenal growth, from a local small manufacturer of telephone exchange switches to one of the designated national champions in China's ICT sector, exemplifies how Huawei interacted with regional dynamism as well as industrial transformation at the national level. In this sense, Huawei's relation with the local and national states constitutes unique characters of the "Huawei model," which also further illustrates the complexity of China's ICT development pattern.

As a key part of the country's opening-up policy, the establishment of SEZs was designated to attract foreign capital and technologies by offering foreign investors favorable conditions such as unlimited supplies of cheap labor and preferential tax rates. Shenzhen, a once obscure small town proximate to Hong Kong, was transformed quickly into a center of China's outward-looking economy and "the vanguard of China's urban reform." Since 1979, Shenzhen Municipal Government has expressed the imperative to embrace the bandwagon of information revolution to promote its FDI-driven economic strategy. Drawing on the so-called front shop and back factory (*qiandian houchang*) model, Shenzhen emerged as a center for export-oriented ICT manufacturing in its early stage of reform, with Hong Kong acting as a financier in the "front shop" and Shenzhen as a manufacturer and assembler in the "back factory." By the end of 1985, the output of Shenzhen's electronics industry had reached ¥1.4 billion, with a 113.5 percent increase from 1979, accounting for 49.7 percent of Shenzhen's total industrial output. The exports had reached ¥120 million, accounting for 11 percent of the electronic output value, and the number of Shenzhen electronics enterprises had increased from 1 in 1979 to 170 in 1985.[55] However, the overwhelming majority of these enterprises were primarily engaged in assembly, processing and packaging, and compensation trade (*sanlaiyibu*).

Starting in 1986, Shenzhen Municipal Government scaled up investment in and policy support for the high-tech sector in concordance with the Chinese state's economic restructuring toward ICT-led developmental strategies. In February 1987 the Shenzhen government issued the "Tentative Provisions on Encouraging Technology and Science Personnel to Establish Non-State-Owned Technological Enterprises," officially lifting control on private ownership in the high-tech sector. This directive stipulated that science and technology personnel were allowed to invest in high-tech companies in the forms of intellectual property, copyrights, or other property rights. At the same time, the government promised to provide these start-ups with a series of preferential policies, such as exemption from enterprise income taxes. This policy stimulated a rapid growth of non-state-owned high-tech enterprises and an influx of private capital into the ICT sector in Shenzhen. As a result of this policy, eighty-five high-tech companies, including Huawei, were formed as "people-run" enterprises in 1987, a term used to describe non-state-run enterprises during the period of transition.[56]

Ren Zhengfei was a representative figure of China's early generation of private entrepreneurs in the reform era. Born into a poor family in the inland Guizhou Province in 1944, Ren attended the Chongqing Institute of Post and Telecommunications in the 1960s. He then joined the People's Liberation Army (PLA) to work as an engineer in the PLA's information technology research unit. During the transition period of the defense conversion projects, Ren was demobilized from the PLA in 1982 and then moved to Shenzhen. Before Ren Zhengfei founded Huawei, he had worked as a manager at an electronics company subordinated to Nanyou Corporation, which was one of the largest SOEs in Shenzhen. Like many other emerging private entrepreneurs during the transition period, Ren left his job at Nanyou and "plunged into the sea" (*xiahai*) to establish a private business. As a typical member of China's "red capitalists," Ren enjoyed a uniquely favorable position in market reforms. His connections with local officials in the post and telecommunications sector helped Huawei acquire some low-end equipment contracts in the initial stage.

Although Huawei was registered as a technology company, initially it had nothing to do with advanced technological research and development. Like many other Chinese ICT companies, such as Lenovo, Huawei started its business in international trade, primarily engaging in activities of retail trade of varied consumer goods in the first few years. However, Ren Zhengfei later shifted the company's strategic focus to the telecommunications equipment market against the backdrop of the unprecedented telecommunications network buildup in the 1980s. He then chose to become a sales agent of a Hong Kong telecom equipment company, Hung Nien Electronics, to sell its small-sized analog private telephone branch exchange (PBX) in Mainland China. This deal became Huawei's first business to step into the telecommunications equipment market.

As Ren correctly anticipated, China's telecommunications market has experienced an exponential rate of growth in the scale of investment and user base since the late 1980s. The fixed-asset investment in telecommunications surged from ¥2.14 billion in 1987 to ¥85.6 billion in 1995 with a fortyfold increase, while fixed-line subscribers also increased, from 3.9 million to 40.7 million.[57] In the early 1990s, the initial installation fees for a fixed-line telephone were as high as ¥3,000–5,000 and sales prices of telecommunications transmission equipment could reach ¥1,000–2,000 per port.⁵⁸ Massive market demand and huge profit returns have turned the telecommunications equipment sector into one of the most commercialized and lucrative industries in the reform era. Benefiting from the booming domestic telecommunications economy, Huawei also prospered quickly in its initial stage of development. Through reselling the imported telecom equipment HAX switch to small enterprises in the mainland market at high prices, Huawei quickly accumulated primitive capital from such speculative activities.⁵⁹

However, Huawei had to face its fiercest competition in the domestic telecommunications equipment market at the same time. Apart from hundreds of Chinese domestic competitors that also served as sales agents of varied low-end imported equipment, foreign telecommunications giants completely dominated the high-end market under the state's pro–foreign investment policy. As industrialized countries had already moved from electronic switching to all-digital systems since the early 1970s, foreign telecommunications equipment manufacturers had made steady strides in advanced switching technology. In contrast, Chinese indigenous telecommunications switching technologies had been caught in a bottleneck ever since China invented the country's first crossbar switch in the 1960s. In order to improve its telecommunications network capacity in a short time, the Chinese government and telecommunications equipment manufacturers chose to adopt a three-stage policy, including (1) direct import of equipment, (2) technological transfer and absorbing, and (3) indigenous innovation, with the hope that the Chinese homegrown firms would eventually catch up with multinational giants.⁶⁰

Before Huawei's entry into the essential telecommunications equipment market, the domestic market share had already been dominated by foreign products thanks to the government's policy of "trading market for technology." In November 1982, China imported and installed the first digital switch system with a capacity of ten thousand ports in Fuzhou, a coastal city of southeastern China, marking a huge leap in Chinese telecommunications network capacity from out-of-date electromechanical networks to digital control. To further lure foreign capital and to boost telecommunications imports, in April 1986 the Chinese government decided to lower tariffs for imported telecommunications equipment; it particularly exempted duties for domestic firms that used World Bank or Asian Development Bank loans to buy foreign equipment. On the other side, foreign governments sought to offer generous loans to China to assist the opening of markets for their vendors. These loans usually came with conditions that required Chinese operators to buy products from creditor countries.⁶¹ For example, in 1988 the Canadian government offered China a twenty-year low-interest loan for assisting the exports of Nortel Networks' products to the Chinese booming market. By 1993 the total "soft loans" used in purchasing foreign digital switches had amounted to ¥760 million.[62]

From the late 1980s to the early 1990s, the Chinese telecommunications equipment market, including both rural and backbone networks, had been occupied by several multinationals, such as Japan's NEC and Fujitsu, the American company Lucent, Canada's Nortel, Sweden's Ericsson, Germany's Siemens, Belgium's BTM, as well as France's Alcatel. This was known as domination by "seven countries and eight product systems [*qiguobazhi*]." These foreign companies not only charged extremely high prices for equipment products and services but also dominated China's telecommunications technology standards. Under this situation, Chinese telecommunications operators could barely adopt unified standards or products due to fragmented markets controlled by different foreign equipment suppliers. As Ren Zhengfei pointed out, Huawei and other Chinese homegrown telecommunications manufacturers had been situated in the most crucial market environment dominated by foreign vendors from the outset, which resembled the era of invasion of the "Eight-Nation Alliance" in Qing China. Ren clearly recognized that technological import and adoption were unlikely to make the country gain independence of industrial and innovation capability. Therefore, Huawei—reflecting the meaning of the company's name referring to "China can"—rearticulated the state's nationalistic developmental discourse with the company's growth mission. Ren believed that the rise of the Chinese technological company was closely tied to the revival of the Chinese nation from its past humiliations and a means to break foreign giants' domination. This belief has been further consolidated as the bedrock of Huawei's corporate culture in its future development.

Meanwhile, apart from direct imports, Chinese policy makers have made a substantial effort for technology transfer since the mid-1980s with an attempt to promote the localization of foreign technology. To facilitate technology transfer and indigenous manufacturing capability, the Chinese government encouraged foreign companies to set up jointly owned companies. Although this approach was implemented, it came with high costs. For example, China's first joint venture in telecom equipment, Shanghai Bell, was founded on extremely unfair conditions with the Belgium telecommunications company BTM. The Chinese partner had to pay BTM high prices for technological transfer fees and key component purchases as well as $280 per port of telecom equipment production.[63] In 1986 China's first production lines of digital switch S1240 were launched by Shanghai Bell. By the 1990s, most of the leading global telecom equipment vendors had established joint ventures in China.[64] For the Chinese government, the cooperation of foreign capital and the Chinese SOEs was devised to help domestic players foster indigenous manufacturing capability and to enable the state to maintain the ownership control in the industry.[65] These major joint ventures picked up market shares rapidly and occupied dominant positions in the early 1990s.

Nevertheless, the process of technological localization through joint ventures was slow, as core technologies and key components were still controlled by a handful of foreign partners. Especially after 1989, the Coordinating Committee on Export Controls (COCOM)—an organization under the control of the United States and its allies during the Cold War—imposed restrictions on high-technology exports from Western countries to China. Although geopolitical tension impeded the Chinese state's effort of technology transfer from the West, it provided an opportunity for indigenous companies' development. A turning point occurred in 1991 when the first Chinese advanced indigenous digital switch, HJD-04, was jointly invented by the PLA Information Engineering University and the state-owned enterprise Post and Telecommunications Industry Corp. (PTIC). This technical progress tremendously boosted Chinese homegrown companies' technological capacity as well as their nationalist pride. To further promote the large-scale commercialization of this product, a state-owned conglomerate, the Great Dragon Group, was founded by grouping eight other SOEs. This state-backed company obtained considerable policy support from the central government in its goal of seizing the market back from foreign rivals.

Following the success of the Great Dragon Group, Huawei decided to shift its focus from sales of PBX to self-invented telecommunications office telephone exchanges in 1992. This indicated that Huawei's business had moved from ICT products targeting small enterprise customers to telecom operators. However, compared to foreign telecommunications giants and government-supported companies, Huawei was completely marginalized in the market. In Ren Zhengfei's words, "Huawei had no capital, no technology, and no 'status' [meaning that Huawei was a non-state-owned company lacking the Chinese government's support]. How could it be possible for a small Chinese firm to survive in the market and grow quickly?"[66] One of the most crucial factors of Huawei's initial success lay in its strategy of exploring alternative markets that had not yet been occupied by transnational corporations and SOEs. China's uneven telecommunications market actually provided Huawei with opportunities for development. As noted by Yuezhi

Zhao, China's unprecedented growth of telecommunications infrastructure in the reform era was compounded by an extremely uneven pattern of network expansion and service provision.[67] Such a disparity inevitably led to the widening urban-rural divide. As of 1993, subscribers of rural residential telephone service accounted for only 18 percent of the country's total telephone subscribers.[68] The national rural-urban gap of telephone penetration reached its peak in 1995.[69] Underdeveloped provinces faced a financial deficit and a shortage of investment to construct their rural lines, because the state excluded rural telephone service from its policy planning and financing.[70]

Apart from the disparity in telecommunications service distribution between rural and urban regions, the single-minded pursuit of modernized technological upgrades also contributed to the unevenness of the domestic market. Due to the disadvantaged status of indigenous manufacturers, the agenda and patterns of China's network expansion and service provision were actually controlled by foreign suppliers. Since the early 1990s, major transnational giants have aggressively lobbied the Chinese government to install fiber-optic cable arteries to upgrade national telecommunications infrastructure in one step. In order to reap more gains and to obtain good records of political performance, coastal provincial governments were eager to revamp existing network equipment with advanced foreign switching technology. But on the other side, the "leapfrogging" plan of systematic network upgrades brought excessive financial burdens for interior provinces that were unable to afford expensive switching systems offered by foreign suppliers. In turn, this widening gap made telecommunications equipment vendors concentrate on lucrative urban markets, excluding rural and remote areas from basic infrastructure development and public services provision.

Contrary to foreign competitors' profit-seeking business strategy, Huawei made a significant strategic decision that had palpable influence on the company's future development. Inspired by Mao's military tactic in the guerrilla war, Ren adopted the strategy of "encircling cities from the countryside" to target rural markets as well as small cities and towns in remote provinces that multinational giants had neglected. In addition, under the decentralized investment regime, local telecommunications operators and authorities were able to make their own choices on equipment purchases. This gave Huawei opportunities to access potential customers in rural markets. In 1992 the company started the innovation and development of digital switches based on the needs of telecommunications infrastructure in underdeveloped areas. To meet the demand in China's unique rural environment, Huawei launched a two-way R&D model to study and solve technical problems by gathering feedback and suggestions from local post and telecommunications bureaus (PTBs). In 1994 Huawei launched the HONET integrated access network and the synchronous digital hierarchy (SDH) product line, becoming the first Chinese firm to install long-distance transmission equipment. In the following year, the advanced digital switch C&C08 ("C" stands for countryside) was introduced in the domestic market, marking a milestone in the company's history as well as in China's telecommunications technology development.

Huawei's self-developed digital switching technology significantly contributed to the development of Chinese telecommunications systems in the 1990s. First, it provided lower prices and better-quality products. By the end of the 1990s, the cost of Chinese switching products had plummeted to twenty-five dollars per port as opposed to five hundred dollars for foreign products. The low-cost supply of core equipment and technology not only accelerated the expansion of China's network infrastructure but also made telecommunications services more affordable for users in underdeveloped areas. Second, apart from the large capacity of Huawei's digital switch, Huawei's switching technology was also compatible with multi-network interoperability, which was easy to upgrade and maintain in multiple operational situations. Contrary to standardized foreign equipment that was primarily suitable in high-end urban networks, Huawei's product possessed strong flexibility and adaptability to multilevel module networking and various service provisions in China's complicated rural environment.

In addition to strong technological capacity, Huawei's considerable success can be attributed to its unique bottom-up market strategy or Maoist "mass campaign" strategy. It helped the company carve out a niche market in the midst of soaring competition. As major multinationals had already monopolized the supply of mainstream equipment, Huawei had difficulty in accessing tier-one telecom operators. At the beginning, Ren had to use personal political connections to obtain contracts from local PTBs. A turning point occurred in 1993 when Huawei successfully deployed its self-developed switch in Yiwu, a small city of Zhejiang Province, which helped the company gain reputation and recognition. Subsequently, a nationwide market network gradually formed. The company's sales staff and technicians penetrated deep into numerous small counties and townships across China to establish their rural bases. For example, Huawei's major foreign rival, Ericsson, had only three or four employees working on telecom networking systems in Heilongjiang Province. In contrast, Huawei sent more than two hundred people to live and work in county towns and small cities across the province starting in the early 1990s.[71] This mass campaign strategy helped the

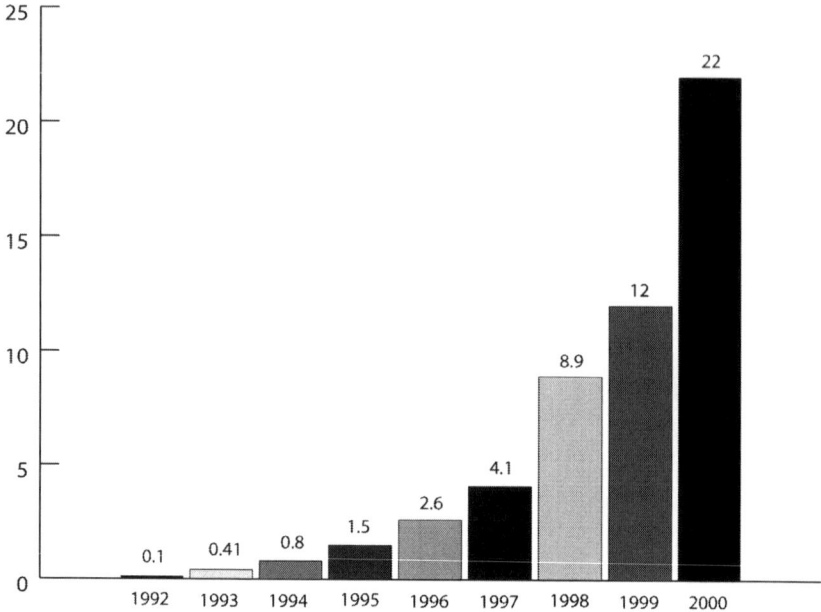

Figure 1.1. Huawei's Annual Sales Revenues, 1992–2000 (RMB billion)
Source: MEI, *Yearbook of Electronic Industry* (1993–2001).

company build up supply chains quickly. In addition, the company chose to ally with PTBs and municipal governments to set up joint ventures. In order to gain support from local governments and telecommunications operators, Huawei promised to allocate 33 percent of its sales profit as dividends to local PTBs' stakeholders. This bottom-up market strategy, which fundamentally distinguished Huawei from foreign rivals' urban-centric approach, helped it gain a firm foothold in marginalized markets. In addition, under the state's auspices of "telephones to every village," starting in the mid-1990s, Huawei became the largest supplier in China's rural telecommunications equipment market in 1995 with annual sales revenue of ¥1.5 billion. Starting in 1997, the central government designated Huawei as a national champion due to the company's significant contribution to China's indigenous ICT development. By 1998 Huawei's revenue had increased sixfold to ¥8.9 billion, the majority of which came from rural areas. At the same time, the company managed to obtain almost a quarter of the domestic market share in public switched telephone networks, overtaking Shanghai Bell as the largest manufacturer of digital automatic switches in China.[72]

Huawei's rise in the 1990s was closely related to the state's policy shift in the telecommunications equipment sector. The embargo initiated by the

West in 1989 not only made the Chinese state realize the strategic importance of commanding core information technologies but also further strengthened the state's determination in breeding its own homegrown companies with competitive capabilities. Fueled by techno-nationalistic discourse, Huawei persistently promoted its corporate image as a source of national pride and institutionalized the nationalistic value of "serving the country through industrial development" (*chanye baoguo*) as well as "rejuvenating the state through science and technology" (*kejiao xingguo*) as the corporate tenet. It is important to note that Huawei's discourse of nationalism was more than a public relations strategy. Throughout Huawei's early stage of development, Ren kept challenging the post-Mao technological development policies that hinged the hope of technological modernization on the acquisition and indigenization of advanced Western technologies. In Ren's words: "If the market was completely lost under 'trading market for technology,' what technology was really mastered? It is painful to realize that without our own core technology the independence of our industry would be only an empty slogan. Without an independent national industry there would be no independence of a nation."[73] In 1994 when Jiang Zemin visited Huawei, Ren explicitly advised that "switching equipment technology was related to national security. And if a nation did not have its own switching equipment, it was like a nation without its own military."[74] Ren's advice was eventually adopted by the central leadership. In 1996 the Chinese government ended preferential import policies for foreign digital switching equipment, and at the same time domestic manufacturers enjoyed discounts on sales-related taxes and priority of government procurement. Under the state's selective import-substitution policy, a few national telecommunications equipment manufacturers, represented by Great Dragon—Datang, ZTE, and Huawei (the so-called *judazhonghua*, according to the first characters of these four companies' names)—have successfully broken the market entrenchment dominated by foreign transnational corporations. By the end of the 1990s, Chinese-made switching equipment had taken 75 percent of the domestic market share in the fixed-line transmission sector.[75] Huawei achieved its tremendous breakthrough in the high-tech market and leaped forward to the next stage of development.

THE SECOND STAGE: DEVELOPMENTAL DILEMMA IN THE NEOLIBERAL RESTRUCTURING

Throughout the 1990s the Chinese ICT manufacturing industry sustained hypergrowth, with annual average growth rates of more than 30 percent. By the end of the Ninth Five-Year Plan (1996–2000), the output of the electronics industry had amounted to ¥1,061.4 billion, accounting for the largest share of the national economy.[76] The fixed-asset investment of the ICT industry had reached ¥97.4 billion, the growth rate of which was three times the rate of gross domestic product (GDP) growth. Fueled by the boom of telecommunications development, the telecom equipment manufacturing sector demonstrated the fastest growth, with the output of ¥24.95 billion at the spectacular average growth rate of 73 percent. Particularly, the output of Chinese-made exchange switches had surpassed 44 million ports, ranking first in the world.[77]

The telecommunications networks expansion was also remarkable as a result of the state's intensified investment. In the first half of the 1990s, China installed more than 73 million phone lines, more than all other developing countries combined.[78] This has made China one of the largest telecommunications networks in the world. By 2000 the number of telephone subscribers (including fixed-line phone and mobile users) had surpassed 200 million, ranking second in the world. Switchboard capacity also leaped from 4 million lines before 1985 to 179 million in 2000.[79] As discussed above, Chinese indigenous telecommunications equipment manufacturers significantly benefited from the state-initiated ICT development and selective import-substitution policy. However, at the turn of the century, the Chinese ICT industry underwent drastic neoliberal restructuring, especially upon China's accession to the World Trade Organization (WTO). This shift in the policy regime brought tremendous challenges to indigenous companies again and directly changed Huawei's developmental trajectories in its growth model and market expansion.

Starting in 1998 a new round of structural reforms was launched to escalate the process of corporatization and deregulation in the telecommunications sector. This dramatically shifted Chinese telecommunications carriers' priority from public service provision to profit-oriented business activities, further institutionalizing the pervasive urban bias in network buildup and undermining the carriers' investment incentive in rural telecommunications development. In addition, a discourse advocating a move from the "telephony era" to the "post-telephony era" came to dominate the agenda of the telecom reform. According to this view, the priority of telecommunications development should be given to the provision of more advanced communication services, such as mobile communications for enlarging customer bases in the high-end market over simple infrastructure-building for basic telephony. Under this wave of neoliberal restructuring, the uneven pattern of China's telecommunications development was further entrenched. The promise of making "telephone access in every administrative village" in the Ninth Five-Year Plan eventually turned out to be a failure. By the end of 2000, only 82.9 percent of administrative villages across the country had telephone access, nearly 20 percent short of the state's target.[80] Rural telephone expansion further stagnated in the 2000s with a slow rate of increase at the beginning of the Tenth Five-Year Plan (2001–2005). As a result, telecommunications operators largely ignored the demand for network infrastructure equipment in rural areas, which further squeezed Huawei's market growth and revenues. Although Huawei's strategy of "encircling cities from the countryside" to some extent incorporated Ren's initiative of serving the goal of communicative equality, market pressures compounded by profit incentive forced Huawei to shift the company's focus from rural markets to urban areas. Since 1998 Huawei has gradually obtained contracts from first-tier operators in developed regions, generating considerable profits from the surge in urban demand. By 1999 Huawei's profit had amounted to ¥1.7 billion, far outperforming other Chinese indigenous ICT companies and ranking at the top of the list of "China's 100 Strong Electronics Companies."[81]

Though Huawei and other Chinese manufacturers had dominated the digital switch market by the end of the 1990s, the profit margin for sales of fixed-line switching was in decline. The growth rate of fixed-line telephone subscribers also slowed considerably. Meanwhile, as part of the neoliberal reform agenda, the Chinese government made special efforts to reduce cross-subsidization in telephone service rates with an attempt to promote domestic competition. In 2000 the Ministry of Information Industry (MII), the State Development and Planning Council, and the Ministry of Finance (MOF) jointly announced cuts of more than 50 percent to telecom service fees and the elimination of fixed-line telephone installation fees.[82] The increasingly saturated market, along with the speedy decline of profit in the fixed-line telephone segment, drove foreign manufacturers to withdraw from the Chinese digital switching equipment market and to cultivate new areas of capital accumulation. As noted by Zixiang Tan, foreign multinational corporations may have strategically chosen to sacrifice the market share of low-end, mature products in exchange for predominant positions in high-end products.[83]

Meanwhile, China's telecommunications market expansion has also been driven by the unprecedented growth of mobile networks and services. The first generation of Chinese mobile communication services started in 1987 in Guangdong Province with an initial 700 subscribers. Since the early 1990s, mobile communication has been regarded as "the priority of all priorities" in the national development plan.[84] As a result of escalated mobile network expansion, Chinese mobile phone subscribers increased from 3.63 million to 84.53 million, with an annual growth rate of more than 80 percent from 1995 to 2000.[85] By July 2001, the number of China's mobile phone users had reached 120.6 million, surpassing that of the United States and constituting the world's largest mobile phone subscriber base. By the end of 2003, Chinese mobile phone users had increased to 230 million, surpassing fixed-line telephone subscribers for the first time. The increasing demand also diverted huge investment from fixed-line network to mobile network sectors.

Although the explosive market expansion made China an indispensable growth engine of the world's ICT industry, Chinese indigenous telecommunications equipment vendors had to face head-to-head competition in terms of transnational rivals. As part of the negotiations on its accession to the WTO, China agreed to open up the telecommunications sector and liberalize its trade and investment regime. In 1995 the State Council approved the catalog of industries opening up for foreign capital, encouraging foreign direct investment in telecom-related products. Moreover, according to the terms of the WTO Information Technology Agreement, China promised to eliminate import duties on a large number of ICT products, including mobile telecommunications equipment. This rule led to a considerable influx of foreign advanced mobile communication products that neither indigenous companies nor joint ventures had the capacity to produce at that time.[86] In addition to trade liberalization, China has also gradually lifted foreign ownership control in the telecom manufacturing sector. These liberalization policies have directly exposed indigenous firms to international competition.

At the same time, transnational vendors sought to explore the booming Chinese market as a powerful impulse to renew capital accumulation. Leading global manufacturers increased investment in China through large-scale mergers and acquisitions (M&A). For example, in 2000 Alcatel spent $312 million to buy a controlling share of Shanghai Bell. In 2001 America's Emerson Network Power acquired Huawei's subsidiary for $750 million, making it one of the largest M&A deals in China's ICT industry at that time.[87] Other transnationals such as Ericsson and Motorola also sharply increased their capital and R&D inputs in the Chinese market.[88] The involvement of FDI constituted a dominant force in restructuring Chinese ICT market structure.

China's neoliberal reform became tangled with the market imperative of transnational business power and struggles from domestic players. Such political-economic dynamics rendered China's telecommunications industry more conflicts in policy making and market competition. At the core of these struggles was the deployment of mobile network standards. In 1994 Guangzhou became the first city to launch the Global System for Mobile Communication (GSM)—the second generation of mobile communications backed by Europe, with foreign vendors such as Ericsson, Nokia, Motorola, Siemens, and Alcatel dominating the supplies of essential equipment ranging from base stations to terminal devices. In the following year, China Unicom and China Telecom announced the adoption of the European-backed GSM standard under the lobbies of leading European equipment manufacturers such as Ericsson, Nokia, Siemens, and Alcatel.

In tandem with the state's developmental plan for mobile communications, Huawei also started the research and development of GSM equipment in 1995. For Huawei, the fixed-line sector has reached a "market growth ceiling," yet the future of the emerging mobile communications market seemed to be unlimited during the transition period. However, Huawei's long march into the mobile network market was fueled with obstructions and difficulties. As Ren Zhengfei recalled, "[At that time] we only had R&D capabilities in the fixed-network communications domain. The threshold to mobile communications technology was unprecedentedly high."[89] At the beginning, only a dozen people were engaged in R&D activities of the GSM system, the capability of which was significantly weak compared to foreign companies' large R&D teams. In 1997 Huawei released China's first independently developed GSM system and initially deployed the commercial trial network in Inner Mongolia in 1998. At the same time, Huawei won the first commercial GSM network contract in Gansu—the less-developed province in the interior region—to replace Ericsson's equipment.[90] To strengthen technological capability, Huawei later teamed up more than five hundred scientists, researchers, and engineers and spent more than ¥1 billion in the GSM system development.

Unlike the fixed-line network market in which local PTBs had financial autonomy in making purchasing decision, the mobile network construction and the procurement of telecom equipment were completely controlled by provincial telecom operators. Until 1999, when China expedited the nationwide expansion of its GSM network, Huawei was allowed for the first time to enter the technical bids for provincial GSM projects. Despite foreign vendors' predominance in the supplies of GSM equipment, the Chinese government became deliberate in supporting homegrown manufacturers in the mobile network sector. In Fujian Province, for example, the supplies of GSM network equipment had been dominated by Nokia's imported products. The extremely expensive foreign equipment sold in the Chinese market even drove the importers to smuggle mobile telecommunications goods to gain huge profits. After the bust of the most notorious "Yuanhua Smuggling Case" in 1999, which involved the smuggling of Nokia's GSM equipment worth $60 million, Fujian telecom operators became more inclined to purchase indigenous firms' products.[91] This case was also a turning point for Huawei to tap into the mobile communications markets in China's coastal provinces. Xi Jinping, who was then the governor of Fujian Province, declared, "Fujian authorities treated Chinese and foreign equipment equally. Chinese mobile communication equipment manufacturers are able to compete on the same stage as global companies. I hope Huawei could . . . contribute to Fujian's network construction and our own country."[92] In 1999 Huawei won a ¥300 million GSM contract in Fujian, the largest contract awarded to domestic Chinese telecom equipment manufacturers at that time. The company was later involved as one of the primary suppliers of Fujian's GSM expansion project. The much lower prices Huawei offered helped Fujian telecom operators reduce the budgets of the investment from $500 million to less than $410 million.[93]

However, foreign vendors that had withdrawn from the fixed-line telephone equipment market came to launch price wars against Huawei in order to prevent Chinese firms from entering the new lucrative market. Because these foreign manufacturers had not only advanced infrastructure-building capacity but also dominated the 2G handset market, they were allowed to use extremely high profits from sales of handset products to cross-subsidize the high costs of the network equipment sector. After Huawei released its 2G network products, foreign vendors gradually reduced the price to ¥900 per line, far lower than Huawei's ¥1,200 per line. Noticeably, after a surge of foreign capital in the mobile equipment manufacturing industry, the cost-competitive advantage that Chinese indigenous manufacturers had enjoyed in the fixed-line digital switching market appeared to be irrelevant in the emerging mobile communications market. In 2000 Chinese manufacturers acquired only 3 percent, 5 percent, and less than 7 percent of the home market share for GSM transmission towers, mobile switches, and handsets, respectively.[94]

To overcome this challenge from leading global vendors, Huawei again implemented the strategy of "encircling cities from the countryside" to explore market opportunities. Specifically, the company invented a GSM scheme called the "Edge Network." This innovative solution had the advantages of large-scale coverage, low cost, and high speed in comparison with foreign products. It also allowed telecom operators to provide 2G mobile service coverage in vast rural areas and unconnected communities that were perceived as "dead zones of telecommunications networks." Huawei's GSM base stations, which featured flexibility in onsite installation and deployment, were widely deployed in Guizhou, Hunan, Sichuan, Liaoning, and other underdeveloped regions. Nevertheless, the policy of urban bias excluded Huawei from the mainstream mobile equipment market and trapped the company in a long-term period of losses in the domestic wireless sector. By 2005 Huawei and other Chinese vendors had accounted for less than 10 percent market share in the domestic GSM equipment market.[95]

Under pressures from the US government and telecommunications firms, in 2001 China Unicom officially introduced the US-based CDMA (code division multiple access) standard for high-end markets with an initial investment of ¥24 billion on network build-out. Different from the open GSM system, CDMA charged equipment manufacturers excessively high royalties for networks and handset production. As a result, Qualcomm, the owner of the majority of CDMA standard patents, along with other North American–based licensed manufacturers, such as Motorola, Lucent, and Nortel, dominated China's CDMA market. As the enclosed CDMA system set a high barrier to new market entrants, the state-backed ZTE was the only Chinese manufacturer that had the capacity to provide a full range of CDMA equipment and network solutions, including base stations, mobile switches, intelligent networks, and mobile phones. Despite foreign domination in the home market, ZTE gradually established an enviable position in CDMA markets along with its global expansion. By the end of the 2000s, ZTE had become one of the largest suppliers in global CDMA markets. The company acquired one-third of the Chinese market and topped global CDMA markets, with a 30 percent market share.[96]

In contrast, due to the lack of capital and R&D input, Huawei's initial development in CDMA technologies was much slower than its foreign and domestic rivals. By 2007 the company's home market share had been less than 2 percent. To pick up the market share in this most lucrative communication sectors, Huawei launched bloody street battles with foreign manufacturers and ZTE in the late 2000s when Huawei had already achieved a considerable success in oversea markets. In 2008 China Telecom spent the huge amount of ¥110 billion acquiring CDMA services from Unicom. In order to occupy an advantaged position in the bidding for China Telecom's CDMA projects, Huawei offered extremely low prices for selling its network equipment, only one-twentieth of Alcatel-Lucent's bidding price and one-tenth of ZTE's price.[97] Through the most crucial price wars, Huawei managed to acquire 30 percent of China Telecom's contracts (see fig. 1.3) and the opportunities to enter some strategic cities such as Beijing, Guangzhou, Tianjin, and Shanghai.[98]

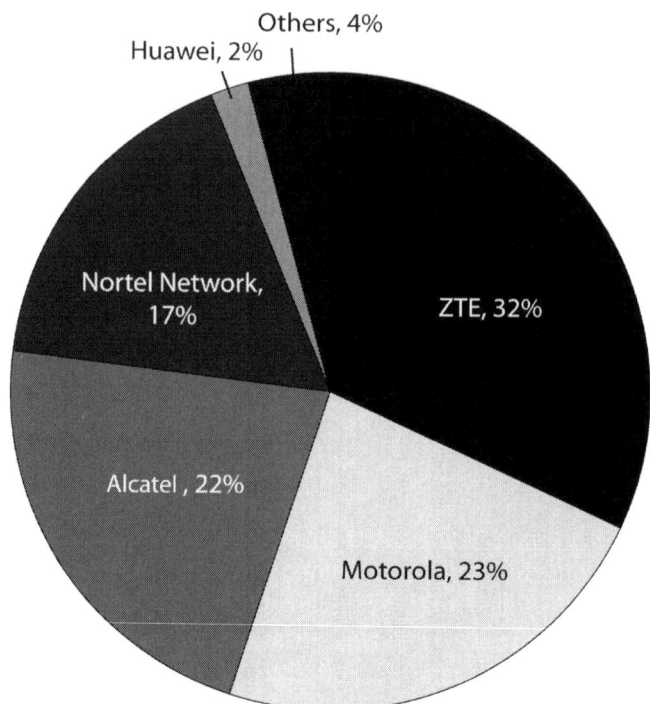

Figure 1.2. China Telecom's CDMA Equipment Market Share, 2007
Source: China Telecommunications website C114.

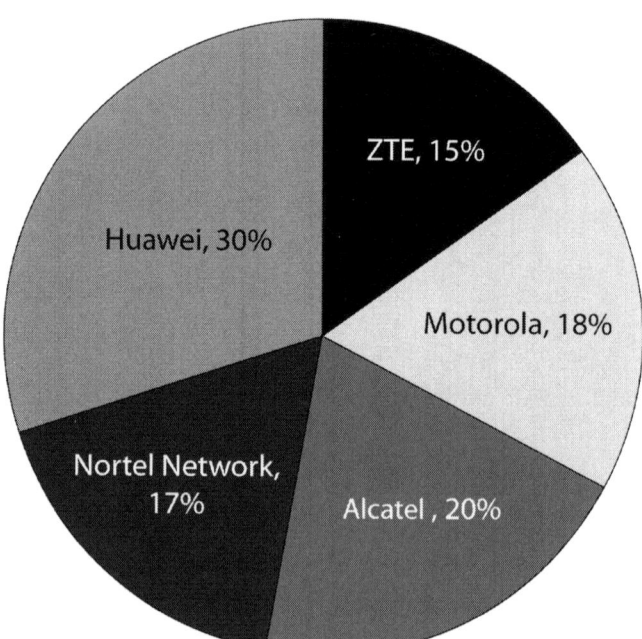

Figure 1.3. China Telecom's CDMA Equipment Market Share, 2008
Source: China Telecommunications website C114.

Huawei's move from a manufacturer of low-to-medium-end products to a supplier of equipment for China's backbone networks exemplified the dilemma and struggle that Chinese indigenous firms faced in the country's structural transformations. Noticeably, China's overheated telecommunications market expansion during the 2000s not only drove redundant investment in wasteful network resources but also led to an oversupply of telecom equipment capacity. This period became a critical juncture for Huawei to adjust its mode of internal accumulation amid the crisis of overcapacity to regain its domestic market status.

THE THIRD STAGE: REGAINING DOMESTIC MARKET STATUS IN THE POST-CRISIS ERA

In view of the extremely uneven mode of China's ICT development and the erosion of the home market by multinationals, Huawei was forced to escape from the domestic market and shift its focus to overseas expansion. Driven by strong international demands and China's outward-looking initiatives during the boom years, Huawei's revenues and profits have significantly increased since 2000. Although the telecom industry experienced a major downturn after the dot-com bubble, Huawei sustained its strong growth thanks to its expansion into developing nations. By 2005 Huawei's overseas sales had accounted for 58 percent of its total sales, exceeding its domestic sales for the first time. Though Huawei's internal accumulation grew steadily, the FDI-dependent policy underpinning China's neoliberal-oriented telecom reform became the greatest challenge to Chinese indigenous firms. The "historical loss of the domestic 2G market" especially exemplifies the failure of China's liberalized industrial policy, which made it more difficult for the country and its domestic players to reverse technological dependence.[99] To overcome such difficulties, Huawei started to make some strategic changes, aiming to recapture its power in the domestic market and rebuild its advantages in internal accumulation.

While Huawei has gained tremendous manufacturing capability and achieved enormous success in the telecom equipment market, the core of global competition in the ICT industry has changed from manufacturing to networking innovations, making the cost-efficient advantage Huawei gained in the fixed-line and 2G mobile network era less competitive. The change also fueled Huawei's restructuring for its developmental strategies, moving from a telecommunications equipment manufacturer to a leading ICT solution provider. It means Huawei was no longer constrained in low-end and low-value-added mass production but tended to extend its control over the whole value chain ranging from ICT equipment production to customized services. The company's strategic change was in accordance with the Chinese state's most recent industrial restructuring plan, which endeavored to reach a self-sufficient innovation trajectory. This trend of restructuring was exemplified in China's initiative of developing its homegrown standards, a "delinking strategy" to nurture Chinese indigenous technological standards on the one hand and to further promote domestic firms by fostering a relatively independent domestic market on the other.[100] Though Huawei's investment in the 3G indigenous TD-SCDMA (time division synchronous code division multiple access) standard was limited due to its pragmatic attitude toward this questionable technology, there is no doubt that the buildup of "a China-only accumulation regime" provided vast opportunities for Huawei and other Chinese indigenous firms to regain their domestic market shares, which had been ceded to foreign rivals in the 2G era. In 2010 three domestic companies, ZTE, Huawei, and Datang Telecom, gained, respectively, 34.2 percent, 31.0 percent, and 13.4 percent market share in the China Mobile TD-SCDMA market, creating a competitive advantage as well as full-range value chains in the 3G market.[101] In this process of technical standard setting, Chinese indigenous ICT firms not only acted as equipment suppliers but also became involved in the activities of standard innovation and infrastructure buildup.

During the transition from 3G to 4G, Chinese indigenous manufacturers have gained early advantages in the domestic 4G market from the outset. In December 2013 the Chinese self-developed 4G standard TD-LTE (time division long-term evolution) license was first issued. In order to nurture the indigenous standard, the Chinese regulator purposely delayed licensing the European-backed FDD-LTE (frequency division duplex long-term evolution) until 2015. Meanwhile, the Chinese government has aggressively promoted the TD-LTE standard outside of the country, which has brought about broader support for the locally developed standard on the global scale and has allowed Chinese telecom equipment companies to expand rapidly in the global LTE markets. Benefiting from the Chinese government's protectionist policies, Huawei has become one of the largest LTE network equipment providers in the world, paving the way for its 5G network construction in the global scale.

The "China-only accumulation regime" policy in the ICT sector has seemed to pay off toward the 5G era. Unlike 2G, 3G, and 4G, China is far ahead of the global 5G race, in which Huawei has already claimed leadership in multiple areas of core technologies. As an integral part of China's economic restructuring agenda, 5G, along with 5G-related applications, was embraced as a "strategic emerging industry" and a "new area of growth" in China's Thirteenth Five-Year Plan (2016–2020). What matters is not only the strategic development of 5G technology per se but 5G-related industrial chains that were interwoven with the Chinese state's initiative in nurturing technological edges and market frontiers. In this process, domestic players, including Huawei, have played a critical role in establishing China's 5G leadership.

In fact, Huawei began its 5G R&D as early as 2009, far ahead of the Chinese state's national plan for 5G development. By leveraging the company's R&D capabilities, Huawei took the lead in China's 5G Promotion Group to complete a domestic 5G R&D trial, significantly outperforming other rivals. However, Huawei's predominance in 5G areas has given rise to widespread security concerns from Western countries. Despite the controversy surrounding Huawei, the company has continued to lead the way in the domestic market by aligning with the Chinese state's systematic efforts of economic restructuring.

As analyzed above, the rapid growth of Huawei can be attributed to the impetus of China's telecommunications revolution from the late 1980s onward. The explosive expansion of China's network construction made the carrier network business the company's most lucrative segment. However, excessive and blind investment in network upgrades vis-à-vis the increasingly saturated market has inevitably led to the crisis of overcapacity in the carrier network business. Moreover, tensions between national security concerns and the rules of neoliberal competition also exploded into economic and political conflicts in international markets, which led to unilateral protectionist measures in some countries. All of these factors posed challenges to Huawei's steady growth in the network business and thereby motivated the company to expand its operations to the segments of enterprise business and consumer devices.

In the area of enterprise business, while Huawei remained far behind its main foreign competitors, such as Cisco, the company has claimed strength in more recent years by focusing on high-value industries and the most innovative ICT technologies, including cloud computing, big data, software-defined networking, and the Internet of Things (IoT).[102] This rapid growth came about as a result of increased capital spending from the transnational business classes that were clamoring for the buildup and enlargement of enterprise networks and for an ICT-enabled industry ecosystem. As Schiller argues, the process of "attaching profit imperatives to connectivity" generated new sites of commodification that formed and stimulated market growth.[103] This "recomposition" of network ecosystem provided vast market opportunities for ICT companies to assume the role of suppliers of network "plumbing." Apart from market demand, Huawei's growth in the domestic enterprise segment was also a result of the Chinese state's policies for protecting the country's network sovereignty. Especially in the aftermath of Edward Snowden's revelation,[104] network security has become a key concern for the Chinese state to reshape its ICT-related industrial strategies. There has been a trend toward the government's choosing to replace foreign suppliers with domestic firms in strategic sectors such as public safety, finance, transportation, and energy in order to ensure the state's control over backbone networks and information. As a result of this policy trend, Huawei has quickly gained local market share at the expense of that of foreign rivals. Some US multinationals, including Cisco, Apple, IBM, and Qualcomm, nevertheless, are facing considerable revenue decline in the Chinese market.

Another significant change of Huawei's capital accumulation was is its strategic focus on the consumer device business segment since 2012. As consumer devices began to have tremendous impact on the recomposition of network commodity chains, consumer demand for ubiquitous access to network services generated a new profitable site of capital accumulation.[105] Unlike other leading global brands that built upon a large user base, Huawei only started its handset manufacturing business in 2003. Before Huawei created its own brand of consumer devices, the company primarily played the role as an original equipment manufacturer (OEM) for leading global brands, such as Motorola and Siemens, as well as for major telecom operators, including Vodafone, PCCW, and eMobile. The explosive expansion of mobile communications in China in the early 2000s motivated many other Chinese domestic electronics manufacturers, such as TCL, Haier, and Lenovo, to rush into the handset market. However, these domestic manufacturers relied heavily on the practice of importing key components and assembling them into branded final products, which entrenched them in the downstream position of the global supply chain.

Huawei, however, fostered a business model that was completely different from that of its peer vendors. Since 2012 Huawei has been motivated to develop its own branded consumer devices because of the serious challenge to its carrier network business segment. Along with its advanced hardware manufacturing capabilities, Huawei leveraged its expertise in network technologies as well as innovation in core chipset technologies and design capacity. Instead of providing low-margin "cheap" devices, the company determined to renew its focus on the high-end market to build up a globally recognized brand. The strong technological competences combining its

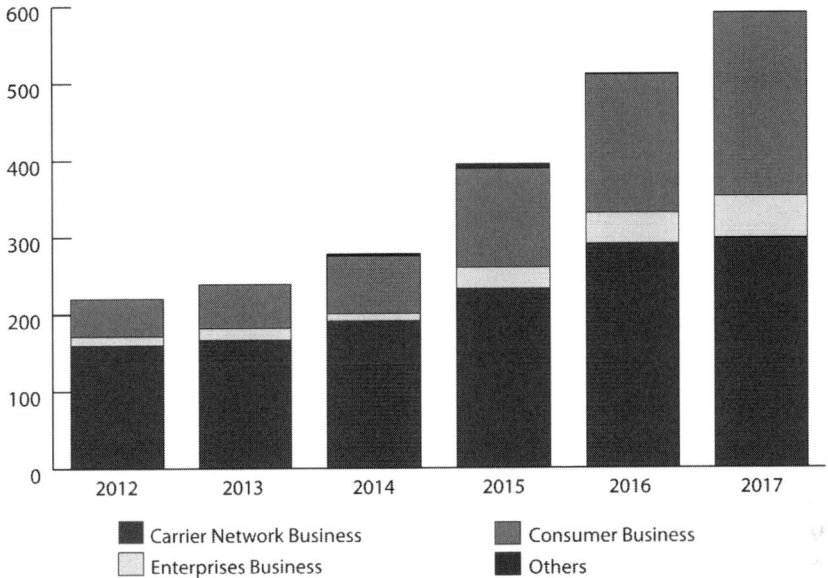

Figure 1.4. Huawei's Revenue by the Business Segment from 2012 to 2017 (RMB billion)
Source: Huawei Annual Report (2012–2017)

strengthening marketing strategies enabled the company to expand rapidly in the consumer device market. The sales revenue of Huawei's consumer business segment grew from ¥48.4 billion in 2012 to ¥348.9 billion in 2018, which has become another major source of revenue and profit for the company.[106] Huawei and other domestic newcomers, including OPPO, Vivo, and Xiaomi, dominated the Chinese smartphone market with more than 65 percent market share in 2019.[107] The changing market dynamics generated more market opportunities for Huawei and other domestic players to catch up and foster a competitive advantage. This not only enabled Huawei to set the pace for recomposition around consumer demands, but it also reoriented the company's mode of internal accumulation by leveraging the domestic demand-driven growth model.

Conclusion

This chapter places the story of Huawei against the backdrop of China's historical industrial development, which was rife with twists and contradictions. To some extent, Huawei's developmental trajectory exemplifies Chinese homegrown ICT firms' endeavors, hopes, and dilemmas in the process of China's ICT-driven development. At the same time, it is worth emphasizing that paradoxical state policies also created a distinct internal accumulation regime for Chinese corporate players. The entangled relations between the Chinese state, Chinese companies, and transnational capital are illustrated in Huawei's development.

The rise of Huawei was deeply rooted in China's digital "leap forward" strategy. It came to symbolize a continuity of China's nation-centric developmental inspiration and the legacies of self-reliant development and was enmeshed with the country's aspirations of reintegration into transnational digital capitalism. The unleashed market imperative coupled with the state's catch-up initiative has created an unprecedented opportunity for the growth of domestic ICT firms. Huawei was clearly the key early beneficiary of the state's market-oriented industrial restructuring and telecommunications revolution starting in the 1980s. But at the same time, the Chinese state's pursuit of the developmental strategy through exchanging market access for technology access has led to the loss of China's burgeoning markets to foreign companies and stifled fledgling Chinese domestic firms in their initial stage of development. This uneven mode of development has further generated structural dependence on imported technology and foreign capital, shaping China's ICT industries in a way to "serve as a downstream industrial cluster in the globalized chain of production."[108]

Despite these substantial development dilemmas, Huawei still managed to adopt an alternative mode of development to break away from technological dependence by leveraging its research and development capacities as well as its distinct market strategies. The unevenness in China's domestic market, which was primarily characterized by the concentration of foreign capital in the urban high-end market, motivated Huawei to explore alternative markets in the rural region. It also helped the company gain some maneuvering space and establish a distinct capital logic of internal accumulation. It is important to note that the state's import-substitution policy in the fixed-line equipment sector also contributed to Huawei's growth in this relatively mature market segment. However, the deepening neoliberal reform, especially the Chinese state's aggressive initiative to leapfrog into the era of mobile communications since the 1990s, has led to the consolidation of foreign giants in the domestic ICT market, which also directly engendered threats to domestic corporate players in rapidly expanding markets. The eroding market space as well as competitive pressure forced Huawei to explore overseas markets to evade foreign rivals at home and create a new growth engine abroad. The Chinese state's "going-out" policy, as well as the massive demand from the international market, then served as a catalyst to Huawei's international expansion. To some degree, Huawei's choice of internationalization at the beginning was merely a defensive strategy against transnational capital power rather than a preemptive or aggressive strategy driven by an expansionary initiative. This "inside-out" strategy constituted one of the distinct characteristics of Huawei's transnationalization. In the next two chapters, the trajectory of Huawei's expansion into the global South and global North is unfolded in detail. The formation of its transnational accumulation regime, expansionary patterns, and implications are discussed.

Meanwhile, in parallel with Huawei's success in overseas markets, the company began to give more priorities to the domestic market, especially to China's burgeoning enterprise and consumer markets in recent years. It is important to remember that the Chinese state's efforts in restructuring and realigning its ICT sector after the financial crisis of 2008 have created indispensable conditions for the rapid growth of Chinese indigenous firms in their home market. Specifically, the state's project that aimed to foster the domestic demand-driven mode of development to some extent motived Huawei to shift its strategic focus from international markets to the home market, or an "outside-in" trajectory, in the current stage of development. On the other hand, the Chinese state's initiative in regaining technological sovereignty, in conjunction with domestic corporate players' cooperation, is conferring more market power on a handful of Chinese ICT conglomerates by way of foreign multinationals' declining influence in the Chinese market. In the post-Snowden era, Huawei might face more opportunities and possibilities in its domestic accumulation along with the Chinese state's ongoing process of industrial restructuring.

CHAPTER 2

Going Global
Outward Expansion into the Global South

Huawei's development was fueled by numerous contradictions in its cycle of internal accumulation. The influx of foreign capital and technology squeezed market share and posed a serious threat to the survival of Chinese indigenous ICT firms. In addition, China's ICT market was caught by the crisis of overcapacity, which pushed domestic players to explore alternative spaces for capital accumulation. The "attracting-in" policy merely represented one side of the Chinese state's initiatives for its reintegration into the global economy. The ultimate end was to "go out" by nurturing a number of national champions that could compete in international markets with the world's leading transnationals. At the forefront of this policy agenda emerged a number of ICT companies that were conceived as significant forces of China's outward-looking initiatives. The following two chapters focus on the expansion of China's corporate power in the South and the North via an analysis of Huawei. After an overview of the evolution of China's external economic policies and the formation of the country's going-out strategy, this chapter provides a detailed account of the initiatives and patterns of Huawei's outward expansion in the global South. A discussion on broader implications of China's role in reshaping global information infrastructure is further unfolded to capture the geopolitical-economic transformations of the global communications order.

The Evolution of China's Foreign Trade and International Investment Regime

The growing presence of Chinese transnational corporations in international trade and investment has increasingly grasped the world's attention. However, a large number of existing studies merely focus on micro-level firm strategies of internationalization, failing to incorporate an analysis of institutional foundations and geoeconomic factors that shape the drivers and instruments of Chinese firms' outward expansion.[1] It should be noted that the growth of Chinese enterprises and their transition into TNCs are closely related to China's global strategic balance in the ever changing international environment. The firm-state relationship is even more significant when considering the far-reaching influence of the globalization of corporate China.[2]

FROM SELF-SUSTAINING MODE TO "OPENING-UP" PROCESS

As discussed in chapter 1, Soviet technology imports jump-started the initial development of China's electronics and telecommunications industries in the 1950s. Nevertheless, foreign trade played a peripheral role under China's self-sufficient mode of economic development throughout the Mao era. With the moral and political value of "Third World internationalism" advocated by Mao, "preinternationalization activities" were established in the form of economic and technical aid to third world countries.[3] By the end of the 1970s, China had spent an average of at least $350 million a year on foreign aid.[4] More important, China's involvement in third world countries' struggle for their independent development and its political alliance with these countries left tremendous legacies for China's reintegration into the world economy and paved the way for Chinese firms' engagement in these areas.

Since 1978 the opening-up policy has been embraced as one of the fundamental principles of the country's developmental strategy. Nevertheless, over the past several decades, the attracting-in policy has actually become a predominant form of China's external economic policy and a driven engine of Chinese economic development, which not only completely replaced Mao's "self-reliant" tenet but also paved the way for greater unevenness in the domestic development. The pragmatic principle of "win-win" development in foreign policy, together with China's embrace of globalized capitalism, came to superimpose over the deep-rooted ideology of Mao's "Third World internationalism." Accordingly, the country's foreign diplomacy strategy has gradually moved away from "economy serving diplomacy" to "diplomacy serving economy."⁵ Under pragmatic foreign policy, the volume of foreign aid to developing countries declined dramatically while the value of China's reception of foreign aid from Western countries and institutions significantly increased.

During the 1980s, the outward economic activities of Chinese firms were mainly constrained in foreign trades and project subcontracting that did not involve large-scale capital investment. China's first export of electronics products can be dated back to 1956, but the categories of export products and destination markets were limited. By 1980 the actual value of electronic goods exports had been under $10 million.⁶ Low-tech products, such as radios, telephones, and electronic tubes, were primarily exported to Hong Kong and Southeast Asian countries. In April 1980 the state-owned China National Electronics Import & Export Corporation (CEIE) was established, monopolizing imports and exports of electronics goods and overseas engineering projects. During the early 1980s, state-owned electronics companies were the primary actors to undertake the country's foreign trade activities.

FDI-DEPENDENT, EXPORT-ORIENTED FOREIGN TRADE REGIME

During the market reform era, foreign trade, especially export-oriented trading activity, was advocated as one of the most important strategies to promote China's ICT industry. With regard to the relationship between domestic demands and overseas exports, Li Tieying, then minister of the electronics industry, emphasized that China's ICT production had to give priority to "foreign markets first and then domestic" (*xianwaihounei*).⁷ In 1993 the new minister, Hu Qili, further declared, "China's ICT industry has to be market oriented, to integrate the domestic to international markets, to promote the internal growth through external markets, and to accelerate the fast growth of the industry."⁸ This development strategy has become a bedrock principle of China's ICT industry, further consolidating China's market-oriented and export-led development regime.

Under these guiding principles, China's exports of ICT goods witnessed impressive rates of growth for decades. The value of China's ICT goods exports escalated from $10 million in 1980 to $591.2 billion in 2010, accounting for 37.5 percent of China's total exports.⁹ Noticeably, the sector of telecom equipment consisted of the largest share of China's ICT exports. In 2010 China exceeded the European Union (EU) to become the largest exporter of telecom equipment products. China's share in world exports of telecom equipment reached 38 percent in 2013.¹⁰

It appears that the ICT sector has become a leading industry supporting China's export-oriented trade regime and the country's leading role in a globalized digital economy. However, China is far from becoming a global technology power in light of its extremely uneven ICT trade system. The growth of China's ICT trade was primarily driven by foreign-invested enterprises (FIEs), including wholly foreign-owned enterprises (WFOEs), joint ventures (JVs), and foreign cooperative JVs. Especially after China's accession into the World Trade Organization, FEIs have accounted for over 80 percent of the country's ICT exports, nearly all in the forms of export processing and assembling.[11] However, it is important to note the tendency that China's domestic firms, especially private firms, have experienced inexorable growth in their exports. In 2013 the export value of domestic firms amounted to $195.8 billion, contributing to 27.5 percent of total exports. Noticeably, the exports by indigenous private firms increased 55.4 percent, consisting of the strongest force of growth in all sectors of exporters.[12]

China's emergence as a key player in global ICT production and trading structure has complex implications. First and foremost, China's integration into the global ICT industrial order has increasingly changed the regionalization of the country's ICT industry value chains and intra-trading relationships. Since the 1970s, Asia has already emerged as a pivotal pole of ICT production and an important trading center. Within these regional networks, China has increasingly assumed a role of "nodes" or pivotal points of these networks by overtaking labor-intensive manufacturing activities from other traditional Asian export manufacturers such as Japan and the four Asian Tigers (Taiwan, South Korea, Hong Kong, and Singapore). Meanwhile, Asian markets have also become the top export destinations of Chinese ICT products. Such regionalization of industrial networks has led to "a new logic of transnational integration based on geographical specialization and tightly linked international sourcing."[13]

In addition to Asian markets, China played the role as a main supplier of American and European ICT consumer markets, becoming the head of a team of "servants" engaging in low-cost and labor-intensive ICT production and exports to the West.[14] This asymmetric North-South production and trade system increased the risk of fragile prosperity for both China and its Asian neighbors. Although some leading Chinese indigenous ICT firms, including Huawei, have attempted to counterattack Western high-end markets in recent years, they have been facing unexpected challenges and difficulties. In order to get rid of such trade dependence, the Chinese state has made massive efforts to alter the composition of the trade structure and to explore alternative export markets. Chinese firms' going-out into the global South thereby became part of China's outward expansion initiatives.

FROM ATTRACTING-IN TO GOING-OUT STRATEGY: THE INSTITUTIONAL FRAMEWORK FOR CHINESE FIRMS' OUTWARD EXPANSION

Under the attracting-in strategy, China has become the largest recipient of foreign direct investment. In contrast, China's outward foreign direct investment (OFDI) regime evolved at a slow pace. In 1979 the State Council permitted Chinese companies' OFDI as one of the Fifteen Measures of Economic Reform. In 1984 the Ministry of Foreign Trade and Economic Cooperation (MOFTEC, today's MOC) enacted the first regulations on OFDI. Moreover, the regulations on foreign exchange relating to overseas investment were published in 1989. Since then, the policy and administrative framework of China's OFDI regime has been established.

Although President Jiang Zemin first came up with the concept of the going-out policy in the Fourteenth Chinese Communist National Congress, in 1992, the primary task of economic development during this stage was still placed on attracting-in activities. It was not until 1997 that Jiang further reiterated the strategic significance of going-out policy, claiming that attracting-in and going-out were two integral components of China's opening-up policy and that they should be complementary to each other. In 2001 the Chinese government established the going-out policy as a national strategy and incorporated it in the Tenth Five-Year Plan for the first time. Under this strategy, the state encouraged Chinese companies with competitive advantages to invest and set up multinational operations abroad, fully taking advantage of "two resources and two markets" (domestic and foreign resources and markets). China's ICT sector was promoted as one of these strategic industries to fulfill the state's going-out initiatives. In 2005 the Ministry of Commerce and the MII jointly launched a directive to "promote Chinese information industry's 'going-out' projects,"[15] with an aim to change the growth mode of China's foreign trade and to explore international markets for domestic ICT firms. Chinese leading ICT firms, including Huawei, ZTE, and Lenovo, were at the forefront of the country's going-out policy in the realm of the information industry.

Since the early 2000s, a series of preferential treatments and instruments have been implemented to support Chinese firms' outward expansion. In late 2005 a special fund for Chinese OFDI was set up by the Ministry of Finance to provide grants and subsidies for Chinese firms, such as medium- and long-term loans on preferential terms and investment insurance. Huawei was one of the beneficiaries of this government-supported fund. Moreover, the state also provided Chinese investors with a lower lending rate credit fund on OFDI projects. At the international level, the Chinese state has also been seeking international protection mechanisms through setting up bilateral and multilateral investment treaties and regional cooperation systems to create a preferential international environment for Chinese companies' overseas activities.

As a result of these going-out preferential policies, Chinese capital's outward investment activities were rapidly unfolding. Since 2007 China-based OFDI has increased dramatically with greater growth rates than that of inward FDI. In 2015 OFDI by Chinese enterprises in overseas markets stood at $145.67 billion, which made China the world's second-largest outward investor behind the United States. It was also the first time Chinese outward FDI exceeded its inward FDI, which means China has become "a capital exporting country" in its true sense.[16]

However, in 2017 China's outward FDI declined for the first time since 2006. After more than one decade of rapid growth in the country's OFDI, the Chinese government has gradually addressed concerns over irrational overseas investments in some "non-strategic industries," such as capital outflows in the sectors of real estate, entertainment, hotels, cinemas, and entertainment. Outbound investments by non-state-owned enterprises that have low long-term solvency were also restricted by the Chinese government, which was used as a measure to protect the country's financial security from potential economic risks. In the meantime, the strengthened US-China trade tensions led to Chinese investors' dramatic pullback in the United States. In 2017 Chinese firms' investment in the United States plunged to $29 billion, a 35 percent drop from 2016.[17] In the same year, the value of Chinese acquisitions in the United States dropped by 90 percent compared to the previous year.[18]

However, the Chinese government still encouraged foreign investment in strategic industries that were critical to the country's economic restructuring. A few companies in ICT manufacturing and information services, which have been assigned central positions in China's industrial upgrade, bear strategic importance for the Chinese state to export its overcapacity abroad and to strengthen its control over the transnational network infrastructure. Meanwhile, the US-China trade war also had a ripple effect in changing the pattern of China's OFDI. There were signs that Chinese outbound capital has increasingly been redirected from the United States to some other destinations, especially to the Belt and Road countries. According to the MOC, the new investment in fifty-nine countries along the Belt and Road routes reached $14.36 billion in 2017.[19] At the same time, the value of the newly signed contractual projects in the sixty-one Belt and Road countries

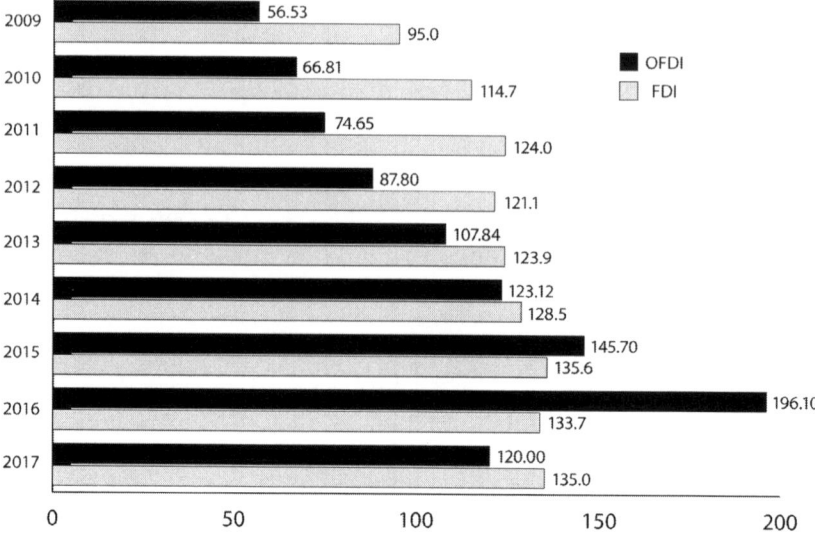

Figure 2.1. China's Inflow/Outflow FDI (US$ billion)
Source: Ministry of Commerce, "Report on Development of China's Outward Investment and Economic Cooperation." (2009–2017).

amounted to $144.32 billion, accounting for 54.4 percent of China's total value of overseas contractual projects.[20] Besides the investment increasing in the Belt and Road Initiative, a growing proportion of China's outbound capital has been diverted into Europe, reaching the highest level of records in 2016. The flows of Chinese capital in the European ICT sector reached €4.8 billion in 2017.[21] The change of China's FDI model suggests that a "de-Americanization" trend of foreign trade and foreign direct investment relations is likely to come about.

THE PATTERNS OF CHINESE FIRMS' OFDI

In foreign direct investment literature a number of theories have been developed to discuss motives of FDI, including resource-seeking, market-seeking, and efficiency-seeking FDI.[22] These theories provided a starting point to explain and generalize motives behind multinationals' OFDI decisions. However, moving from firm-specific initiatives, the state-business alliance that underpins China's going-out regime presents a predominant feature of Chinese firms' OFDI. The formation of China's going-out regime provided a variety of tools to assist Chinese firms in gaining their international presence and prestige. In turn, the expansion of China-based firms to some extent was tied to national interests and the state's initiatives and strategic planning. In general, Chinese firms' outbound investment activities can be characterized by the following patterns, which to some degree align with traditional international business theories yet present some distinct sectoral features at the same time:

1. *Natural resource-seeking activities.* This initiative has become a leading form for Chinese state-owned giants' outward expansion in resource-rich countries across Africa, Latin America, and beyond. In some cases, some Chinese OFDI projects, such as Chinese firms' overseas telecommunications projects, were provided to underdeveloped countries in exchange for natural resource acquisitions. But in more recent years, the pattern of China's outward investment has gradually shifted from acquisitions in the energy sector to manufacturing and commercial services (including ICT-related services), which has constituted a significant new trend of China's OFDI activities.[23]
2. *Market-seeking OFDI through setting up marketing and sales networks abroad.* This form of OFDI activities is usually undertaken by Chinese companies to facilitate their exports to larger markets. The market-seeking motive underpins much of Chinese TNCs' international investment behavior. However, it is important to note that Chinese TNCs' exploration of overseas markets is not simply driven by a firm's portfolio investments but is a response to domestic overcapacity crisis in some industries. As discussed in chapter 1, the unevenness of China's telecommunications equipment market has become a key motive for indigenous companies such as Huawei and ZTE to seek alternative markets for its export-driven strategy.
3. *Efficiency-seeking OFDI.* Apart from establishing sales networks to promote domestic exports, the Chinese government also encouraged Chinese firms with competitive advantages to relocate their operations and productions activities, especially their processing and assembly lines, to lower-cost regions. The government's OFDI report shows that in 2010, 28.6 percent of Chinese enterprises investing abroad were concentrated in manufacturing, accounting for one of the largest categories of Chinese OFDI activities.[24] The MOC confirmed that most of the manufacturing activities were related to ICT enterprises.[25] For example, Huawei has set up large-scale production lines in emerging markets in Brazil, Mexico, and Hungary.[26] Some Southeast Asian countries, such as Indonesia, Vietnam, and Thailand, have also become the most popular destinations for Chinese firms' outbound investments for manufacturing relocation. In addition, Chinese firms have significantly increased

their leverage in Africa. In 2016 China's OFDI stocks of manufacturing in Africa amounted to $4 billion.[27] This implies that a new China-centered and -leading "flying geese model" is forming in the restructuring of the globalized production network. However, it should be noted that China's restructuring on the global scale is no longer entrenched in downstream manufacturing activities. Instead, those technology-intensive, knowledge-based firms that already achieved a certain level of competitiveness in such fields as computers, telecommunications equipment, and electronics equipment manufacturing started to engage in value-added activities in international markets.

4. *Strategic asset-seeking motive.* Chinese firms' OFDI activities have been increasingly motivated by the search for capabilities and competencies, which primarily directed China-based capital toward developed countries. This type of investment often intends to acquire proprietary assets, including access to knowledge stocks and expertise, branding assets, local distribution systems, and managerial expertise. This motive has led to a surge of China's outbound merger and acquisition activities by Chinese firms. In 2016 the M&A value completed in the sector of information-related services grew 214 percent, at a record high of $30.1 billion, becoming the largest sector of the country's overseas M&A.[28] Chinese information-related firms have made a large number of high-profile overseas acquisitions in more recent years. For example, after acquisition of IBM's personal computer (PC) business, Lenovo spent $2.3 billion on IBM's low-end server business and purchased Motorola Mobility from Google for $2.91 billion. China Huaxin, a state-backed ICT firm, bought the enterprise network division of Alcatel-Lucent for €202 million. China Mobile, one of the world's largest mobile carriers, invested more than a billion dollars in telecom companies in Pakistan and Thailand. China's internet giants—Baidu, Alibaba, and Tencent, collectively known as BAT—have aggressively escalated their outward investment in acquiring upscale R&D capacities despite their weakness in overseas market access.

5. *Capital raising/investment activities.* The liberalization of international capital flows has augmented the pace and scale of Chinese ICT firms' capital investment. Capital raised in volatile global financial markets via highly publicized initial public offerings (IPOs) has gradually become a driving factor for Chinese firms' going-out strategies. In US stock markets, the listings of China-based technology firms have grown at an incredible pace since 2008, making up nearly 70 percent of total Chinese stocks.[29] Apart from capital raising activities, a large number of

Chinese ICT firms turned to outbound equity investment as a primary means of OFDI to penetrate overseas markets. For example, China Mobile has accelerated its outbound investment through enlarged capital investment to participate in some countries' telecommunications operating businesses. Chinese firms' active approach to capital investment and integration into the global financial network indicates a new trend of China's OFDI pattern—the combination of financial and ICT capitals—in Chinese firms' going-out initiatives.

In line with China's push to increase OFDI, the Ministry of Industry and Information Technology (MIIT) set up specific strategic goals in relation to Chinese ICT firms' going-out strategy—that is going-out of Chinese products, technology, and standards, as well as services—to improve China's position in global production and value chains.[30] As a leading force of China's corporate globalization, Chinese telecommunications equipment manufacturers have made impressive achievements in their going-out process. According to the MOC reports, Chinese telecommunications equipment exports have experienced rapid growth, with a 46 percent annual growth rate since 2000.[31] In 2014 the OFDI flows in the field of telecommunications reached $14.78 billion. More than 650 Chinese ICT firms had set up foreign subsidiaries by 2014. Alongside exports and outbound investments, Chinese telecommunications equipment manufacturers also assumed a major role as infrastructure construction contractors throughout much of the world. In 2014 Chinese ICT firms won $15.9 billion in overseas construction contracts in the field of telecommunications.[32]

In some specific areas, Chinese ICT firms have achieved remarkable successes: the output of Chinese communications terminal devices has accounted for 90 percent of global production; wireless network equipment has taken almost 30 percent of global market share;[33] seven Chinese ICT multinationals, including Huawei, Lenovo, Xiaomi, TCL, OPPO, Vivo, and ZTE, were ranked on the list of top ten global smartphone vendors in 2018.[34] In addition to ICT firms' activities of internationalization, the companies have been assigned a new role in facilitating other Chinese firms' going-out strategies by providing more-encompassing ICT-related services with global reach. Corporate ICT, such as cloud computing, big data, and web-based IT applications, has been given an unprecedented emphasis in retooling China's traditional industry and supporting Chinese firms' global expansion. This strategy, which was officially dubbed "borrowing boats to go to sea," has underpinned the strategic importance of Chinese ICT companies in the globalization of China's corporate power.³⁵ If the explosive demand from transnational business in China gave rise to the first wave of China's domestic ICT development in the reform era, then the Chinese government's going-out strategy since the 2000s has pressed Chinese indigenous ICT firms with competitive advantages to compete on the global scale, which promoted a new round of prosperity in the ICT sector. Firms like Huawei took up a central position in China's strategic initiative. However, have Chinese ICT firms really possessed technological and market prowess as this evidence indicates? What are the contradictions and ramifications arising from Chinese ICT firms' going-out strategy? The complexities of China's corporate globalization may be further illustrated through the example of Huawei's internationalization at the firm level, which may provide distinct experience as well as lessons for Chinese multinationals in the making. More important, Huawei's distinct trajectory of internationalization marching from global South to global North is of strategic significance in examining the geopolitical-economic factors that shaped Chinese firms' going-out strategies.

The Particularity of Huawei's External Accumulation

Huawei's first step of internationalization started in 1996. In 2005 the company's overseas sales outstripped its domestic sales for the first time. From 2004 to 2017, Huawei's global sales revenues rose from $5.58 billion to $90 billion.³⁶ After more than two decades of global expansion, Huawei has deployed its products and services in more than 170 countries, serving nearly one-third of the global population. As an example of China-based capital's outward expansion, Huawei conducted its outward investment activities in distinct ways, which are less likely to be identical to how they were made by Western TNCs.

NATIONALISTIC AND GEOPOLITICAL INITIATIVES UNDERPINNING HUAWEI'S INITIAL INTERNATIONALIZATION

In traditional TNC theories, a TNC usually turns to the strategy of internationalization only when it has already established its dominance at home.³⁷ This model is useful to explain grown-up TNCs, especially those from developed countries in their domestic business cycle. In contrast, most China-based ICT firms chose to launch internationalization in their immature stage of development as a direct reaction to the increasingly competitive domestic market in their country. As analyzed in chapter 1, Huawei has encountered the most crucial competition from the outset. On the one hand, the domestic high-end urban market has been monopolized by foreign competitors for a long time, which directly threatened domestic firms' survival in the telecommunications equipment market. On the other hand, China's institutionalized policy bias against the vast countryside resulted in a skewed development policy and market activities, which further deprived Chinese ICT firms of growth opportunities in the alternative market. Such structural imbalances in China's ICT industry have become a bottleneck for Huawei's sustained growth in the domestic market and pushed the company to initiate its internationalization strategy. When Huawei came to such a critical juncture of development, Ren Zhengfei predicted, "If we cannot build an internationalized team in three to five years, we will come to a dead end when China's economy becomes saturated."[38] In this sense, Huawei's initial attempt of exploring international markets was driven by the proactive strategy to evade the risks of China's structural imbalances instead of an aggressive motive for market expansion.

At the same time, many other Chinese ICT firms that had obtained certain shares in the domestic niche market also looked outward for international expansion. As early as 1990, Shanghai Bell became the first Chinese company to export modern telecommunications equipment abroad. A further step was achieved by ZTE in 1998 when the company defeated other Western TNCs and acquired a $97 million contract from Pakistani telecom operators, which was the first international contract obtained by the Chinese ICT firm.[39] In the same year, ZTE invested $8 million to set up a local factory for equipment manufacturing and technology transfer in Pakistan. In contrast to these domestic state-owned players that had tremendous policy support, Huawei's plan of internationalization was launched in relatively disadvantaged conditions. Although Huawei's products and services already received high recognition in China's domestic market, they still had very low global appeal in international markets because of the deep-rooted stereotype concerning the poor quality of Chinese products. Chinese manufacturers in the high-tech sector were also discredited for their inferior manufacturing and innovative capabilities.

To offset such a skewed image, Ren Zhengfei emphasized strengthening Huawei's voice as well as Chinese indigenous firms' images in international markets. In 1994 Huawei participated in an international telecommunications exhibition in Beijing. This event was symbolic for the company because it was the first time Huawei appeared on the international stage to represent a Chinese brand in the high-tech sector, which also raised attention from the Chinese leadership. When Chinese vice premier Zou Jiahua visited this exhibition, he commented, "Huawei has made all of the Chinese people proud."[40]

Since then Huawei has successfully established itself as a national brand, aiming to spearhead the cutting-edge innovation and technology development of China's national industry.

In 1995 Huawei's import-export department set up its first overseas subsidiary in Hong Kong, a market adjacent to Huawei's headquarters, mainly taking charge of Huawei's international supply chains and settling foreign exchanges, which were still restricted in Mainland China at that time. During the same period, many other Hong Kong–based enterprises had increasingly looked inward to explore the Mainland Chinese market and had sought low-cost supply of manufacturers upon Hong Kong's return to China. This linkage provided more opportunities for Chinese firms to connect with broader international markets. The Hong Kong market became the most desired international outlet for China-based capital's outward expansion during the late 1990s. Huawei's first overseas contract benefited from such mutual political-economic relationships. In 1996 Huawei acquired a fixed-line equipment contract from Hutchison Telecommunications, which was Hong Kong's second-largest telecommunications operator, owned by billionaire Li Ka-shing. In only three months, Huawei completed Hutchison's fixed-line upgrade projects, much faster than the anticipated time estimated by other European vendors. Yet the price Huawei offered was only half of its competitors' bidding. Huawei's success in bidding was not only based on its low-cost, high-quality products; noticeably, its technology could be scaled to meet the demand of network communications in one of the world's most densely populated areas.

Huawei's entry into the Hong Kong market represents the normal pattern of most Chinese manufacturers' going-out process—that is, to take a few neighboring and ethnically similar countries as their first step to tap into broader global markets. Huawei's further extraterritorial expansion actually followed a more richly complex and conflicted path in which geopolitical-economic conditions have increasingly become pivotal factors for the company's going-out activities.

As in China's domestic market, Huawei's outward expansion had to face head-to-head competition from a handful of leading telecommunications TNCs like Ericsson, Alcatel-Lucent, and Nokia, which have already established entrenched positions in developed countries and regions. Under their domination, it was impossible for an unknown Chinese corporation to gain entry opportunities into these areas. To escape from the dilemma existing in both the domestic and foreign markets, Ren revised the strategy of "encircling cities from the countryside"—namely, "encircling developed markets from emerging markets" in the company's trajectory of internalization. Following Huawei's entry into Hong Kong, the company's international business was later extended to Russia in the late 1990s, the process of which was facilitated by the Chinese government's involvement.

Huawei's decision to enter the Russian market was closely tied to China's foreign policy in the post–Cold War era, especially in a larger geopolitical context after the collapse of the Soviet Union. The turmoil of the 1990s in Russia had thrown the country into a decade of deep recession, which crippled the country's network-building capacity. At the same time, Western governments and their military allies sought to reshape Russia into a capitalist model toward a market economy and capitalist democracy. Ren Zhengfei clearly recognized the influence of US dominance in the global political-economic order and further elaborated the initiatives of Huawei's extraterritorial expansion in relation to China's geopolitical strategy. He commented: "The US offered Russia the 'shock therapy,' which made the Russian economy collapse. They kept baiting you to follow their policies by raising new conditions. . . . The US strategy has never changed, including provoking Japan, suppressing China, supporting Taiwan independence, creating the discourse of 'China's threat,' and provoking China's neighboring countries' hostility against China. All of these reflect the American ambition of dominance in the world."[41] To ward off such a threat from US hegemony, Ren Zhengfei further declared, "The strategic partnership relationship between China and Russia will be in line with the two countries' fundamental interests and national security. . . . China's foreign policy is successful. Huawei's transnational marketing should follow the path of China's foreign policy."[42] Ren stressed that Huawei's entry into Russia was not only driven by the corporate profit-seeking motive but was also in accordance with the state's geopolitical interests to undercut US hegemony and the influence of its client states in Asia-Pacific areas.

Huawei's assertion to align with the Chinese state's foreign policy won the central government's support. In the process of Huawei's initial internationalization, the Chinese government played a critical role in assisting the company's entry into these emerging markets. As early as 1995, the Chinese government introduced a large volume of Huawei-produced C&C08 digital switches to some former Soviet countries through bilaterally diplomatic activities and aid programs. In April 1997, Russia and China signed a "Joint Declaration on a Multipolar World and the Establishment of a New International Order" as a foundation of the Chinese-Russian strategic partnership against US unipolar hegemony. Under this inter-state relationship,

Ren accelerated the company's expansion into the Russian market. In the same year, Huawei allied with Russian telecommunications equipment vendor Beto Konzem and Russian Telecom to establish the Beto-Huawei Joint Stock Company, which was Huawei's first foreign direct investment. When Chinese state councilor Wu Yi visited Huawei in July 1998, she claimed that MOFTEC would create all kinds of favorable conditions to help Chinese multinational companies explore overseas markets and engage in global competition and cooperation.[43] Under the state's policy support, Huawei quickly gained a rapid market growth in Russia. By 2001 Huawei's sales in the Russian market had reached more than $100 million. And by 2003 the company had made more than $300 million in sales revenues in the Commonwealth of Independent States (CIS), becoming one of the top multinational telecommunications equipment suppliers in this region.[44]

Although Huawei's international investment at this stage was motivated by a strong nationalistic drive and highly dependent on inter-state strategic relations, it is undeniable that its extraterritorial investment increasingly merged with other fractions of the transnational capitalist class to create "unified networks of common TCC concerns."[45] Taking the Russian telecom market reform, for example, Huawei and other Western multinationals, such as Nortel, Alcatel, Siemens, and NEC, have engaged in the sweeping privatization of Russian telecommunications enterprises starting in the 1990s to acquire a significant position in the country's telecommunications sector by way of partnerships or joint ventures. In this sense, despite the proclaimed "nationalistic" initiatives underpinning its outward expansion, the Chinese TNC acted in a way similar to that of other Western counterparts by forging bonded relationships with the local oligarchic and elite classes. To some degree, Chinese capital played the role of both a participant and a beneficiary of global neoliberal transformations.

China's foreign diplomatic relationship with third world countries provided favorable external conditions for Huawei's extraterritorial expansions in the global South. The company began its business ventures in the Middle East, Southeast Asia, Africa, and Latin America in the late 1990s. In 1998 Huawei entered other Asian countries, including Yemen and Laos, through international bidding. The following year, the company set up its first office in Brazil, starting businesses projects in Latin America. Beyond these regions, Huawei's expansion into Africa represented a significant part of the company's broader global expansion and generated a mixture of outcomes in relation to the presence of China's corporate power in the global South.

"THE ENEMY RETREATS, YET WE ADVANCE": AN AGGRESSIVE INTERNATIONAL EXPANSION IN THE EARLY 2000S

Huawei's large-scale international expansion began at the threshold of the new twenty-first century when the global ICT industry was beset by a deep crisis of overcapacity. From 2000 to 2002, major Western telecom equipment giants experienced a sharp decline in revenue and profit margin. As a response to this deep crisis, these companies underwent extensive corporate restructuring, including withdrawing from low-profit markets, cutting R&D spending, and slashing employment.

Thanks to China's relatively independent market mechanism and the state's capacity to support the hypergrowth model of the ICT industry, Chinese telecom equipment companies experienced less damage than their Western rivals in this wave of global digital depression. However, they still faced a confluence of challenges to renew their capital accumulation in China's domestic market. From 2000 forward, the compound annual growth rate of Chinese telecom fixed-asset investment decreased from 24.9 to 2.1 percent.[46] In view of sharp declining profits in the telecom market, Ren Zhengfei explicitly warned that Huawei was facing a "chilly winter" in the domestic market.[47] In contrast with strategic downsizing plans adopted by Western rivals, the company adopted an aggressive strategy to explore new international markets as a major driver of sales growth and to expand spending on the company's R&D activities. This strategy actually drew lessons from Mao's military guerrilla warfare tactic of "the enemy retreats yet we advance [*dijinwotui*]."

Although Western multinationals chose to withdraw from low-profit markets, their presence in these regions still possessed unparalleled leverage, posing an obstacle to Huawei's entry. As Ren Zhengfei said, "All of [our] fertile lands have been occupied by Western companies. Only in those remote, turbulent regions with adverse natural conditions where they entered at a slower pace and had less investment did we have a window of opportunity."[48] This insight shaped Huawei's internationalization trajectory: march into less-developed countries before venturing into developed markets. Since 2000, Huawei has accelerated its pace of international expansion by entering Southeast Asia, the Middle East, and Africa in succession, marking the company's transformation from a China-based vendor to a global player. To advocate for the company's large-scale overseas expansion and to mobilize more employees to work in overseas branches, especially in underdeveloped countries with extremely harsh conditions, Ren said, "We have to work hard for our country's prosperity, for our nation's rejuvenation, for Huawei's development and our own happiness. . . . We have to shed tears and sweat on the five continents, for our country's future, and for getting rid of the humiliation caused by the Opium-war and the invasion of the Eight-Nation Alliance one-hundred years ago."[49]

It seems that Huawei's motive of business internationalization was coated with the discourse of nationalism as "both a means of political legitimacy and a corporate PR strategy."[50] However, it is important to underscore that Huawei's appeal to nationalism also strengthened its corporate identity as a Chinese national champion in the era of globalization and distinguished the fraction of the transnational capitalist class with Chinese nationalist characters from other capitalist blocs. The revolutionary tradition of thrift and hard work (*jiankufendou*) was also evoked as a fundamental work ethos to constitute Huawei's distinct corporate culture. To further provide detailed insights into the particularity of China-based enterprise's capital accumulation and the dynamics of China's going-out strategy, the following sections discuss Huawei's significant inroads into African and Latin American markets.

HUAWEI'S EXPANSION INTO AFRICA

Along with the path of Huawei's outward expansion, the company's presence and success in Africa have increasingly obtained global visibility. In 1998 Huawei first entered African markets by starting operations in Kenya. After two decades, Huawei has become the largest telecom equipment supplier on the continent. By 2012, Huawei's sales in Africa had topped $4 billion across more than forty African countries, establishing strategic partnerships with twenty mainstream telecom operators.[51] In moving from an unknown brand to a dominant player on the continent, Huawei's developmental path reflects the peculiarity of Chinese capital's outward expansion and a broader political-economic significance in relation to the global reach of China's corporate power.

Since the late 1990s, Huawei's entry into Africa has coincided with sweeping neoliberal transformations across the continent. As a result of the coercive structural adjustment programs imposed by the International Monetary Fund–World Bank and Western donors, more than twenty African countries introduced market liberalization and opened up their basic telecom service markets for foreign capital from 1995 to 2000. The large-scale liberalization led to the influx of transnational telecom operators, most of them from Europe and the Middle East, into African telecom markets. By 2005, more than thirty transnational telecom giants, including Britain's Vodafone; France's largest mobile operator, Orange; Portugal Telecom; and Kuwait's Mobile Telecommunications Company (MTC), had established cross-border operations in Africa. Among them, six mainstream transnational telecom operators, including South Africa–based Telkom, Vodafone and its subsidiary Vodacom, MTC, Orange, and Egypt-based Orascom, dominated 65 percent of African telecom service markets,[52] leading to the monopoly of market power by these leading transnationals. By 2006, over 55 percent of African countries had partially or completely implemented privatization of their telecom sectors.[53]

On the side of the telecom equipment market, major traditional Western TNCs, such as Ericsson, Alcatel-Lucent, and Nokia-Siemens Networks, dominated the market with their well-established "incumbent advantages," which were built upon generations of their engagement in the continent dating back to the colonial period of primitive accumulation. Moreover, their close strategic partnership with Europe-backed telecom operators further consolidated their leading positions in the market. A senior Huawei market manager working in Africa revealed that African telecom operators, especially those backed by Europe-based FDI, were more willing to hand over purchase contracts to European telecom equipment manufacturers (author interview). For example, he explained, Luxembourg-based company Millicom International Cellular (MIC), one of the largest mobile operators in Africa, has developed a long-term partnership with Ericsson. Under such domination by "the white old boy club," Chinese companies, as latecomers, were completely excluded from the market at the beginning. But Western telecom equipment companies that sought to pursue maximization of profit found underdeveloped African telecom markets less attractive than high-end developed markets, because the telecom infrastructure buildup across the African continent might require huge investment yet end up with low-profit return. This lack of European vendors' market imperatives provided Chinese companies with an opportunity to enter the market. As the manager recalled, Huawei was awarded a major contract from MIC to deploy a brand-new GSM network in the Democratic Republic of Congo in 2006, marking a milestone of Huawei's expansion in African markets. However, the primary reason behind Huawei's success was Ericsson's withdrawal from the bidding due to the project's low profit return. This example is illustrative of the distinct logics of capital accumulation by "varieties of capital."[54] In contrast with Western companies' profit-making motive, Chinese capital is more interested in long-term returns through in-depth engagement. Thus, Huawei has been pursuing other types of strategic objectives instead of short-term profit-making activities—that is, to open up new markets entrenched by Western multinationals first and then further extract surplus value from subsequent network upgrades and services in the long haul.

Another key element of Huawei's competitive advantage over Western giants lay in its pricing strategy. My interviewees revealed that Huawei managed to achieve tremendous margins by offering 10–15 percent lower prices than those of Western rivals (author interviews). For example, in Nigeria, one of the largest telecom markets in Africa, Huawei's product prices were more than 40 percent lower than the prices of Ericsson and Alcatel-Lucent. Huawei's pricing advantage can be attributed to the company's low costs of labor input. At the same time, because African telecom development was far behind the rest of the world and its market demands remained at a low level, Huawei was able to export outdated, low-cost surplus products to those underdeveloped countries and yield high profit to sustain its hypergrowth in Africa. In this sense, Huawei has turned African markets into an outlet of its surplus product exports from China. For example, Huawei had been at a disadvantage in the war over the CDMA market since the early 2000s, occupying a relatively low share of China's saturated market. But the company adopted the export strategy in international markets and rapidly picked up market share in Africa. Now Huawei has become the largest CDMA equipment supplier in sub-Sahara African markets.[55]

Apparently, Huawei's pricing strategy became a key factor for its initial success in Africa. But the market competition also forced rivals to ally and launch price wars against Chinese companies. The price gap between Huawei and other Western companies has been reduced in recent years. While Western companies learned to cut prices and compress their profit margin to counterattack Chinese companies, Huawei started to focus on innovation and comprehensive solutions for the demand of local markets. The company no longer prioritizes the goal of "making it cheaper" but "making it better" (author interview), with considerable efforts to change the image of Chinese manufacturers from producing low-cost, low-quality goods to providing innovative customized telecom solutions. Huawei's eco-friendly strategy of "going green" solutions can be viewed as an example of such a strategic shift. These solutions actively promoted energy-saving base stations in Africa, which can use solar or wind energy to replace the consumption of coal and electricity to save more than 47 percent of energy usage compared to regular towers. Moreover, the power of such a base station can cover the telecom networks of several villages, preventing a waste of infrastructure construction. By the end of 2007, Huawei had deployed more than one hundred thousand green base stations across the world, significantly benefiting local ecosystems.[56]

It is important to underscore that Huawei's expansion into Africa is characterized by multilayered activities and processes. Beyond firm-specific advantages and corporate initiatives, Huawei's engagement in Africa incarnated part of China's geopolitical-economic strategy on the continent, with a manifest firm-state nexus in place. The globalization of China's corporate power served to fulfill China's reposition in the new global political-economic order, while in turn the Chinese state also played the key role of vanguard for Chinese companies' expansion in international markets.

Chinese foreign direct investment concentrated heavily on large-scale projects of infrastructure building and manufacturing, which were seldom pursued by Western companies because of low profit return. Besides construction, energy, and mining, telecom is one of the strategic mainstay sectors underpinning China's involvement in Africa. The strategic significance of telecommunications and the Chinese government's role in buttressing Chinese companies' penetration into Africa was underlined in 2004 when Deputy Minister of Commerce Chen Jian stated in the symposia "Chinese-African Ministers of Telecommunications." In Chen's words: "China will further expand telecom cooperation with African countries in line with mutual benefits and common development. Moreover, the Chinese government will support its telecom companies to operate more telecom services in Africa."[57]

The government's role in facilitating Chinese ICT corporate expansion is institutionalized through many venues, which can be seen as part of China's going-out endeavor. At the policy level, the Forum on China Africa Cooperation (FOCAC), founded in October 2000, was marked as a milestone of China's new political-economic engagement with Africa. At the 2006 FOCAC, the Chinese government pledged to "vigorously encourage Chinese companies to participate in the building of infrastructure in African countries, scale up their contracts, and gradually establish multilateral and bilateral mechanisms on contractual projects. Efforts will be made to strengthen technology and management cooperation, focusing on the capacity-building of African nations."[58] In 2015 China and Africa mapped out the "Ten Cooperation Plans" to boost the China-Africa ties at the Johannesburg Summit of the sixth FOCAC, proposing telecommunications infrastructure as a focal area to strengthen China's "infrastructure connectivity initiative" on the African continent.

Under the arrangement of such a policy framework, a large number of business contracts in the area of telecommunications were reached, with the Chinese government primarily acting as a mediator and a bargainer. In 2000, when the FOCAC was founded, Ren Zhengfei accompanied Vice Premier Wu Bangguo on a diplomatic tour to a number of African countries, which laid the groundwork for the company's future business expansion in Africa. Aided by such well-established political links, in 2005 Huawei was awarded a contract worth $200 million to build a CDMA network in Nigeria. In 2006 the Beijing Summit of FOCAC saw the deals between both Huawei and ZTE with Ghana to build that country's national communications backbone infrastructure. In the same year, the government of Ethiopia signed contracts with Huawei, ZTE, and China International Telecommunication Construction Corporation to undertake three major telecom service expansion projects nationwide. These projects, which were also the largest ICT infrastructure construction projects in Africa, were designed to increase these countries' fiber-optic deployment, mobile network expansion capacity, and rural telecom coverage.

In fact, Chinese ICT companies' OFDI on the continent was primarily concentrated in "first-tier countries" such as Algeria, Egypt, Tunisia, and South Africa. Besides the relatively advanced infrastructures these countries have developed, they also served as springboards for Chinese capital to penetrate into the subcontinent regions. At the same time, to cooperate with the state's energy-seeking strategy in Africa, Chinese ICT companies were also encouraged to invest in resource-rich countries such as Nigeria, Angola, Ethiopia, Ghana, and Sudan. A Huawei employee revealed that the company sometimes had to take into account policy signals from the Beijing government because ICT projects in these countries were more likely to acquire the Chinese government's financial support (author interview).

In this situation, the Chinese state can be better seen as a financier for Chinese ICT companies' going-out activities. The state-backed institutions and financing mechanisms provided Chinese companies with cheap finance to invest in capital-intensive ICT projects. One of the most important of these financing institutions is the China-Africa Development Fund (CADF), which was set up in 2007 as a result of the Beijing Summit of the FOCAC. By 2015 this venture capital fund amounted to $10 billion, becoming the world's largest private equity fund investing in Africa. According to the CADF, the financial support for African countries' telecommunications development was one of the key missions of the fund's undertaking. It should be noted that the establishment of such a development fund distinguished itself from China's traditional aids and loans. It identified itself as a profit-oriented PE fund, using a variety of financial tools, such as equity investment and investment in stocks and bonds, to diversify state-backed financial sources. In turn, the fund was guided by the state's going-out initiatives and served as a quasi-commercial financing institution to support Chinese companies' strategic expansion. Such a financing model that combined market-based financial tools and political functions reflected the new tendency of China's going-out patterns. Moreover, beyond the state-backed financing sources, the CADF also cooperated with the pan-African EcoBank to facilitate cross-regional flow of capital.

In addition to the development fund, Chinese companies can access cheap funding from Chinese policy banks such as China Development Bank (CDB) and Export-Import Bank of China (Exim Bank). These financing institutions have allowed Chinese firms to leverage their financing capacity in international bidding by providing their foreign buyers with low-interest loans. For instance, in November 2004 Huawei obtained a $10 billion credit line from CDB and a $600 million line from Exim Bank. After the financial crisis of 2008, CDB declared that it would further support Chinese ICT companies' projects in Africa and extended Huawei's credit to as much as $30 billion in 2009. By the end of January 2010, the loan commitment granted to Huawei by CDB had amounted to $17.4 billion.[59]

These preferential loans were granted not directly to Chinese companies but to their foreign clients for which foreign governments acted as guarantors of loans. For example, Nigeria received $200 million in low-interest loans from CDB to buy Huawei equipment in 2004. In 2010 Exim Bank offered Ghana two concessionary loans worth $30 million and $150 million to construct its e-government projects, in which Huawei was awarded the contract as a key ICT service provider.[60] Across the African continent, Ethiopia was the primary beneficiary receiving the Chinese government's financial support. The country's loans from China for upgrading its ICT projects were estimated at more than $3.5 billion, with ZTE and Huawei serving as primary contractors.[61] Along with preferential loans, Chinese companies were able to provide host countries with packages of aid for infrastructure constructions. This state-backed financing mode, as part of "no strings attached policy," made Chinese companies more appealing than Western investors in African markets. Meanwhile, these packages of aid often led to technology transfer to local communities, revealing a positive spillover effect on local economic and technological development. According to a former vice president of Huawei's regional business, many African countries benefited tremendously from the company's technology transfer programs to develop their own telecom technology capabilities (author interview). He explained that with Huawei's deeper engagement in Africa, a large number of local telecommunications firms have gradually taken over some telecom construction projects and product testing services from Chinese firms to form relatively independent supply chains since 2008. The collaboration between Chinese ICT firms and local business partners provided more alternative opportunities for local communities' development.

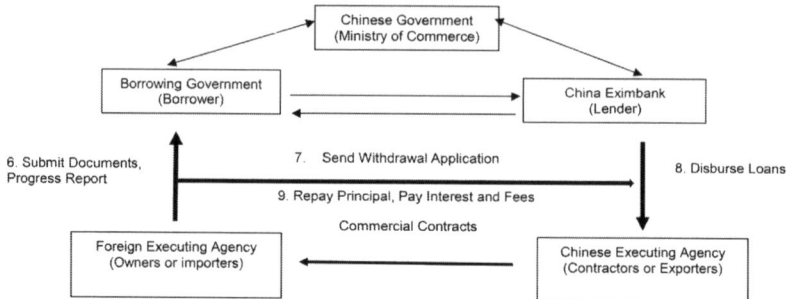

Figure 2.2. China Exim Bank Concessional Loan Cycle
Source: China Exim Bank website, as cited in Deborah Brautigam, *The Dragon's Gift*, p. 143.

Although the Chinese government asserted non-conditionality of these loans, implicit conditions were still applied to guarantee that recipient countries would use the credit to purchase Chinese companies' equipment and services. Moreover, Chinese policy banks would take lenders' future capacity into account when making lending decisions to manage debt sustainability.[62] This mechanism can largely reduce solvency risk for Chinese firms, because the risk is being passed to foreign governments and corporate lenders. In addition, to offset potential risks of repayment, the debt-equity swap was implemented by Chinese investors to secure their status in the process. For example, ZTE would take certain equity shares from the Ethiopian Telecommunications Corporation as a condition of repayment.[63] A Huawei employee also explained that some African countries that had low repayment capability usually signed agreements on resource-backed infrastructure loans with which natural resources were used as guarantee to repay debts (author interview).

From product exports to capital exports, the state capital-backed financing model has become one of the key features of Chinese firms' going-out strategy. It has not only functioned to fund Chinese ICT companies' overseas expansion but also represented a new loan-driven growth model to export China's domestic overcapacity through exchanging loans for markets. Yet in comparison with loans offered by Western countries, the size of Chinese financiers' lending has been relatively small. Moreover, China's approach of financing is not demanding, which makes China's concessional loans more acceptable than those of other Western donors in less-developed countries.

HUAWEI'S EXPANSION INTO LATIN AMERICA

Like its strategy in Africa, Huawei adopted a very similar pattern of entry into Latin America. Because the company's expansion was complicated by crucial impacts of geopolitical upheaval in this region, an analysis of Huawei's engagement with this region identifies the specific challenges and impacts of Chinese ICT firms' outward expansion in different situations.

Since 1999, when Huawei set up its first joint venture in Brazil, the company has established a corporate presence in fourteen Latin American countries, with a total of forty-five hundred employees in nineteen regional offices, three research and development centers, and three training centers.[64] However, due to the dominant influence of its major Western rivals in this region, Huawei's initial presence in Latin American markets was relatively weak. The company's American division merely contributed the lowest amount to the group's revenue and experienced the lowest growth rate.

However, in view of potentially huge profit generating from Latin America's burgeoning markets, Huawei started to accelerate its expansionary strategies in this region. Such corporate efforts were further facilitated by the Chinese government's strategic engagement in Latin America. In 2008 the Chinese government issued its first policy paper on Latin America and the Caribbean, declaring that China would strengthen "practical cooperation" with Latin American and Caribbean countries in information and communications infrastructure development. With the government's advances in this region's infrastructure construction, Chinese ICT companies, represented by Huawei and ZTE, have made remarkable achievements in these emerging markets. Huawei claims leadership in a range of different segments, including being the largest provider for IP DSLAM (internet protocol digital subscriber line access multiplexer) and Next Generation Network applications, second in market share for optical networks, and supplying routers and LAN (local area network) switches for the entire region.[65] The company has also established relationships with major telecom players in the region, including Telefonica, America Movil, Telmex, Millicom, Nextel, TIM, Digitel, CANTV, CNT, and Intel.

In particular, Huawei attempted to focus on Brazil and other large markets as its strategic focus to extend the company's presence in the region. Despite its disadvantaged position in 2G and 3G markets, Huawei picked up market share rapidly during the country's telecom network upgrade from 3G to 4G. According to *China Daily*'s report, the company has won six out of seven 4G mobile network contracts in Brazil.[66] In July 2012 Huawei was selected by the Brazilian government to build up broadband internet infrastructure in rural areas in exchange for tax breaks. In addition, Huawei invested $350 million to build a new technology center in the state of São Paulo, in an attempt to project itself from Brazil into the markets of neighboring countries such as Venezuela, Bolivia, and Columbia.[67] Over the past decade, the company managed to take up to 40 percent of Brazil's network equipment market, with total sales at $1.5 billion in 2014.[68]

Beyond Brazil, Huawei's most significant advances have come in the ALBA (Bolivarian Alliance for the Peoples of Our America) countries, which were primarily driven by the geostrategic relationship between the ALBA nations and China. For the ALBA countries, expansion of economic ties with China helps them fuel an orientation of trade and essential infrastructure away from the United States. At the same time, growing export revenues, loans, and foreign direct investments from China—especially its financial support linked to the provision of Chinese products and services—have allowed these countries to finance and sustain their "Bolivarian Socialist" projects in the region.[69] For example, Venezuela received China's credit loans to purchase 3 million Chinese electronics appliances to support the state's social program "Mi Casa Bien Equipada" (My Well-Equipped Home), through which consumer electronics products were distributed to lower-income households at heavily discounted prices. In the strategically high-value-added ICT sector, the Chinese telecommunications firms Huawei and ZTE have come to occupy a major role in serving these ALBA nations' public service programs with the support of local governments. In 2007 Huawei was awarded multiple large contracts by Venezuela's state-owned telecom enterprise CANTV to extend the national fiber-optic network to remote rural areas of the country. The company has also worked with Digitel, which was awarded a license to develop rural telecommunications infrastructure in the central region of Venezuela, to deploy 3G and 4G networks in the country. In Bolivia, Huawei acquired the contract from the Bolivian national telecommunications firm Entel in 2011 to build wireless infrastructure in underdeveloped areas. In addition, Huawei has also made important advances in Ecuador. According to a report by the Peruvian newspaper *El Comercio*, Huawei won 61.4 percent of contracts from the National Telecommunications Corporations of Ecuador,[70] becoming a primary provider of the country's 3G and 4G infrastructure services.

R. Evan Ellis, a researcher of Latin American studies, argues that beyond commercial interests, the position of the People's Republic of China in Latin America has been publicly trumpeted as a "geopolitical alternative" to the United States by the new generation of Latin American populist leaders.[71] Although the presence of Chinese telecommunications firms in Latin American markets is still relatively weak in comparison with traditional Western players, there is no doubt that the expanding engagement of China's corporate power in this region's strategic ICT sector will increasingly play an important role in reshaping these countries' economic policies and political projects.

Beyond Unified Capitalist Interests: The Varieties of Chinese Capital

The analysis above touches on the peculiarity of the Chinese ICT firm's outward expansion patterns in comparison with foreign vendors, which is mainly characterized by the logic of encompassing accumulation and the strategic relationship between the Chinese state and firms.[72] Nevertheless, extant discussions concerning the rise of Chinese capital tend to commit to a misunderstanding that sees outbound Chinese investors implement the same logic of capital accumulation. As sociologist Ching Kwan Lee argues, the generic term "Chinese capital" is not a unified concept. It actually "masks a hierarchy of capitals of varying status, resourcefulness and connection to the Beijing government."[73] Likewise, Huawei's patterns of outward expansion and its logic of capital accumulation are not identical to those of other Chinese firms.

According to Lee's definition, at the top of the pecking order are state-owned or state-controlled companies. Below these are private companies of varying sizes.[74] Such hierarchical differences are illustrated in the story of Huawei and ZTE. During my interviews, all Huawei employees commented that Huawei's business model was far different from that of ZTE due to their dissimilar ownership status. One former Huawei sales manager working in Kenya and Tanzania said the state-controlled shareholding company ZTE generally had more policy support from the Chinese government than that of Huawei (author interview). For example, there were some cases where the Chinese government directly helped ZTE introduce new foreign clients and negotiate for their contracts. Intergovernment cooperative projects were more likely granted to ZTE instead of Huawei. The interviewee further explained that the "advanced" status ZTE enjoyed was also reflected in that company's chances of acquiring state-backed funding. It was said that ZTE had more opportunities to access large amounts of financing packages from the central government and policy banks than did Huawei. For example, based on Chinese-Ethiopian governments' bilateral agreements, ZTE became the exclusive telecom equipment supplier for Ethiopian Telecom in 2006 with the $1.5 billion financial support provided by CDB. In the interviewee's words: "ZTE has fostered a privileged relationship with the Chinese government because of its state-backed status. Of course, this also determined that ZTE's business activities had to assume certain political tasks. In contrast, Huawei's identity is more complicated. Its relationship with the government was not as close as that of ZTE but it was still promoted as a 'brand' of China, representing Chinese identity in the eyes of foreign clients" (author interview).

In comparison with ZTE, which focused more on public relations with foreign governments, Huawei's business activities were client-oriented. Instead of complete dependence on the government's grants for foreign contracts, Huawei's sales teams directly targeted potential clients—mostly telecom operators—to make sure that the company was able to enter the short list of suppliers and then form long-term strategic relations with local telecom carriers. When the company acquired contracts, Huawei sales representatives would persuade buyers to apply for Chinese concessional loans. Then the company's public relations (PR) teams in Beijing would propose the projects to the MOC and policy banks to appraise and approve the request-based loans. One of my interviewees commented that Huawei's bottom-up, client-centered business model strikingly contrasted with ZTE's top-down model, but it was also this pattern of investment that made the company's overseas contracts and revenue less secure and stable than those of ZTE (author interview).

Although Huawei and ZTE both represent the rise of "Chinese ICT multinationals," the expansion of their corporate power does not necessarily serve unified Chinese capitalist interests. The emergence of these two Chinese telecom giants did not lead to the cluster and synergic effects in their business expansion. Otherwise, they were always in direct competition with each other in multiple business areas and markets. According to an interview conducted with a ZTE employee, the company has always seen Huawei as its top adversary (author interview). In some cases, these two firms have tried every means to undercut the other's prices to win contracts. A Huawei employee claimed that wherever Huawei was present there was competition from ZTE and that the real threat for Huawei came primarily from ZTE (author interview). In turn, Huawei took action to counterattack its rival in some of the markets. In Ethiopia, Huawei seized a large share of the telecom market from ZTE, which had been the sole provider of Ethiopia's telecom carriers. In Kenya, ZTE's contracts for providing IT security solutions to Kenya's "Safe City" program—an artificial intelligence–enhanced system for police surveillance and monitoring—were handed over to Huawei.[75] The tensions arising from two China-based transnational capitalists defied the homogenized nation-state framework and the concept of "unified national interests" to some degree. As William I. Robinson argues, "Transnational capital is heterogeneous and internally divided and has no unambiguous boundaries demarcating it as a specific fraction."[76] The domicile of TNCs in the same home country does not necessarily mean the formation of unified class interests or identical business patterns.

However, it is important to note that the formation of competitive blocs of transnational corporations does not prevent fractions of the transnational capitalist class from using state apparatuses to achieve their class interests, nor from formation of a particular national identity embedded in their cross-border capital expansion. The Chinese state has also made an effort to strengthen the solidarity of Chinese capital in their going-out process in order to advance China's political agenda. For example, the Chinese ambassador to Nigeria has mediated in the vicious competition between Huawei and ZTE and persuaded them not to launch price wars against each other but to unite and resist against foreign rivals together (author interview). In this sense, the Chinese state not only served to ease the tensions and conflicts existing in the segments of Chinese capitalist groups; it also played an important role in organizing and mediating varieties of Chinese capital for advancing China's nation-state interests.

The hierarchical structure and varieties of Chinese capital are also reflected in the supply chain of ICT products and services. At the top of the chain are Chinese ICT transnational corporations like Huawei that can directly acquire contracts from telecom operators and obtain huge profits from delivering products and service solutions. Otherwise, those construction companies, which undertake the most difficult tasks of network infrastructure building, are situated at the bottom of the supply chain. As most telecom operators in less-developed countries were not equipped with network-building capabilities, they generally required equipment providers to undertake the whole supply chain ranging from construction of base stations to supply of consumer-end products. To fulfill such a form of package deals and reduce costs, Chinese ICT companies usually subcontracted construction and engineering projects to other Chinese capital–backed companies. The majority of these subcontracting companies were provincial state-owned telecom engineering companies affiliated to national backbone construction enterprises such as China's post and telecommunications construction companies, the China Railway Construction Corporation, and China State Construction (author interview). Many of them were originally sent by the Chinese government in the 1990s to build foreign-aid telecom projects. With the Chinese state's acceleration of its going-out strategy in the field of ICT, these subcontractors were encouraged to become involved in commercial projects in order to cooperate with Chinese telecom equipment providers and were primarily responsible for telecom networks construction projects, base station construction, signal testing, network maintenance, and other after-sale technical services. Thousands of skilled engineering workers were dispatched from China to accomplish hard work in extremely harsh conditions. These construction and engineering workers accounted for a large proportion of Huawei's labor force as outsourced labor. On the Huawei side, the company set up a project management department to take charge of subcontracting bids and supervise subcontractors' projects. To force down prices, Huawei periodically called for bids to choose subcontractors that could offer competitive prices under fixed-term contracts, which indirectly squeezed subcontractors' profit margins. Despite the large profit returns of telecom infrastructure projects, the lion's share of profit was actually taken by contractors. This unequal relation further enforced the hierarchies of Chinese capital along the supply chain.

Geopolitical-Economic Implications of Chinese ICT Companies' Expansion in the Global South

The Huawei story reflects the fact that China is rising as an indispensable actor in restructuring the global ICT infrastructure networks system by exporting China's experience and undercutting Western dominance in the traditional political economic order. China's ICT corporations also played an important role in integrating peripheral countries into the telecommunications boom or the widespread digital revolution. Mesmerized by the "information superhighway" imperative, less-developed countries deeply embraced the encompassing logic of digital capitalism by promoting the deployment of ICTs and informatization of the entire socioeconomic spheres. Over the past decade, Africa has become one of the fastest-growing telecommunications markets in the world, a boom largely powered by Chinese ICT companies. Notably, Huawei in particular has built 50 percent of African's wireless base stations, fifty 3G networks in thirty-six African countries, 70 percent of the continent's 4G networks, and fifty thousand kilometers of fiber cables across the continent.[77]

Inspired by China's massive success in the ICT sector, some African countries were enthusiastic to copy the same feat to improve their local telecommunications infrastructures and to increase the capacity of transmission networks. For instance, China's "Eight Vertical and Eight Horizontal" (*bazong baheng*) backbone networks—the country's "Great Digital Leap Forward" project that connected all provincial capitals and dozens of medium- and large-size cities through eight vertical and eight horizontal routes—has set an example for Africa's ICT development. Africa's information superhighway projects, which were also dubbed the "Eight Vertical and Eight Horizontal" plans, proposed to invest $15 billion to build terrestrial cable networks across the continent to connect forty-eight countries along eighty-two large cities with two hundred thousand kilometers of optical fiber.[78] Chinese ICT companies, including Huawei, became major contractors of such ambitious projects.

Chinese companies' participation in construction of networks in underdeveloped countries has significantly addressed the issues of ICT-related inequality in the region. Taking Ethiopian telecom services, for example, the country had the second most expensive broadband services in the world before Chinese companies entered the market. With the participation of Chinese telecom equipment vendors in the country's broadband program, the country's internet costs have been reduced considerably while penetration rates of internet access have increased.[79] On the western side of the African continent, internet services were exclusively controlled by Western telecommunications companies led by AT&T, Sprint, Vodacom, and Verizon, which together constructed a patchy network within countries and across borders.[80] Huawei's senior manager in West Africa claimed that "many African countries are still dependent on just one or two underwater cables connected to Europe, which are very vulnerable to external disruptions" (author interview). In Guinea, one of the least connected West African countries, with an internet penetration rate of only 2 percent, the local government chose to cooperate with Huawei to build the country's very first fiber-optic cable network. This project will not only make Guinea the first West African nation to benefit from broadband coverage, but it will also expand the country's ICT applications to public services that benefit schools, local administration, public health, and others. By assisting African countries in such telecom projects, Huawei helped these countries strengthen their local autonomy in owning and building the ICT backbone infrastructure.

Despite the unprecedented growth of Africa's landlines across the continent, a huge digital divide still exists because of the unequal distribution of submarine cables (see fig. 2.3). Since 2008 a resurgence of capital investment ($2.9 billion) has been directed to new cables to and around sub-Saharan Africa.[81] In this new wave of investment, Chinese firms have emerged as active investors and builders in the new cable projects, contributing to redistribution and rerouting of transnational material infrastructure. Huawei in particular has begun to venture into the submarine cable area by establishing a joint venture, Huawei Marine Systems, with the British company Global Marine Systems since 2008. From 2008 to 2018, Huawei Marine deployed over fifty thousand kilometers of submarine cable, including twelve submarine cable systems in Africa (see fig. 2.4).[82] In 2015, backed by investment from

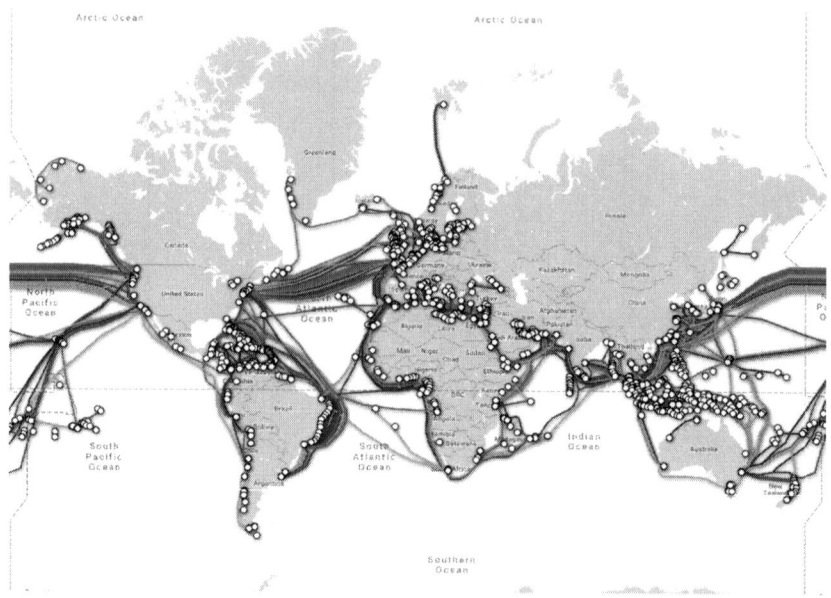

Figure 2.3. The Global Submarine Cable Map
Source: TeleGeography website, https://www.submarinecablemap.com/#.

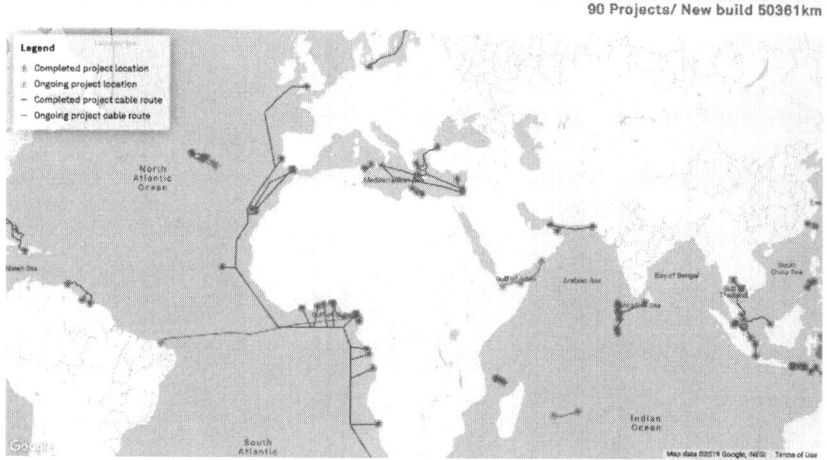

Figure 2.4. Huawei Marine Submarine Cable Projects
Source: Huawei Marine website, http://www.huaweimarine.com/en/Experience.

China Unicom and Cameroon telecommunications operator Camtel, Huawei Marine was awarded the contract to construct the Cameroon-Brazil Cable System (CBCS). The transatlantic CBCS became the first direct submarine cable that connected Africa and South America without diverting to Europe.[83] Another of the flagship projects Huawei Marine was involved with was the Pakistan East Africa Cable Express (PEACE) cable system connecting China, Pakistan, the Middle East, Europe, and Africa. As part of China's Belt and Road Initiative, this project reflects China's quest to offer a China-centered exterritorial communications network along the Belt and Road route. The deployment of fiber backbone systems in the least connected, worst served regions has made mobile and internet services more affordable and accessible in these countries.

As many communication scholars have documented, the struggle for the control of international communications infrastructure—submarine cables in particular—underpins the focus of global power shifts. In *The Undersea Network*, digital media scholar Nicole Starosielski argues that intense competitions in cable technologies "involved negotiation between existing routes of empire, emerging forces of infrastructural decentralization, and a new club system of cable laying."[84] More recently, traditional players have slowed down their pace of expansion and even stopped their investment in new cables due to limited profit returns, along with declining shares of global internet traffic in developed countries. Demand for Chinese investment and construction, however, has surged in underdeveloped countries. Huawei's elevated role in undersea cable construction provided these countries with an alternative to challenge the domination of American-led consortiums and to construct a relatively independent infrastructure for global connectivity. Although Huawei reportedly planned to sell its majority stake in Huawei Marine to Hengtong Optic-Electric Co.—one of China's biggest manufacturers of optical telecommunications network products—due to US sanctions, the growing presence of Chinese companies in the "new club" has fundamentally changed the traditional order of global telecommunications infrastructure.[85]

Conclusion

Huawei's case provides a rich context for the discussion of the nature and implications of China's corporate globalization. The salient presence of Chinese firms in the global South has raised heated debate at home and abroad. On the one hand, China's official rhetoric portrays the country's role as an egalitarian partner based on the "win-win" development model, seeking to legitimize the penetration of China's economic power into these regions and to ease the tensions between China and host countries. On the other hand, a view calling for China's greater power projection is emerging inside China's policy-making circles.[86] Especially China's BRI reflected the country's ambition in restructuring the global geopolitical economic order. At the core of this strategy was the goal to enlarge Chinese outward investment in the requisite infrastructure development, including telecommunications infrastructure, in developing countries. In addition to capital expansion, people upholding this perspective called for strengthening the state capacity and military forces to protect Chinese capital abroad in order to consolidate the country's influence in the South. However, the extensive global expansion of Chinese firms also raised criticism from the West, condemning the rise of "global corporate China" as a new force of neo-imperialism.[87]

These arguments and controversies actually focused on a pivotal question with regard to the implications of China's corporate globalization: Has China played a role as a colonizing power or an egalitarian partner of globalization? This question should be assessed in relation to who benefited from the transnationalization of Chinese capital and what was at stake. It is important to bear in mind that neither biased nor idealist rhetoric is adequate to grasp the nature of Chinese capital's outward expansion. As Barry Sautman and Yan Hairong note, China's role in the global South should not be reduced to either "China is the best" or "China is just like the rest."[88] The complexity of Chinese capital should be understood in terms of its peculiar logics and practices.

The way Chinese capital behaves abroad more or less mirrors the "externalization of China's domestic developmental difficulties, challenges, and problems,"[89] such as severe exploitation of labor forces, devastating ecological and environmental conditions, and crucial market competition. In the process of external capital accumulation, the behavior of Chinese firms was to some extent similar to that of their Western counterparts in extracting natural resources, displacing local industries and markets, and establishing oppressive labor regimes. These particular patterns of capital accumulation represented the destructive logic of capitalist growth and revealing contradictions of Chinese capital's expansion.

But Chinese firms also distinguished themselves from Western investors in their business patterns. As Lee argues, Chinese capital actually followed the pattern of encompassing accumulation, which means the motive of Chinese capital's accumulation was not taken purely on grounds of profitability.[90] In contrast, the outward expansion of Chinese firms somewhat conveyed a compelling geopolitical aim. According to Huawei, the company's going-out strategy was to assist the country to regain its political and economic influence in the new era of globalization. Such an initiative was in line with China's strategic goal to shape the country into a responsible stakeholder of the global system. Serving as an arm of China's global reach, Chinese capital as such is highly politicized with strong nationalistic identity.

In response to the Western discourse of "China's threat," it is argued that China's going-out approach is not developing toward colonialism or imperialism. First, far from extraction of massive "imperialist rent," returns for Chinese companies' overseas investment in developing nations has remained relatively low compared to their business in other regions.[91] Telecommunications infrastructure projects, which were deemed as a "white elephant," a term used to describe unprofitable but costly investment, have been neglected and even abandoned by Western investors decades ago. Chinese companies actually filled the vacuum by providing more cost-efficient ICT infrastructure to those less-connected regions.

Moreover, China's strategic partnership with third world countries and their economic cooperation were built upon their shared experiences and legacy of anti-imperialism, anti-colonialism, and anti-hegemony. China's commitment to mutual benefit, equality, and respect for sovereignty also laid a durable foundation for its in-depth cooperation with these countries. Therefore, the presence of Chinese corporate power in third world countries is not a zero-sum game. China's historical experience and development model resonated powerfully with third world counterparts, which made China's distinct approach more appealing to them. Many developing countries were eager to translate the Chinese model into their own process of development, in hopes that their engagement with China would be more practical than their past experiences with the West. This factor made Chinese firms more acceptable in third world countries.

In addition, China's investment and foreign aids were largely spawned by efforts to address a variety of requests and needs from those host countries and to support local approaches for development. China's engagement in the global South is characterized by a top-down approach through which "co-operation has invariably been directed towards the states."[92] This approach ensured the capacity of local states in implementing national ICT strategies and the application of ICT in a variety of socioeconomic spheres, which significantly facilitated these developing countries' digital transformation.

Second, unlike other conditional foreign direct investment from the West, Chinese FDI often comes in a package of aid, including debt cancellation, soft loans, technological aid, and investment in public infrastructure construction.[93] Besides financial support, other innovative forms of cooperation, such as human resources training, education resource input, and technological transfer, were implemented to promote development in third world countries. The combination of foreign aid and business investment in underdeveloped countries provided an alternative model of South-South cooperation, which was based on the principle of co-development with local communities. This principle was also articulated in Huawei's official corporate discourse, particularly in its "Corporate Social Responsibility" statement, which highlights the goal of "building an equitable, sustainable and balanced model of information society" with local stakeholders.[94] Since the early 2000s, Huawei has established more than seven technical training centers in Africa, seeking to train ten thousand ICT professionals for Africa and to facilitate ICT technological transfer in local communities. Starting in 2015, Huawei implemented the "Future Seed Plan," with the goal of training over one thousand African university students within five years.[95] To implement the Chinese government's foreign aid policy and the International Telecommunication Union's strategy of a "Connecting Africa" program, Huawei not only committed to basic telecom service in major cities but also made a significant effort to improve such capabilities in rural areas and to bridge regional and international ICT gaps on the continent. There is no doubt that the presence of Chinese ICT capital plays a significant role in building third world countries' ICT capabilities and improving local ICT services.

However, Huawei's expansion into third world countries was not free of frictions or contradictions. Ongoing labor protests against Chinese investors were on the rise within some host countries. Inter-state competition within the global South also generated obstacles to Chinese companies' cross-border operations. Huawei's experience in India was illustrative of such frictions. Huawei has become a long-established supplier for all of India's major telecom operators since 1999. The availability of Chinese cost-effective equipment allowed major Indian telecom operators to expand their regional backbones and network access at relatively low costs. Despite the shared economic interest between Chinese ICT vendors and local business players, the inter-state rivalry deriving from geopolitical tensions and ideological differences between these two countries prompted the Indian government's ban on Chinese manufacturers, including Huawei and ZTE. The profound division within the third world bloc might pose a serious challenge to the presence of Chinese capital in the global South.

China's growing influence in the global South has reshaped the geopolitical-economic power structure, resulting in heightened tensions between China and Western countries. The US reorientation toward a new approach to Africa—a strategy to counter China's influence in this region—signals a US policy shift toward China on multiple geopolitical and economic fronts. There is no doubt that the current US-China confrontation will create more obstacles to the expansion of China-based capital. This contradiction has already been reflected in the Huawei case and will be further examined in the next chapter.

The implication of Chinese ICT firms' presence in the global South is complex. The case of Huawei illustrates a peculiar logic, pattern, and ramification of Chinese capital's outward expansion. We can hardly say it provides an alternative mode of transnational capital accumulation to the neoliberal logic or merely acts as an agent of the Chinese state's imperialist power. Nevertheless, it is for sure that Huawei, which has emerged on the world stage as a major player on par with the world's leading firms and an equal partner in local communities, represents an important symbol of the globalization of corporate China.

CHAPTER 3

March into the Global North
Opportunity or Peril?

As a result of the strategy of "circling cities from the countryside," Huawei has gained a firm foothold in emerging markets since the early 2000s. However, the company has still sought vast opportunities in developed countries where telecommunications markets are larger and more lucrative. The company's penetration in the South can be viewed as a springboard for its further plan of expansion into developed countries, which prepared the company to foster competitive edge in international markets. But in contrast with the company's massive success in the South, Huawei's march into the global North was faced with numerous difficulties and challenges. This chapter looks at Huawei's presence in two different regions—the European and US markets—to examine the dynamics and limitations of Chinese capital's expansion into the global North. The conflicts and contradictions arising from the Chinese ICT firm's counterflow into developed countries underscore inter-state and inter-capitalist competition and the potential for Chinese capital to challenge the US-led global capitalist order in the centers of the capitalist system.

Over the last decade, major global telecom equipment giants have experienced several dramatic changes of restructuring. Traditional Europe-based transnational companies undertook mergers, cross-border investments, joint ventures, and alliances with extra-regional TNCs to consolidate their domination in the market. In April 2006, France-based Alcatel merged with US-based Lucent, paving the way for Alcatel's expansion into the American telecom market. In the same year, Finland's Nokia and Germany's Siemens merged their network telecom equipment businesses in a joint venture. But this merger did not last, and Nokia bought out the shares of the joint venture from its German partner in 2013. In the following year, Nokia sold its mobile businesses, which had been the company's most profitable business unit, to Microsoft. But two years later Nokia's devices business was sold again to Foxconn's subsidiary. To strengthen its core businesses in the telecom network market, especially in reaction to heightened competition from new market players such as Huawei, Nokia announced its acquisition of Alcatel-Lucent in April 2015. Such a "mega-merger" changed the market structure and dynamics dramatically, stimulating a new wave of industrial restructuring. In November 2015, Ericsson and Cisco, two tech giants in the telecommunications sector, decided to establish a strategic partnership to merge the services of telecom networks and data communications as a response to rising competition from Huawei and the merged Nokia-Alcatel-Lucent conglomerate. Nevertheless, it should be noted that restructuring through convergence and "deconvergence" is primarily a corporate response to market failure and a scheme of battles for position in the industry rather than a solution to the systematic crisis. Such a pattern of capitalist restructuring is primarily driven by the long-established transnational powers that tend to sustain their dominance in the face of new market comers. To the greatest extent, the scene of global restructuring in the telecom industry has set the backdrop for Huawei's march into developed countries.

Although Chinese ICT corporations have displayed considerable appetite for participating in transnational capitalist markets, they encountered numerous conflicts and obstruction from capitalist rivals and states. The arrest of Huawei CFO Meng Wanzhou in 2018 as well as a US trade ban are the latest examples that demonstrated the escalated confrontation between the United States and China, especially in the race for 5G. Some observers even predicted that the conflict around Huawei signaled an "iron curtain" falling across the global high-tech domain.[1] In this sense, Chinese capital's integration into global capitalist networks is not as smooth as that of the country's counterparts in the West. The following sections provide the stories of Huawei's entry into European and US markets, revealing the twists and turns of Chinese capital's counterattack against its Western rivals. Some key questions remain to be answered in this chapter: How did Huawei open up mainstream markets dominated by traditional Western ICT giants? Is Huawei's entry mode different from its practices in the global South? Why did Huawei encounter completely different outcomes in European and US markets? Has the rise of Chinese ICT corporations changed the geopolitical economic dynamics in the global North?

Turning Europe into a "Second Home Market"

As discussed in chapter 2, Huawei's internationalization started from Russia in the late 1990s, which profited considerably from China-Russia strategic diplomatic relationships. By taking a firm foothold in the Russian market, Huawei planned to enter advanced Western European countries through peripheral markets. Huawei's strategic interests in the European market were based on several considerations.

First, driven by ongoing technological upgrades and supply demands, the European ICT market has undergone qualitative growth for decades, constituting one of the most important growth engines in the global ICT industry. Western Europe had the most sophisticated ICT infrastructure and networks in the world, spearheading the development of the global ICT industry for a long time. The region not only took a lead in 2G mobile communications technologies with a decade of domination by its GSM standard, but it also stayed far ahead of the United States in 3G services. In the field of internet services, broadband development has also become a priority of the Europe 2020 strategy. Despite a decade's stagnation, Europe still managed to sustain most advanced research and development in the ICT sector. The strategic significance of the European market for Huawei lay not only in the company's profitable market potential but also in its sophisticated R&D capacities and resources.

Second, Huawei's decision to enter into the European market was symbolic, signifying the company's leap from a Chinese low-end, low-quality telecom equipment provider to a transnational firm with a place in global high-end mainstream markets. But on the other hand, Europe is also the home turf of several incumbent telecom manufacturing giants, including Ericsson, Alcatel, Nokia, and Siemens. They have taken competitive advantages in key areas. For example, Alcatel is strong in the fixed network business, Ericsson has outstanding performance in the mobile sector, and Siemens is solid in the optical networking sector. The predomination of these telecom giants set a high entry barrier and posed numerous challenges to outside players, constituting an enclosure in high-end markets.

ENTRY MODE

The process of Huawei's expansion in the European market has unfolded with the recession and restructuring of the European economy since the 2000s, a backdrop that granted Huawei unprecedented opportunities to step into mainstream markets at an especially propitious moment. Toward the end of the twentieth century, some key European telecom operators started to invest heavily in advanced wireless technology, but the burst of the internet bubble in 2001 led to large-scale recession across Europe. From 2001 to 2004, the European telecom industry was trapped in a severe debt crisis. By the end of 2002, the asset liability of key European telecom operators in Germany, Britain, France, the Netherlands, and elsewhere had climbed from 120 to 210 percent, while aggregate liability had amounted to €251 billion.[2] Incumbent operators beset by the debt crisis were compelled to cut costs on equipment procurement, while Huawei's low-cost yet high-quality products and services were able to meet such demand during the crisis.

Although the structural crisis provided Huawei with an opportunity of entry, the path toward acceptance and recognition in developed markets was difficult. Therefore, the company's entry mode in Europe was different from its practices in developing countries where state-backed financing and diplomatic activities played important roles. In Western markets, however, Huawei's state-supported background generated persistent criticism because of the company's alleged relationship with the Chinese government.

In the initial stage, Huawei actively looked for local vendors to form joint venture companies and establish cooperative relations to break into local markets. To obtain opportunities of cooperation, Huawei intended to serve as an original equipment manufacturer, trade agent, and low-end supplier for European firms that were already entrenched in the upscale market. Among these incumbent European vendors, only Siemens, which had a well-established relationship with the Chinese government, was willing to cooperate with Huawei (author interview). In 2003 Huawei and Siemens signed a cooperative contract under which Huawei franchised Siemens as the sole agent to sell Huawei's Quidway routers and switches in global markets. In return, Siemens would assist Huawei in selling the latter's data communication products, such as routers and other telecom equipment, in the European market through Siemens' sales networks. To increase the company's presence in high-end markets, Huawei participated in several eye-catching telecom exhibitions to display the company's innovative products and solutions, which to a large extent changed the "low-quality" image of a Chinese brand and raised the attention of mainstream operators.[3] The company also invested intensely in its PR activities to lobby local customers for creating brand recognition.

Huawei's encroachment into the European market was incremental, especially when facing the full force of competition from its European rivals. Starting in the role of low-end original equipment manufacturer and supplier, the company eventually achieved a breakthrough in 2004. In April of that year, Sweden-based Banverket Telenät selected Huawei among fourteen bidders to deploy Ethernet and broadband services for its rail sector across Sweden, where Ericsson, one of the largest telecom equipment vendors, is headquartered. Though it was only a small-scale contract in a marginal field, it was the first time a Chinese telecom equipment manufacturer managed to break into the Nordic telecom market. In December 2004, Huawei acquired a WCDMA (wideband code division multiple access) 3G contract from the Dutch mobile operator Telfort to build a nationwide 3G network that can be managed to migrate with its existing network, built by Ericsson. This deal marked a substantial milestone in Huawei's expansion in developed countries, indicating a Chinese company's breakthrough in the mainstream market where the dominant 3G standard originated.

IN-DEPTH ENGAGEMENT IN THE UPGRADE OF EUROPEAN TELECOM NETWORKS

When Huawei achieved its initial breakthrough in Europe, the company encountered a setback in the United States at the same time. In 2003 Huawei was blocked out of the US market because the company was sued by Cisco for the violation of intellectual property. This setback became a watershed for Huawei's strategy of outward expansion. Since then Huawei has shifted its strategic focus of internationalization from the United States to the European market, launching a turf war against global giants in this region. In 2004 the company set up a European headquarters in the UK, which later became its largest overseas branch.

At such a turning point, the European telecom market has also experienced a new wave of industrial restructuring, which posed challenges to and opportunities for Huawei's development in this region. Since 2005 the European telecom market has gradually recovered from the internet bubble, but key operators still faced considerable strain from the profit-making imperative. From 2007 to 2009, most large network operators witnessed negative growth, while their costs of marketing, management, and administration continued to grow at a rapid rate.[4] Moreover, with the saturation of the fixed-line market, most countries planned to escalate the network services upgrades, migrating fixed-line networks to wireless networks.

Key operators' initiatives with technological upgrades gained staunch support from the EU. The EU blueprint Europe 2020, launched in 2010, further called for investment in the construction of the "Future Internet" as a priority of European long-term ICT development. For example, the UK telecommunications company BT Group, one of the largest telecom operators in the world, launched the nationwide 21st Century Network (21CN) program to begin the process of network convergence. It intended to transfer BT's fixed-line telephone networks to an Internet Protocol (IP) system, combining data, voice, video, and web services over one converged network. More important, this scheme of network convergence enabled telecom operators to provide more integrated solutions for interconnected multisite operations of transnational corporations. As Dan Schiller observed, "By integrating forward into internet service and backward into backbone networks . . . the largest network operators staved off threats to their core business of connectivity and elbowed their way toward the center of the new network architecture."[5] However, the conflict between declining profits and the imperative of network expansion has become a primary obstacle to further industrial restructuring. One of the biggest challenges of Europe's broadband development lay in the large-scale replacement of outdated network infrastructure with innovative broadband applications. Under the plan of Next Generation Networks (NGN), traditional circuit-switched telecommunications networks and services had to be gradually upgraded to IP-enabled networks. To accommodate the ongoing reconfiguration of networking technology and the pressure of heavy investment, the demand for flexible technological upgrades and cost reduction became a priority for European mainstream operators to achieve migration plans.

In order to respond to this market demand, Huawei developed a set of "brand-new overall fixed network solutions" based on its progressive fixed network experience to construct new converged networks. In 2005 Huawei launched a "New Fixed Network" campaign in thirteen European countries to promote its innovative solutions for the NGN project. In the same year, BT selected Huawei as one of the eight preferred telecom equipment vendors to provide access and optical transport equipment for the 21CN rollout project, worth $19 billion. This deal was groundbreaking for Huawei's expansionary strategy in Europe. In 2008 Huawei topped the global broadband equipment IP DSLAM (digital subscriber line access multiplexer) market with a 32.9 percent global market share, while the European market contributed to one of the largest proportions of Huawei's market share.[6] Huawei has now become the key supplier of the NGN backbone projects for operators around Europe.

GRASP THE "TIER-ONE" OPERATORS

In the mobile network field, because China's 3G licenses had not been issued until 2009, Huawei had to explore overseas 3G markets to grasp the fast-growing opportunity ahead of its domestic agenda. Europe, which spearheaded global 3G network development, was perceived as the most attractive market for expansion. The primary goal of Huawei's business strategy in the European 3G market was to acquire contracts from the European tier-one operators, with an attempt to get access to these operators' controlled markets and to further achieve global reach in other areas.

With the trend of business consolidation, a few pan-European operators, such as Vodafone, Orange, Telefonica, and T-Mobile, dominated over 90 percent of European markets. By appropriating Mao's revolutionary tactic, Ren Zhengfei suggested that Huawei should grasp "the principal contradiction and the principal aspect of a contradiction" in its internationalization by targeting these tier-one operators.[7] To obtain the entry opportunity, Huawei chose to adopt the role of low-value-added equipment supplier for these giant operators at the beginning. In November 2005, Huawei signed a strategic partnership agreement with Vodafone, marking a milestone of Huawei's advance in the tier-one markets. As one of the world's largest mobile operators, Vodafone has established a series of criteria for selecting its core suppliers. After two years' strict assessment of Huawei's capability in terms of manufacturing, R&D, marketing, management, finance, and information security, Vodafone eventually chose Huawei as one of the preferred global suppliers of its short list, on which only Ericsson, Nokia, Siemens, and Lucent were included. However, Vodafone's endorsement did not necessarily lead to Huawei's establishment in the core 3G equipment market. The role Huawei served as an OEM actually constrained the company's autonomy in developing its own business capacities and entrenched the company in the low-end supply chain. In February 2006, Huawei obtained a strategic 3G handset contract from Vodafone. Under the agreement, Huawei served as an original design manufacturer (ODM) to provide Vodafone-branded consumer 3G handsets across twenty-one countries. This contract can be seen as a purchasing strategy by Vodafone that used Huawei's presence to put pressure on other European suppliers to meet Huawei's low prices.[8] The ODM model not only enabled Vodafone to avoid "co-branded" fees paid to European vendors but also strengthened its control over the whole telecom market chain from backbone infrastructure to device provisions. For Huawei, it was the first time the company's consumer devices entered the European market. However, this entry mode has come at the expense of Huawei's own brand in the market, and the company's profit-making space has also been tremendously squeezed by local carriers.

Huawei's strategic advance in the European 3G market was further made in those peripheral countries controlled by the tier-one operators, which allowed the company to climb up the supply chain from a low-end handset supplier to a key equipment and solution provider in core business areas. As these operators set high barriers to non-European firms in core countries, Huawei had to detour its expansionary trajectory by "circling core countries from peripheral ones." Due to the uneven growth within European fragmented markets, 3G services in peripheral countries were at a relatively low technological level and a small business scale. Such discrepancies generated opportunities for Huawei to break into the European 3G equipment market. In 2006 Huawei passed Vodafone's testing on its 3G network equipment and gained Vodafone Spain's contract to deploy the High Speed Packet Access networks. In the next year, Huawei was awarded the contract to build 70 percent of Vodafone Spain's 3G network. Under Huawei's deployment, the performance of Vodafone Spain's mobile network was enhanced by 30 percent.[9] Following the large-scale network expansion in Spain, Huawei was awarded the contracts by Vodafone to deploy other subnetworks in Greece, Romania, Iceland, and Hungary. Huawei's success in these marginal markets paved the way for its expansion into core countries. In 2007 Huawei won the bid from telecommunications company O2 Germany to upgrade the previous supplier's equipment by using Huawei's innovative 2G/3G dual-mode base stations, which were capable of meeting the need for coexistence of 2G/3G networks. This deal was significant for Huawei, because by then the company had successfully established partnerships with all of the European tier-one operators.

Huawei's rapid growth in market share was a clear indication of its strong presence in Europe. Even during the economic recession, Huawei still managed to speed up its penetration into European markets and sustained strong growth. In 2008 Huawei's sales in Europe increased by 42 percent. In the same year, the company acquired $3 billion worth of contract sales in this region, accounting for 10 percent of European contract sales.[10]

In the post–2008 crisis era, major European operators have substantially increased spending in network migration from 3G to 4G in order to create new demand in previously mature and saturated markets. Huawei launched an aggressive 4G rollout plan across Europe to catch up with this wave of restructuring, which was warmly welcomed by European operators. The company even took a lead in 5G research by developing core technological components of the European 5G infrastructure, becoming one of the key contributors of the EU 5G Infrastructure Public Private Partnership program (5GPPP). Huawei's entry into this lucrative, cutting-edge market has intensified the fray with other European rivals and led to the fast-eroding dominance of these European companies in the telecom equipment market.

R&D INVESTMENT AND ASSET-SEEKING ACTIVITIES

The process of corporate transnationalization often went through different phases, including exporting products; establishing overseas manufacturing for local markets; and linking sales, manufacturing, sourcing, and R&D processes in an integrated circuit of global production and capital accumulation.[11] Huawei's international expansion has primarily followed such patterns and trajectories. As Huawei has evolved from a junior manufacturing partner to a key ICT equipment provider, the company's presence in Europe has no longer been confined to the provision of low-cost equipment products but has extended to various value-added business initiatives, such as the acquisition of R&D capability and strategic assets.

Since its entry into Europe in 2000, Huawei has been seeking to establish large R&D networks on the continent, fully taking advantage of the EU resources in science and technology development. Since 2007 Huawei has considerably increased its investment in European R&D operations, with a 24 percent annual growth rate. In 2012 the company's European subsidiaries invested more than €3.6 billion on R&D and more than €14.5 billion in total over the past decade.[12] In 2015 Huawei announced the launch of the European Research Institute in Belgium, running eighteen R&D branches in Germany, Sweden, Italy, France, Belgium, the UK, Ireland, and Finland.[13] These research institutes took advantage of local R&D capabilities and performed basic and applied research in different specialized fields. Huawei's Europe-based R&D facilities have become a backbone of the company's global technological research networks and a test field for its most advanced ICT technologies. In addition, Huawei set up eighteen collaborative innovation centers with local mainstream operators across the EU, cooperating with partners in some national or EU-backed research projects. Huawei's increasing investment in European R&D facilities indicates that the company has gradually fit into the local innovation system and acted as a knowledge contributor, establishing itself as a key player within the "bedrock of the science and technology landscape in Europe."[14]

At the same time, Huawei's foreign direct investment in Europe underwent a dramatic increase. Especially after the European debt crisis, Chinese investors seized opportunities to buy into cash-strapped European industrials and assets. The increasing flow of Chinese investment into the ICT sector coincided with the EU's endeavor to rebuild its high-tech industry. In the framework of the Digital Agenda for Europe, for instance, ICT was given unprecedented priorities.[15] As part of this agenda, the Connecting Europe Facility project, which was designed to contribute to the competitiveness of the European economy and interconnection of pan-European networks, set aside €9.2 billion to support the investment of ICT development in the EU. Huawei's huge direct investment has been channeled into such endeavors to support the priorities of the ICT-led restructuring. Huawei scrambled to leverage its roles in Europe's ICT development and constituted itself as "a legitimate contributor to the policy-making process."[16] The escalation of the company's investment scale and scope, on the other hand, fully exemplified the heightened degree of Huawei's transnationalization and the deep integration of Chinese capital in the regional and global economic systems.

Given the increasingly important role Chinese ICT firms have played in the restructuring of the European economy in the post-crisis era, Europe provided a much friendlier place than in the past for Chinese transnational corporations to expand and penetrate. Chinese telecom equipment firms have reportedly spent more than three times as much in Europe as in the United States.[17] In 2012 Huawei announced a further investment of $2 billion and promised to double its current workforce to fourteen thousand employees in Europe. Huawei has become the second-biggest Chinese investor in Europe, just behind global automotive group Zhejiang Geely (which owned the Swedish carmaker Volvo), and is the biggest employer among all Chinese TNCs operating in the region.[18] As a Huawei executive claimed, Huawei intends to turn Europe into the company's "second home market" and a stable engine of profit growth.[19]

CHALLENGES AND TENSIONS

In spite of the significant success Huawei has achieved on the continent, the company's expansion has also encountered immense challenges and tensions. One big challenge was the prevailing concern about the company's Chinese identity and its relationship with the Chinese government and the military. To consolidate the company's position in the global North, Huawei attempted to blur its Chinese identity in its discourse and conformed to more universal market norms advocated by Western countries. Ren Zhengfei even claimed that Huawei wanted to be viewed as a European company in an effort to receive recognition and trust from the West.[20] Along with Huawei's deeper integration in Western markets, Ren has further suggested that the company must reject "parochial nationalism" for the sake of internationalization. This change of corporate discourse is in striking contrast with Huawei's expression of nationalism in its early stage of international expansion. It also underscores the company's intention of acquiring a legitimate status in global markets, while acquiring recognition from the West is seen as the prerequisite to achieve this objective.

Although Huawei received a warmer welcome in Europe than in the United States, the company's growing presence and rapid expansion has still raised considerable tensions and disputes within the EU. In 2012 the EU trade commission launched an anti-dumping and anti-subsidy investigation into Huawei and ZTE, alleging that the Chinese vendors were being subsidized by the Chinese government through its preferential cheap loans, which enabled the Chinese companies to undercut the European champions' prices and create a "distorted playing field" for Chinese TNCs in their overseas expansion. The EU trade commission sent a warning letter to Chinese president Xi Jinping, urging the Chinese state and corporations to change their practices. The EU executive further declared that the Chinese vendors had to increase 29 percent of their products' prices and urged the Chinese government to guarantee 30 percent market shares for European companies in the Chinese market.[21] This anti-dumping action against Huawei and ZTE was intended to shield the European strategic sector from the rush of Chinese rivals and bring Chinese players in line with international market rules. But Europe-headquartered vendors such as Ericsson, Alcatel-Lucent SA, and Nokia Siemens Networks feared that the EU's protectionist action would cause the Chinese government's retaliation on their business in China, which might make them lose more opportunities in China's lucrative market.

Despite the prevailing concern about the expansionary power of Chinese capital, division emerged among EU member states and different capitalist blocs, reflecting the entangled interests and conflicts among various power blocs, including states, supranational powers, and fractions of transnational capitalists. For example, some states linked Huawei's business expansion in Europe with security issues. The UK government, nevertheless, had explicitly expressed its support for Huawei's presence in the country before the US ban, hoping to attract Chinese investment for local economic recovery. The David Cameron administration especially and explicitly claimed that economic growth powered by the development of the technology "should not be subsumed beneath national concerns,"[22] a view that starkly contradicted other Western nations' skepticism. Such a pragmatic stance explained why the deal to establish Huawei Marine, the joint venture partnered by Huawei and UK-based Global Marine Systems, in one of the most sensitive ICT areas was approved by the UK government in 2008. During the UK's "golden era" with China, the UK had been a major buyer of Huawei's telecommunications gear and one of the most important business partners in the EU. Huawei alone has also pledged to increase investment to £3 billion in the UK between 2018 and 2022.[23]

Growing geopolitical rivalry between the United States and China, especially the controversy over Huawei's 5G technologies, has complicated Huawei's engagement in Europe and added uncertainties to Europe's 5G deployment. In fact, US-led calls for a ban of Huawei 5G technologies received mixed responses in Europe. On the one hand, European countries were eager to integrate 5G to boost their digital economy. According to an estimate from the EU, the introduction of 5G could bring €113 billion in economic growth to the EU's automotive, health, transport, and energy sectors by 2025, but it would also cost Europe €56.6 billion on 5G network construction.[24] As Europe's 4G already lagged behind its competitors in Asia and the US, the introduction of 5G was perceived as a crucial agenda for European countries to catch up amid increasing global competition for the next generation of telecommunications technologies. In the race to 5G, Huawei is taking a lead in multiple areas, far ahead of its European competitors. In view of the economic stakes, excluding Huawei from key European markets will be likely to deter the progress of the 5G rollout across Europe and substantially increase the cost for European operators to build their 5G networks.

But on the other hand, the concern over Huawei's threats to national security has overridden economic and technological consideration across some European countries, giving rise to the calls for protecting Europe's digital sovereignty by reducing Chinese companies' deep involvement in the buildup of Europe's ICT infrastructure. In particular, the UK government's "golden era" policy with China was disrupted amid increasing geopolitical tensions. The UK-based operator BT, one of the first European tier-one operators to establish partnership with Huawei, announced that it would remove Huawei's technology from its core networks under US pressure. Vodafone also followed the US ban, confirming that it would restrain its involvement with Huawei in the UK. ARM, a UK-based chip designer, suspended its business ties with Huawei, leaving Huawei's semiconductor business in peril. Although the EU's quest for strategic autonomy by reducing dependence on the United States and advancing independent industrial policies has become a pressing political issue across the continent over the past decade, Europe's current lack of ability, especially its lack of critical military capabilities, made the reality fall short of its political ambition.

On the side of Huawei, Europe still constituted one of the most important international markets. As of January 2019, Huawei had won thirty 5G contracts in the world, including eighteen in Europe, nine in the Middle East, and three in the Asia-Pacific region.[25] The company had 35 percent of the market share in Europe. Some European countries, such as France, Spain, and Italy, as well as smaller network carriers, were still willing to preserve their partnership with Huawei and embrace the company's advanced 5G technologies.

In spite of the rapid integration of Chinese ICT capital in regional restructuring and the globalized capitalist system, territorial logic still plays an important role in both restraining the expansionary nature of globalized capital and reshaping the modes of capital accumulation. The following section describes Huawei's expansion in the United States and exemplifies how the interplay of geopolitical pressures and inter-capitalist rivalry has influenced uneven capitalist development and the struggle of neoliberal capitalist blocs.

Insurmountable Obstacles in the United States

The United States enjoys the world's largest ICT market, containing a massive ICT investment and user base. Its ICT funding has far exceeded that of China, Japan, the UK, and Russia combined.[26] The large market size became a compelling motive for Chinese firms' expansion into the United States. On the other hand, US-based TNC giants have preemptively occupied leading positions and established long-standing strength across numerous transnational markets, such as corporate data communication, semiconductor, mobile equipment, software, and cloud computing, which has posed a barrier to foreign rivals' entry into their home markets. Moreover, the US state-corporate alliance also scrambles to suppress any "hostile," non-US-based capital by wielding the powerful state apparatus, which can be viewed as part of the US effort to maintain its leadership in the global capitalist system. US confrontation over Huawei through a series of arbitrary actions signals the US move to contain China's business and technological power. Huawei's encountering of setbacks in the United States sheds light on such tensions between the US hegemonic power and the corporate power of newly emerging markets.

AGGRESSIVE ENTRY MODE: INTER-CAPITALIST COMPETITION AND ALLIANCE

Huawei's engagement in the United States can be traced back to the early 1990s. As early as 1993, Huawei established a subsidiary called "Ranboss" in the United States. This subsidiary, which was later renamed "FutureWay," has been developed into one of Huawei's most important R&D centers in its overseas markets. Before Huawei started its large-scale internationalization, this subsidiary primarily served to procure advanced ICT products in the US market. During the Clinton administration, Huawei reportedly spent $685,700 to purchase high-performance computers from Digital Equipment Corporation; $300,000 from IBM; $71,000 from Hewlett-Packard; and $38,200 from Sun Microsystems.[27] In addition, Huawei also bought $500,000 worth of telecom equipment from its major rival, Qualcomm.[28] In 2001 Huawei established its North American headquarters in Plano, Texas, indicating the company's strategic move to explore the world's most advanced ICT market.

Although had Huawei marked its footprints in emerging markets and in Europe since the early 2000s, the United States remained the last untapped market for the company. As the US government set insurmountable barriers to foreign vendors in the domestic network infrastructure market, Huawei instead chose the burgeoning field—the enterprise business, such as corporate routers, switches, internet access points, and corporate networks—as a beachhead into the US market. This meant Huawei had to launch head-to-head competition with Cisco—the world's largest supplier of business network equipment—in its home market. Before Huawei entered the United States, the two companies had already competed in China's booming market. In spite of its role as a market latecomer, by 2002 Huawei had already taken up a 25.4 percent market share of China's router markets, next to Cisco's 51.8 percent. In China's low-end market, Huawei's market share reached 35.1 percent, narrowing its gap with Cisco's 46.4 percent.[29] To some extent, Huawei has posed a direct threat to Cisco.

After gaining a firm foothold in China's market, Huawei was ambitious to expand its enterprise business in the United States. It adopted a low pricing strategy again, offering prices 30 percent lower than those of Cisco and other Western rivals. In addition, in the early 2000s the company launched an aggressive advertising campaign across the United States to build its corporate image. One advertisement features Huawei products against the background of the Golden Gate Bridge in San Francisco, a reference to the Cisco system. The text reads, "The only difference between us and them is price," an underlying meaning that indicates the company's competitive advantage in its cost-effective products and solutions. However, Huawei's aggressive market strategy raised persistent counteraction from the rival. Cisco's first reaction was to negotiate with Huawei by promising to provide Huawei with OEM subcontracts for its low-end product manufacturing, but the condition was to force Huawei to give up its high-end products under its brand and withdraw from the US market.[30] Huawei refused this request.

To expel the Chinese competitor from its home market, Cisco launched another war against Huawei in 2003 by suing the company for infringement of intellectual property. Cisco claimed that Huawei infringed on its patents and stole its source code in Huawei-produced routers and other networking equipment. The company also lobbied the US government to enact more intrusive policies over property protection to guarantee and privilege US-based companies' interests. In reaction to Cisco's unresolved lawsuit, Huawei chose to cooperate with another American enterprise network supplier, 3Com, to establish a joint venture. The alliance helped Huawei reshape its market strategy in North America and allowed both vendors to compete effectively with their common rival—Cisco. Despite the different origins of these two firms, their shared interest in capital accumulation served to bond diverse national blocs of capital together and to contest with other factions of capital in the market. In this case, the involvement of 3Com in the disputes actually helped Huawei increase its bargaining power in settling the lawsuit.[31] In July 2003 Cisco and Huawei finally reached an agreement. Cisco agreed to drop the lawsuit, but Huawei was forced to remove almost all of its router products from the US market.

The conflicts with Cisco frustrated Huawei's expansionary initiatives in the United States. As a result, Huawei had to change its aggressive entry mode in the States, turning to other US companies for cooperation. This strategy compelled Huawei to give up its own brand in North America and adopt the forms of OEM and joint venture to reroute the path toward the enclosed market. In 2006 Huawei collaborated with Motorola on 3G technologies, undertaking manufacturing subcontracts for Motorola's 3G wireless equipment. But such an alliance was shallow and unstable when conflicts occurred among different factions of capitalists. In 2010 Huawei and Nokia-Siemens competed to acquire Motorola's telecom network equipment business, but the European giant eventually won the deal for $1.2 billion. This acquisition directly led to the termination of Motorola's collaboration with Huawei. After the announcement of this acquisition, Motorola immediately launched a lawsuit against Huawei for alleged theft of trade secrets, with an attempt to attack one of the biggest potential rivals in North America for its new partners.

OBSTACLES ERECTED BY THE US STATE APPARATUS

In addition to inter-capitalist competition, Huawei also faced formidable obstacles erected by interlocked US state apparatuses that tended to articulate the presence of Chinese capital with the threat of national security. In line with the government's policy, US mainstream media took advantage of their discursive power to distort Huawei's corporate image, linking the expansion of Chinese ICT capital with the discourse of the "China threat," especially accusing Huawei of its links to China's military. This prevailing rhetoric, which is also representative among US military elites and its ruling class, reflected US fears about the ICT-enabled modernization of China's military forces. The ruling class was also concerned that the increasing involvement of Chinese capital in the lucrative military industry would substantially threaten their immense business profits and margins in the market. In addition, Huawei was under fire from US media for its engagement in some "hostile" countries. In October 2011, the *Wall Street Journal* made a charge against Huawei's business operations in Iran, claiming that Huawei aided Iran's government in nationwide surveillance and censorship.[32] Under immense public pressure from the United States, two months later Huawei announced that it would scale back its business in Iran, promising not to seek new customer contracts but to limit commercial activities with existing customers. This accusation seems to have set the scene for the controversial arrest of Huawei's Meng Wanzhou in 2018. Along with the pullback from Iran, Huawei's operations in Cuba, Syria, Libya, and other "politically sensitive countries" have also been disrupted. According to an employee who had worked in Skycom Tech, Huawei's Hong Kong–based subsidiary company accused of breaching US sanctions on Iran, Huawei's operations in these "hostile" countries had to be carried out in a covert manner in order to avoid unreasonable accusation from the West, especially from the United States (author interview).

As Ren complained, "For years some of the Americans and media have persistently distorted facts and attacked us."[33] The media rhetoric that resonates the discourse of US extraterritorial network policy primarily serves to consolidate US political control and economic strategic interests when facing the threat of foreign capital. As a significant constituent of American hegemony, US mainstream media's discursive power not only plays a crucial role in defining "rules of law" but also creates "a world after its own image" to sustain its supremacy in the global political economic order.[34]

It should be noted that the difficulties Huawei faced were more than media distortions and pure competition with its peer rivals. Under the US government's direct intervention, Huawei underwent a series of setbacks in the American market. In 2008 the company was forced to drop a bid for purchasing a controlling stake in 3Com. The US government claimed that this deal would give China access to the anti-hacking technology used by the US Defense Department. Eventually the American firm Hewlett-Packard won the bid for acquisition of 3Com, while Huawei lost its most important partner in the US market. Likewise, in 2011 Huawei's purchase of the assets of American server company 3Leaf was also blocked. The Committee on Foreign Investment in the United States (CFIUS) declined the transaction due to "concerns of national security." In the telecom infrastructure segment, Huawei remained confined to the periphery of telecom businesses. For decades the company has been completely excluded from purchase lists of US top-tier carriers, including AT&T, Sprint, T-Mobile, and Verizon. In 2010 Huawei was close to winning the bid from Sprint Nextel, America's third-largest mobile operator. Huawei's solutions for Sprint's wireless network upgrade projects could have helped the carrier save more than $800 million in costs. But according to a Huawei employee who worked at the company's North American branch, the deal suddenly came to a deadlock because of the US government's intervention (author interview). And the operator eventually opted for another homegrown vendor.

In response to the American government's unfair treatment, in 2011 Huawei's deputy chairman, Hu Houkun, released a lengthy open letter to rebut the groundless allegations against Huawei, calling for a formal investigation of Huawei's operations in order to dispel the concerns about Huawei's threat to US national security. As a direct result of this open letter, the US House Intelligence Committee launched a yearlong investigation of Huawei and ZTE. However, contrary to Huawei's expectation, the investigative report not only concurred with the allegations against Huawei in terms of its potential threat but also further urged the US government system and private-sector entities to shun these two Chinese companies from the US market.[35]

In fact, US discourse on national security was grounded in several concerns. First of all, it underlay the domestic realist concern that considered telecommunications architecture and cyberspace as new frontiers of interstate wars and as "nationally bounded territory in need of defense."[36] US military elites had specific concern about foreign suppliers' unauthorized access to US public and private network systems.[37] This has become the key excuse for the US government to block foreign ICT capital from the supply chain of domestic critical infrastructure. The setbacks Huawei has been encountering in the American high-tech market can be seen as a result of US defensive operations in managing potential threats of network security.

Nevertheless, US network policy initiatives in the most recent decade have not only focused purely on defensive strategies but also tended to foster more offensive actions to maintain US dominance in the high-tech areas. One of these crucial measures was to ramp up the range and depth of surveillance via big-data processing capabilities. Moreover, US unilateral dominance in the extraterritorial cyberspace hardens US offensive efforts to build a global invasive network of surveillance. Its operations of unscrupulous surveillance have gone far beyond the rationale of "antiterrorism," penetrating deeply into other countries' critical infrastructure networks as well as foreign firms' corporate networks through state-firm partnerships. The US authorities and media have charged that Huawei-made telecom equipment was devised to allow unauthorized access by the Chinese government and the military. Ironically, it is the US National Security Agency (NSA) that has reportedly launched major cyberattacks against Huawei since 2009. In early 2009 the US spying program hacked into servers of Huawei's central office in Shenzhen, which allowed the NSA to gain access to Huawei's email archives and information about the company's major customers. The NSA also obtained the individual source code of Huawei-made products, allowing US officials easy access to any network using Huawei's equipment. A classified NSA document leaked by Edward Snowden further revealed the reason behind the US agency's cyberattack: "Many of our targets communicate over Huawei-produced products. . . . We want to make sure that we know how to exploit these products—we also want to ensure that we retain access to these communication lines, etc."[38] As Huawei Rotating Chairman Guo Ping stated in the *Financial Times*, "[Huawei] hampers US efforts to spy on whomever it wants."[39] The full-scale assault on Huawei reflects the United States' fear of losing control over its global surveillance networks, especially when Huawei's gears are gaining wider adoption on the global scale. It also reveals the US double standards in defining "national security."

Furthermore, with the growing geopolitical tensions, the Trump administration has intensified the fight against Chinese high-tech companies. In August 2017 the US government formally initiated an investigation into China's practices related to technology transfer, intellectual property, and innovation under Section 301 of the Trade Act of 1974. In March 2018 the Office of the United States Trade Representative published a report of its findings, declaring that China's industrial upgrade plan "Made in China 2025" (MIC2025) would pose a threat to the US economy and technology. Following the Section 301 report, President Trump signed a memorandum on March 22 to impose tariffs on Chinese imports, primarily targeting China's strategic areas in MIC2025.

In fact, before the full-scale trade war launched by the Trump administration, the US government had already taken heightened control of Chinese investment in the high-tech industry. Three months earlier, in January 2018, the

US government blocked the $1.2 billion acquisition plan of Ant Financial—a Chinese electronic payments company affiliated with Alibaba—to buy the American money transfer company MoneyGram. Upon the failure of this acquisition, President Trump issued an executive order in March, blocking the Singapore-based microchip maker Broadcom proposal of a $117 billion buyout of Qualcomm on grounds of national security. The US officials warned that the proposed takeover would weaken Qualcomm and give Chinese rivals like Huawei an advantage.[40] If these incidents offered early signs of a US move to contain China's ICT companies, the US government's ban on ZTE in April shows how the United States stepped up its drive to confront China. Although the US government later lifted the ban, the action was followed by the trade war and blatant attacks on Huawei. In May 2019, when the tit-for-tat trade war between China and the United States was escalating, Trump signed an executive order declaring a national emergency, barring US companies from using telecommunications equipment made by manufacturers deemed a national security risk. Following the order, the US Commerce Department announced it would add Huawei to its export blacklist, the Entity List, aiming to smash the Chinese ICT giant's global supply chains. After the blacklisting, a few high-tech companies, such as Google, suspended their business with Huawei, which involves the transfer of hardware, software, and technical services.

Behind such arbitrary actions was the US attempt to wage an economic war to crack down on China's rise and assert US dominance in the global political-economic order. Following US operations, some US allies, such as Australia, also invoked protectionist policy excluding Huawei from their network construction plans due to "security concerns." Australia has repeatedly banned Huawei from taking part in its national infrastructure projects, such as the National Broadband Network projects. An undersea cable project deployed by Huawei Marine that would connect the internet between Solomon Islands and Australia was also blocked by the Australian security agency. The officials of the Five Eyes, the Western intelligence alliance including the member nations of the United States, the UK, Australia, New Zealand, and Canada, reportedly met several months before the Huawei arrest and reached an agreement to counter Huawei's global reach.[41] The unprecedented arrest of Meng was symbolic to reveal the United States' extraterritorial power to exercise universal jurisdiction beyond its territory. As Schiller argues, the United States has the ability to project power into the domestic space of other countries and to affect their decision-making process.[42] As a rule maker, the United States applied its power at the national and international levels to pursue its double standards: to promote liberalized expansion for its home-based capital abroad and to launch protectionism to exclude rivalries at home.[43] Therefore, the simple-minded rhetoric of "national security" is limited to capturing inter-state conflicts and new forms of imperialism in the network age. In digital capitalism, critical ICT infrastructure has become one of the fundamental elements of network sovereignty. The US effort to sustain its leadership in digital capitalism is illustrated in its coercive actions against rival capitals and states, which can be viewed as an extension of the US imperialist power in the network age. As a Huawei executive commented, Huawei has become a "negotiating pawn" between the United States and China. The US government's ban on Chinese ICT capital under the logic of "national security" is nothing more than a means to restrain the rise of China's "national comprehensive strength."[44]

Apart from the realistic concern related to nation-state interests, the discourse of "national security" also intertwines with a tension of inter-capitalist rivalry. In the 4G era, American companies such as Apple and Qualcomm have become the biggest winners, playing critical roles in revolutionizing the ecosystem of wireless industries. Apple, for instance, established a vertically integrated value chain ranging from proprietary equipment to software systems and from services to distribution channels.[45] The significant economic edge these companies enjoyed enabled the United States to surpass Europe in becoming a dominant leader in the transition from 3G to 4G. But Chinese companies with core technologies and strong innovation capabilities, such as Huawei and ZTE, have posed real threats to US companies, especially in the backdrop of the global race to 5G technologies. In fact, the focus of 5G mobile communications is more than the evolution of technologies enabling accelerated telecommunications connection; the focus is also on the massive transformations of business and technological ecosystems that revolutionize geoeconomics of the ICT development. Apart from advancements in network equipment and hardware devices, the changes of 5G ecosystems redefine network connectivity by supporting some strategic industries and applications such as self-driving cars, virtual reality, and the Internet of Things. The 5G revolution will also bring promising revenue streams to ICT companies. Yet the rise of China in 5G, which is mainly led by Huawei's technological innovations in hardware, has undercut US companies' monopoly profit in the redistribution of the profit chain. In this sense, the US attack on Huawei was more provocative to protect American companies' interests and the home-based industrial ecosystem in strategic areas.

However, for those Chinese manufacturing companies entrenched in the low-end value chain, the US government was more positive about and tolerant toward their entry. For example, Chinese PC producer Lenovo encountered fewer obstacles and oppositions than Huawei when acquiring American companies' assets such as IBM's PC business unit and Motorola's handset division. This is largely because the ICT manufacturing business in the United States has been facing shrinking margins in the last decade, and many American high-tech companies were eager to seek a restructuring strategy by getting rid of low-value-added business and shifting to high-end internet-based applications. Chinese companies' acquisition of American companies' outdated business was actually congruent with the benefit of the US industrial restructuring.

LOCALIZATION AND BUSINESS STRATEGIC ADJUSTMENT

In response to coercive actions from the US government-corporation power complex, Huawei had sought changes in terms of the corporate structure and market strategies to conform to US policy requirements and economic interests. After the US Congress published the investigative report against Huawei, the company released a Cyber Security White Paper in September 2012 to respond to the US government's accusation, promising to improve the company's cybersecurity operations and calling for consensus of international standards based on a broader, collaborative, and rationally informed dialogue.[46] This report clarified Huawei's connection with the Chinese government and military and implicitly challenged US-dominated standards on cybersecurity. To concretize the company's effort on the protection of cybersecurity, Huawei also promised to publish original codes of all of its equipment to the US government. In addition, Huawei sought to localize the American branch's operations to act like an "American company" and to engage closely with US political institutions and partner companies, in an attempt to gain recognition from the public and private sectors. In 2012 Huawei announced that it awarded three-year procurement contracts worth $6 billion to three US semiconductor companies—Qualcomm, Broadcom, and Avago—promising to create tens of thousands of job opportunities for the American ICT industry. A Huawei employee working at the North American branch revealed in an interview that since 2012 the company has called back a large number of Chinese employees from the US-based branches and substantially extended the number of local employees to fulfill its commitment to the creation of local employment opportunities (author interview). After the Meng arrest, Huawei sought an interim agreement with Qualcomm to pay the latter $150 million royalties each quarter. Meanwhile, Huawei tended to recruit more American executives who had former working experience in other Western TNCs or US government institutions in order to transnationalize its managerial strata. In addition, the company hired an army of outside and in-house lobbyists, including key former politicians in the US government, and expanded its large spending on lobbying in Washington, DC.

However, Huawei's transnationalized effort in the United States appeared futile. The company's sales in the segment of the infrastructure business and enterprise networks business sharply declined in the US market after the 2012 congressional report. Huawei's revenue in North America accounted for the lowest share of the company's overall revenue. To eschew the controversy of national security concerns and revive the market strategy in the United States, Huawei entered the consumer business with a focus on lower-margin sales of its branded mobile devices using Google's Android operating system after 2012, shifting the role from a critical infrastructure equipment supplier to a consumer device maker. In addition, because the software operating system is still mastered by the American company, Huawei's expansion in the consumer market seems to pose less of a threat to American firms and the country's network security. Despite dramatic growth of Huawei smartphone sales globally, its market share in the US market was far behind other smartphone giants, such as Apple, Samsung, LG, Motorola, and HTC. Google's move to restrict Huawei's access to its service could further bring catastrophic consequences to Huawei's overseas smartphone markets.

In view of the insurmountable obstacles and unfair treatments in the United States, as early as 2013 Ren Zhengfei announced that "Huawei is exiting the US market." He explained that "it is not worth it if [Huawei's involvement] causes problems for US-China diplomatic relations."[47] Since then Huawei has gradually scaled down its US operation. After the ZTE ban in 2018, Huawei reportedly scheduled its own withdrawal from three US offices and closed factories in the United States.[48]

Although Huawei was banned from US federal agencies and tier-one operators, an overlooked fact is that Huawei's cost-effective telecommunications gear was highly sought after among a significant number of rural telecommunications operators. In the US rural telecommunications market, Huawei offered 20 to 30 percent lower prices of high-quality networking gear than its competitors, helping some smaller US telecommunications companies to provide landlines, mobile service, and data coverage to the poorest and most remote areas in the country.[49] For some rural telecommunications operators, Huawei was the only telecommunications equipment supplier to support their wireless network. The US federal government's sanction against Chinese telecom equipment manufacturers would bring a detrimental impact on these operators and their wireless services in rural, underserved areas across the country. According to the Rural Wireless Association (RWA), an American trade association representing rural wireless carriers, at least 25 percent of its carrier members would be seriously impacted by the government's ban on Huawei. It would cost these carriers as much as $1 billion for the replacement of their telecommunications equipment.[50] The RWA and some smaller rural carriers have been lobbying the Federal Communications Commission (FCC), urging the American government not to adopt rules that restrict Huawei's presence. There is no doubt that US protectionist policy, driven by the realistic concerns and big capitalists' imperatives, was at the sacrifice of local carriers' interests and the universal public service, which will deepen the divisions within the US market.

The Chinese government's central leadership had made efforts to intervene in and ease the tensions between Chinese ICT companies and the US government before the US-China trade war. As part of these efforts, in 2015 Chinese president Xi Jinping began his first visit to the United States by organizing a China-US tech summit in Seattle, with the goal of seeking out an ally with US tech giants and quelling or containing the US government's sanctions on Chinese high-tech firms. Meanwhile, US internet companies such as Facebook, Google, and Twitter have also been clamoring for improving access to China's huge digital markets. However, the deep-seated divisions over a range of issues—from trade disputes to cyber-commercial espionage—continued to set the scene for US-China confrontation. Moreover, the changes in power politics have complicated the inter-state and inter-capitalist competition between China and the United States. The aggressive policy the Trump administration pursued forced the Chinese government to slip into the "conflict zone mode" amid the US-China trade war tensions. This incident also led to diplomatic disputes between China and Western countries, a tough stance that the Chinese government rarely adopted to intervene in a business foreign affair in order to support its national champion. Within China, the US arrest of Meng and the trade ban provoked a widespread nationalist backlash against US "imperialist" action and nationalist support to Huawei.

The irreconcilable conflicts compelled the Chinese government to readjust its geopolitical strategy. Likewise, Huawei opted for a strategy of "delinkage" with the US market. As Ren Zhengfei claimed in an interview with the BBC, "There's no way the US can crush us." He further quoted Mao in Huawei's strategy: "If the lights go out in the West, the East will still shine. And if the North goes dark, there is still the South. America doesn't represent the world. America only represents a portion of the world."[51] Under consistent attack from the United States, Huawei decided to turn defense into counterattack by taking legal action against the US government, signaling the company's more aggressive stance against the United States and its determination in reducing dependence on Western markets. At the same time, Huawei's "delinking" with the United States might make the company adjust its strategic focus to accommodate China's thriving market. China's reorientation toward a "domestic growth-driven model" actually "granted some maneuvering room to Chinese capital."[52] The Chinese state's capacity in reserving and cultivating its national market might enable Huawei to adjust its trajectory of development from "going out" to "going back" to its rapidly growing home market.

Conclusion

The outward expansion of Chinese capital from peripheral countries to core countries is consistent with the Chinese state's initiatives of pushing for deeper integration into global capitalism. The penetration of Chinese ICT capital into traditional core countries is somewhat posited as an essential step to enhance China's position in the global order. It is important to point out that the process of such a "counter capital flow" is not friction-free. It is rife with inter-state and inter-capitalist tensions. As Robinson emphasizes, the conjunction of geopolitical and structural analyses must be informed in order to understand the growing conflicts between traditional core countries and rising powers in the global South.[53] The Huawei case illustrates the intensifying geopolitical-economic struggle over the control of network infrastructure and information sovereignty. Underlying this struggle is a new form of "territorial logic" in the age of digital capitalism—that is, securing the commanding height of information technologies and cyberspace warfare to ward off threats and to ensure greater security. China's proliferating efforts of nurturing globally competitive ICT firms and pursuing their extraterritorial expansion can be viewed as part of such a logic to secure greater political and economic power in the global capitalist system.

Besides the tensions of the territorial logic, the contradictions embedded in Huawei's expansion also demonstrated inter-capitalist competition. The conflict between China's emerging corporate power and the traditional core powers can be seen as a form of competition between capitalists for repositioning in the ranks of the transnational capitalist class. But given intertwined interests of different blocs of the transnational capitalist class in the highly interdependent networks of capital accumulation, the United States' drastic move to attack Huawei could in turn damage American firms and the US high-tech sector.

In light of the multifaceted and complicated nature of Chinese capital, it is still too early to predict that the rise of Chinese ICT corporate power would pose any real threat to the West. Although Huawei has successfully broken into Western mainstream markets and possessed competitive advantage in global production, the scale and scope of Chinese TNCs in the ICT sector has "remained below par" with giant Western competitors.[54] The US attacks have exposed the vulnerability of Chinese ICT companies' supply chain, which is highly dependent on US core technologies. Although Huawei has achieved leadership in some fundamental hardware technologies, the role of other Chinese companies in the global ICT ecosystem remains less important than their US counterparts.

Moreover, despite Huawei's "delinkage" strategy in the United States, factions of Chinese capitalist groups, such as the newly emerging internet capitalists, still tend to forge ties with the United States for their expansionary ambitions and converge on a shared agenda of capital accumulation or policy goal. Therefore, it would be a mistake to posit the rise of China's corporate power as a coherent force in challenging the existing US-led political-economic order. There is no doubt that the US approach that resorted to containment and confrontation will create more uncertainties for Chinese ICT companies' global expansion in an increasingly hostile international market. More Chinese companies are likely to be caught up in the geopolitical-economic conflicts between China and Western countries in the transition of global power shift.

CHAPTER 4

From Path-Dependent to Pathbreaking?

Huawei's Technological Capability Development

Apart from Huawei's competence in market expansion, the company's success can be attributed to its self-reliant R&D-oriented strategy. Huawei's pursuit of progress on the technological front is congruent with China's national strategy to strike the "global strategic balance" and the initiative to move from technological dependence to "indigenous innovation."[1] However, the techno-nationalistic initiative is not the sole driving force for Huawei's R&D strategy. The company's keen interests in seeking cooperative, transnationalized R&D networks along with its going-out process constitute a transnational character of its R&D strategy. This path not only contrasts with the state-centered, nationalistic approach but also gives rise to new forms of competition, conflict, and synergy among multiple technological actors within a transnationalized context. In this sense, the tension between the state's techno-nationalistic initiative of pursuing technological leadership and the growing transnational nature of capitalist accumulation has become one of the most prominent themes that define much of China's recent struggle in its developmental trajectory in the network age.[2] This chapter focuses on such underlying contradictions and paradoxical dynamics by looking into Huawei's strategy in technology development and innovation.

As the evolution of China's approach to technological development—from Mao's militarization, to a market-oriented approach, and then to the current inspiration of cultivating indigenous innovation—is shaping local firms' course of technological development, this chapter first provides a historical review of China's evolving technology strategy to understand how the changing policy framework set the scene for the growth of Huawei's R&D capabilities. Then a detailed account of the company's R&D strategies—specifically exemplified in its development in the fields of digital switching technology, telecom standards, semiconductor technology, and patent-oriented strategy—is provided in order to illuminate the incentives and patterns of Huawei's technological and innovative development as well as its dynamic interaction with multiple technological actors.

China's Distinct Trajectory of Technological Development

There has been ongoing theoretical debate about the role of technology in third world countries' social development within the postwar literature. The mainstream modernization theorists view technology progress as the driving force of social transformation and believe that the development of third world countries primarily depends on the importation and diffusion of technology from developed countries.[3] Modernization theories have been under attack from many scholars.[4] From the perspective of the dependency theory, less-developed countries' dependence on the importation of advanced technology from core countries would lead to structural underdevelopment in the periphery. Some radical neo-imperialist writers went further to question the nature of capitalist technology development. As Samir Amin has argued, "Borrowing a technology from the capitalist world is never 'innocent' because this technology supports class relations of production."[5] The critical question concerning development for whom brings the issue of power relations to the discussion of the nature of technology. It rejects the idea of technology neutrality and takes into account broader social, political, and economic factors that shape the politics of technology-led development.

At the same time, the empirical experience from newly industrialized countries complements this theoretical debate, demonstrating the different patterns of technological progress in these countries in comparison with the earlier industrialization of Western countries.[6] East Asian firms generally build up their technical competency through technological learning and acquisition in the globalized production network, moving from simple original equipment manufacturing to original design manufacturing and to original brand manufacturing. However, it should be noted that these countries' technological achievements were primarily built on their linkage with foreign transnational capital. The rise of Asian dragons especially benefited from their "relatively unhindered access to US markets and technology" during these countries' takeoff period.[7] Although China's market reform followed a similar export-oriented path of development, the Chinese state's effort to cultivate domestically accumulated expertise by drawing on self-reliant R&D activities constituted a distinct approach of technology development.

China's technological development has experienced complex policy struggles along with the country's political-economic transformation, a complex process that characterized China's search for an alternative to capitalist technological development. Political scientist Evan A. Feigenbaum highlights the legacy of China's militarization from the 1950s to 1970s in the evolution of China's technology and science development.[8] Under the external Cold War pressure of that time, "techno-nationalism with Chinese characteristics" was embraced as the overarching developmental doctrine in the planning of the national economy, placing much emphasis on "industrial competitiveness, international standing, and economic power."[9] In this regard, technology can be redefined as an intrinsically strategic power struggling for the relative position of the Chinese state in international relations.[10] The development of critical technical infrastructure during this period led to the spin-off of high technologies from military to civilian industries and "trickle-down" from strategic technology sectors to a wider industrial base, which laid a solid foundation for China's technical progress in the reform era. As discussed in chapter 1, Chinese major breakthroughs in the fields of electronics and telecommunications technologies were primarily fulfilled by military-related research institutes and third-front enterprises under the nationwide programs of militarization.

In terms of the organizational style of technology development during the Mao era, the state played a crucial and direct role in mobilizing R&D resources and developing critical technology sectors under the central planning system. However, China's technology development was not confined under the rubric of the state-led militarization, but it also incorporated proletariat class politics.[11] In contrast with the Western elite model, China's socialist pattern of technological development and innovation articulated workers' participation and experience in the manufacturing process. The technology education during this period emphasized workers' knowledge production and technical innovation in working practices. By overcoming fragmented, vertically bureaucratic hierarchies and technocrat politics, ordinary workers who had formed the political identity of "the master of technology" were able to participate in the design of products and to determine how products and technologies were created. Apart from workers' participation in the design-and-production process, such a democratic organizational style presupposed a two-way collaboration and interaction between professional scientists, technicians, and industrial workers. In this context, technical progress strongly reflected the working class's subjectivities and identity politics in the combination of production and technological development. This distinct experience of socialist technological development has also partially been translated into Huawei's R&D practices.

The path hinging on a domestically accumulated self-reliant technology and R&D system constituted the essential experience of China's technological development. However, with the trend of depoliticization in the post-Mao era, the dialectic relation between technology and politics has been overridden by the market mechanism in China's technology policy. A paradoxical path of China's ICT technology development has been contested with heightened uncertainty.

Starting in the early 1980s, the central government set "dual-track" development as a guiding principle of China's ICT technological development. This mode of development involved four essential steps: (1) importing and acquiring advanced foreign technology products, (2) absorbing this knowhow from technology transfer, (3) exploring indigenized technology, and (4) nurturing innovative capacity at the state and firm levels.[12] With regard to the relationship between technology transfer and indigenization, Li Tieying, former minister of the electronics industry, declared, "Importing and indigenization are two sides of the same coin. . . . Importing is to fully utilize the achievements of international technology to promote indigenization. And indigenization is to obtain new development and better economic benefits based on a new technical level."[13]

Despite the state's incentive of promoting indigenous innovation and technology capabilities, foreign technology importation and transfer seemed to be the quickest route to build up the basic infrastructure at the beginning of China's opening-up process. The wholesale import of foreign standardized products, however, was primarily confined in manufacturing, engineering, and installation technology through a "highly formalized and carefully planned process."[14] The so-called technology transfer often includes "know-how" (production engineering) but not "know-why" (basic design, research, and development).

Local technology firms were keen to import proven foreign technologies and products directly in order to obtain profits in the burgeoning domestic market rather than investments in in-house R&D efforts. Instead of focusing on domestically accumulated R&D capabilities, most Chinese indigenous technology firms chose to engage in international trade to create linkages to transnational capital and fulfill the circuit of initial capital accumulation. For example, Lenovo followed a typical *mao gong ji* (trade to manufacturing and then to technology) trajectory. With the influx of foreign capital into China's ICT sector in the 1990s, Chinese indigenous firms were further entrenched in labor-intensive, export-oriented production, lacking incentive in indigenous technological innovations.

Parallel to the outward-looking mode of technological development, the Chinese government strove to revive the national R&D and innovation system by way of the market mechanism. The 863 Plan, a massive military and industrial development plan, was initiated in 1986 to focus on seven strategic sectors ranging from information technology to space technology. As a follow-up policy strategy, the so-called Torch Plan was launched in 1988 to promote commercialization and marketization of China's strategic high technologies. The market-oriented mode of high-tech development also moved from the state-centered approach to the involvement of multiple technological actors consisting of state, multinational corporations, local firms, and universities and research institutes. The R&D activities by indigenous firms, in particular, were embraced as a priority within the national innovation system. In 1997 the National Conference on Technological Innovation promoted the role of enterprises as a key force in national R&D activities. In 1999 the government further required that Chinese high-tech firms had to spend at least 5 percent of their annual sales on R&D. By 2000 spending by enterprises had accounted for 60 percent of China's R&D spending. However, R&D spending by Chinese indigenous enterprises remained at a relatively low level. In 2006 the top one hundred domestic electronics and information enterprises spent an average of about 3.9 percent of annual sales revenue on R&D, far below the goal set by the state government.[15] But over the past decade, China has accelerated its R&D investment in high-tech sectors. In 2013 China overtook Japan in R&D spending and became the second-largest R&D spender in the world, just behind the United States.[16] The country's ratio of R&D spending to GDP had reached 2.11 percent by 2016, the highest among developing countries.

In concert with the state initiative in strengthening R&D capability, local governments also played a critical role in nurturing effective developmental strategies for indigenous high-tech enterprises at the subnational level. Shenzhen, home to Huawei and many other Chinese high-tech giants, such as ZTE and Tencent, has displayed a distinct pattern of indigenous innovation.

Thanks to the decentralization of China's policy planning, local state actors were able to wield administrative power to steer the direction of local economic development. In 1995 Shenzhen Municipal Government issued a "Decision on the Promotion of the Science and Technology Progress," proposing the "strategy of developing the city through science and technology" (*kejixingshi*) as the priority of local development. The information industry was placed as one of the pillar industries in Shenzhen's long-term development.

In the fourth meeting of the Shenzhen Municipal People's Congress, in 2005, city officials announced that Shenzhen would promote and insist on indigenous innovation, with the intent to become an international hub of scientific and technological innovation.[17] As part of China's innovation-driven development strategy, Shenzhen was elevated as the first national innovation pilot city in 2008, pioneering in national R&D activities. Beginning in 2013, Shenzhen spent more than 4 percent of its annual GDP on R&D, far exceeding the international norm for innovative economies. However, in stark contrast to other R&D centers in China, like Beijing and Shanghai, that drew on a top-down approach to technology development and their rich science and technology resource, the "Shenzhen model of innovation" was largely driven by corporate R&D capabilities, characterized by "the four 90 percents" in its innovation system. The term refers to the goal of more than 90 percent of the city's R&D labs, 90 percent of R&D personnel, 90 percent of R&D funding, and 90 percent of patents coming from Shenzhen-based enterprises.[18] In addition, Shenzhen-based companies accounted for more than half of China's international patent filings, with Huawei and ZTE contributing to the largest share of filings.

It is important to note that the Shenzhen model of innovation is also built upon the Pearl River Delta region's manufacturing prowess.[19] This advantage enables the region to master a complete production chain and develop a regional innovation network. For instance, Shenzhen's neighboring city, Dongguan, has increasingly undertaken manufacturing activities from Shenzhen-based high-tech companies based on the Shenzhen-Dongguan "supercity cluster" of the ICT industries. Such a "bottom-up production-to-innovation model" characterizes the Pearl River Delta's pragmatic approach to "independent innovation,"[20] which also laid an innovation ecosystem and institutional arrangement for local ICT companies' development. The industrial policy developed and implemented at the subnational level was the key institutional mechanism for Huawei's success in technology and market expansion.

Despite rapid growth of national technological spending at the national and subnational levels, China's R&D resources are still unequally distributed. With China's integration into the globalized R&D network, foreign multinational corporations have increasingly played an important role in China's R&D activities by setting global R&D centers and appropriating R&D talents in China. In addition, state-owned enterprises possessed advantage in their access to national R&D resources relative to domestic private enterprises. For example, SOEs have a privilege to obtain national R&D funding and projects. Despite the full force of competition, Huawei managed to carve out a distinct path toward technological capability development in the high-tech sector. How can a private firm that started from a sales agent grow into a technological giant in its own right? Huawei's distinct experience might provide special lessons for other Chinese indigenous firms.

Huawei's Technological and Innovative Capability Development

The analysis of China's technological development strategies at the macro level provides a perspective in examining the role of the state and industry policy in shaping a firm's innovation strategies and capabilities. In turn, a close investigation of innovation models and R&D practices at the firm level is useful for understanding the role of the Chinese indigenous firm in driving China's technological upgrading and the development of indigenous innovation.

The source of innovation at the firm level may come from internal efforts, such as in-house R&D activities, or externally from the acquisition of technology.[21] For some high-tech companies, the acquisition of other firms' technological assets, including patents, new technologies, and innovation capacity, might be the most efficient way to accumulate technological capabilities. For example, Lenovo's purchase of world-renowned brands, including IBM's PC business and Motorola Mobility, can be seen as a particular approach to technological acquisition. Even technological giant Cisco relied on the acquisition strategy to strengthen its technological capacity. Starting in 1993, Cisco has accelerated the process of acquisition in numerous market segments—ranging from internet hardware and software to switches and routers—in which Cisco intended to become a market leader. Such a model of growth by acquisition not only enabled multinational corporations to take a shortcut in acquiring technological assets but also allowed them to concentrate on market expansion and consolidate their monopoly over core proprietary technology. Using a different approach to technological development, Huawei opted to build up its own self-reliant technology to sustain the company's long-term development from scratch.

Due to a lack of core proprietary technologies, Huawei, like many other Chinese indigenous high-tech firms, started its business as a sales agent to accumulate primitive capital from the "telecommunications fever" of the late 1980s. However, Huawei quickly realized the importance of building its own proprietary technology in the market. It then established a series of in-house R&D strategies and committed itself to indigenous innovation efforts. For decades, Huawei has maintained its massive investments in R&D, devoting more than 10 percent of its sales revenue to R&D activities annually. From 2005 to 2015, Huawei spent a total of $37 billion on R&D.[22] This amount far exceeded Lenovo's ten-year aggregated R&D investment as well as that of BAT.[23] Noticeably, Huawei's R&D spending paralleled or even outpaced that of the most influential high-tech giants, including Intel, Apple, Facebook, Oracle, Cisco, Nokia, Qualcomm, and Ericsson.[24]

Huawei's transnationalization at the current stage has strived for not only market access but also for building impressive and genuine technological capabilities. With Huawei's internationalization of R&D, the company has set up sixteen major R&D global centers located in India, the United States, Germany, Sweden, Russia, Japan, and Canada, in addition to those in Beijing, Shanghai, Nanjing, Shenzhen, Hangzhou, and Chengdu in China. Different research centers are devoted to specialized R&D activities by taking advantage of local resources.

From a technology follower to a global leader, Huawei's path toward technological progress has been faced with numerous setbacks and difficulties. To gain insights into the dynamics of Huawei's R&D patterns and its interaction with other multiple technological actors, the following section looks into Huawei's specific R&D strategies and innovation activities in its various domains, including its core strength in switching technology, its contradictory role in developing China's indigenous telecom standards, the catch-up strategy in semiconductor technology, and its patents and intellectual property strategies.

BREAKTHROUGH IN DIGITAL SWITCHING TECHNOLOGY

As early as the late 1980s, Huawei had already decided to step into indigenous switching technology innovation. However, Huawei's first self-branded product, the BH01 switch, was actually an assembly product, the components of which were bought from a state-owned enterprise affiliated with the Ministry of Post and Telecommunications. In 1990 Huawei launched its first R&D project, whose primary task was to develop an independent product based on the imitation of the BH01 technology. The R&D team was made up of only six engineers at that time.[25] The developers had to take full responsibility for both hardware and software production, including activities in researching, developing, producing, and testing.

A critical turning point of Huawei's technological development occurred in the early 1990s. Although Huawei had successfully gained a small slice of market share in low-end markets by selling small private branch exchanges to small businesses, its switching technology was constrained in small-capacity applications. When facing critical challenges from technological innovations, a Huawei production worker, Cao Yian, proposed that the company shift its R&D focus to digital switches with large capacity, which can be used in large-scale telecommunications transmission by telecom operators. Huawei's leaders adopted Cao's advice and then turned to R&D in digital switching technology.[26] This decision was significant for Huawei, as it indicated the company's advance in its R&D endeavor, moving away from low-end exchange technology to innovations in core telecom technologies. An ordinary worker, Cao was later promoted to the position of manager of Huawei's digital switch project. This example fully illustrates Huawei's bottom-up approach in decision making, which contrasted with the elite and professional-oriented R&D model.

When Huawei decided to tap into switching technology, China's indigenous digital switching technology had gained a breakthrough by a military research institute—the Center for Information Technology (CIT) in the Zhengzhou Institute of Information Engineering of the People's Liberation Army. During the Maoist era of militarization, the CIT had already deeply engaged in the R&D of China's large-capacity computers, a national defense project that was endorsed by Zhou Enlai in 1968. Under the force of marketization in the reform era, the research institute shifted its focus of technology innovation from military-related computing technology to the booming telecommunications industry by launching the development of the first Chinese self-innovated digital switch, the HJD-04 system. During this process, Professor Wu Jiangxing, who had been a senior engineer in the People's Liberation Army and later the head of CIT, played a decisive role in the R&D and architecture design of the HJD-04 project. Professor Wu had participated in the research of China's first integrated-circuit computer in 1970 and the distributed computer system GP300 during the early 1980s. Based on the advanced computing technology deriving from the legacy of military-related technology, in 1991 Wu Jiangxing and his research team successfully produced the HJD-04 system, the capacity of which parallels that of advanced digital switching technology in Western countries. This innovative system was quickly converted into mass production and commercialization. Meanwhile, the MPT's Luoyang Telephone Equipment Factory (LTEF), previously a three-front telecom manufacturing enterprise, assumed the role as a manufacturer as well as a technical assistant to the CIT in the project.

It should be recognized that the breakthrough of China's digital switching technology largely benefited from the mixed legacy of the country's history of self-reliant technological development. This technological breakthrough also had a trickle-down effect on Chinese indigenous firms such as Huawei in their own R&D efforts. Because Huawei's technicians did not have previous experience in developing advanced digital switching technologies, they mainly depended on the approach of "learning by doing" from scratch. According to these technicians, the process of technological learning was like "crossing the river by touching the stone" (author interview). Based on studies of the HJD-04 system, Huawei managed to develop its own digital switch, C&C08, in 1994, which was also China's second self-innovated digital switch with high capacity.

Huawei's R&D activities were not confined to the laboratory. The technologies they developed fully took into account the reality of China's telecommunications conditions and local network requirements based on technicians' surveys and practical experience in different areas. Apart from the three international gateways, Chinese public telecommunications networks actually varied at five different levels: there were eight level one (C1) transit switching centers in different districts; level two (C2) transit switching centers were located in the capital cities of provinces for provincial transit; level three (C3) networks were used for transit within each province; level four (C4) switches were located at the county level; and level five (C5) network was comprised of terminal switches, including town and village rural telephone lines.[27] Standardized foreign systems were barely able to meet specific requirements at the local level, especially at the county level. Moreover, transmission lines for China's public telecommunications services were intensive because of the high usage of lines in the early 1990s,[28] thus many foreign systems had run into problems. Huawei's R&D otherwise sought to solve such complicated conditions in an attempt to overcome the huge gaps between cities and rural networks. To this end, Huawei R&D teams organized several technical seminars with local PTB officers (C5 level) to determine the demand from rural areas. Apart from the low-cost requirement, China's rural telecom networks also required flexible equipment systems that were suitable for network upgrades and complicated geographical features. Based on this two-way R&D information flow, Huawei researchers and technicians successfully incorporated all of these requirements into the development of the C&C08 switch. This product had a flexible modular design that allowed exchanges to be supplied in the remote region and was easy to expand as transmission demands grew. The small telephone stations it built could also be widely dispersed and easily maintained in the countryside. As Dieter Ernst and Barry Naughton argue, Huawei's innovation change provided "a judicious combination on incremental and architectural innovations that provide integrated solutions throughout the life cycle of communications systems."[29] This foremost innovation accommodating China's local conditions had allowed Huawei to successfully seize the domestic switching market by the late 1990s.

It should be remembered that Huawei's success in indigenizing switching technologies was partly due to the standardization and maturation of switching technologies. Huawei's switch products actually were not new technologies in the strictest sense. China had started its own public digital switching technology in the late 1980s, a decade later than Western countries' investment.[30] Therefore, Huawei merely acted as a follower of incumbent technological players without having to go through some of the pioneering developmental stages. However, there is no doubt that Huawei's R&D activities still represent Chinese ICT firms' distinct approach to technical and innovative capabilities. Their creative effort has not only rested on the modular and architecture designs that is more compatible with local technological, economic, and political requirements but has also explored some alternative approaches of self-reliant technological development.

FROM STANDARD ADOPTER TO STANDARD DEFINER

Huawei's major breakthrough in switching technologies enabled the company to be on par with foreign competitors in the equipment manufacturing capability. But at the same time, the company moved to climb up the value chain by turning itself from an equipment manufacturer to a technology standard definer. This goal was congruent with the Chinese state's pursuit of "the mastery and proprietary control of core technologies,"[31] which was especially illustrated in China's strategy of developing its own wireless telecom standards.

Due to China's increasing leverage in standard wars, the country's initiative in challenging the West-dominated regime of standardization has become a pivotal issue in the geopolitics of global technological development. Meanwhile, firms' involvement in new technological standard setting produces high profits and ensures their monopolistic positions in the market. Standard wars also involve inter-capitalist competing interests. Therefore, the struggle over China's standardization policy can be better seen as a co-evolution process between the firm's strategy and government policy as well as a hybrid of struggles between techno-nationalism and techno-globalism.

The role of Huawei in the struggle over China's standard-setting activities has been complex. On the one hand, Huawei claims to have collaborated with the Chinese state in its national standard strategy in line with particular interests of China's ICT industry and the Chinese state. On the other hand, investing in immature Chinese standards also means substantial risks for Huawei, if limited commercialization of indigenous standards eventually threatens the company's survival. The conflict between the nationalistic commitment and the capital accumulation imperative has become a foremost challenge for Chinese indigenous firms like Huawei. The company's ambiguous attitude toward China's 3G homegrown standard TD-SCDMA and its interaction with multi-actors in this process demonstrates such a tension.

Before China embarked on the project of its own 3G wireless communications standard, the country's mobile telecommunications industry technologies were caught in long-term dependence on foreign standards. In 1987 China started to launch the analog mobile service (1G) by using the Ericsson's TACS (Total Access Communication System) standard. Since then China's analog mobile systems completely relied on direct import from foreign vendors. At that time, Ericsson and Motorola dominated 1G analog mobile communications standards in the world, but the networks and devices of these two companies were barely compatible with each other. In the 2G era, the European policy makers decided to end the fragmented system of incompatible networks and adopted a common standard GSM. The standardization policy generated significant economic benefits to European telecommunications equipment vendors such as Nokia, Ericsson, Alcatel, and Siemens, leading to European companies' domination in 2G technological innovations. In the United States, however, the story of 2G development was different. Regulators in the FCC decided to adopt a laissez-faire approach to 2G development, leaving market players to develop their own standards. In 1991 Qualcomm introduced a proprietary standard CDMA, which was originally used by the US military but later became one of the major commercial standards preferred by some operators. The US 2G policy framework led to a fragmented system of network development that mirrored Europe's 1G experience, leading the United States to lag far behind Europe in 2G market development and in technological innovation. When China moved to the 2G era, the European GSM and US-backed CDMA became two dominant mobile communications standards in China. In the late 1990s, Chinese indigenous telecommunications equipment vendors, including Huawei, ZTE, Datang, and Putian, started to enter the 2G market by adopting the path-following strategy. However, domestic vendors were in a disadvantaged position in the market, as core technologies of 2G standards were completely controlled by foreign giants. In addition, Chinese indigenous companies had to pay tremendously high patent fees to foreign intellectual property owners. Chinese firms had paid about ¥250 billion ($31 billion) for royalty fees in the 1G era and about ¥500 billion ($62 billion) in the 2G era.[32]

The technical inferiority and commercial burdens, along with the state's strategic concerns about national security, became driving factors for China's standard-setting endeavors. The earliest R&D phase of Chinese standards development started in 1993 when CDMAone technology was first introduced to China. This R&D project, which was sponsored by the "863 Program," primarily focused on assimilating imported standards. In 1995 under the support of the MPT, a Sino-US joint venture called Xinwei Telecommunications was established. The new firm then partnered with Datang to develop the SCDMA technology that later became a core part of TD-SCDMA. This project was also incorporated as one of the key R&D programs of the Ninth Five-Year Plan (1996–2000). At the same time, Datang chose to collaborate with Siemens to incorporate TDD and SCDMA systems, which later became the base of China's alternative 3G standard TD-SCDMA.

In May 2000 the International Telecommunication Union approved China's TD-SCDMA as the third 3G standard along with Europe-backed WCDMA and US-backed CDMA2000. However, the core technologies of these three competing standards were built directly on Qualcomm's proprietary 2G standard CDMA. Such competitive technological advantages granted Qualcomm the position of the "gatekeeper" of CDMA technology, which allowed the company to hold nearly all 3G core patents. Competition in standard setting and relevant technologies also reflected in the struggle of global technical governance. To counter the United States' increasing power in 3G standard setting, the 3rd Generation Partnership Project (3GPP), led by the European Telecommunications Standards Institute and European telecommunications companies, was founded in 1998 to promote the evolution from GSM to WCDMA. This Europe-centric standards body pushed the United States to establish the 3rd Generation Partnership Project 2 (3GPP2) in 1999 to develop the CDMA2000-based 3G ecosystem, with Qualcomm playing a dominant role. The competition of these two mainstream standards actually countered the ITU's intention to develop a globally unified wireless communications standard. China's participation in the 3G battles has further intensified such standards wars.

Within China, the development of TD-SCDMA generated massive disputes and divisions among policy makers, standard developers, equipment manufacturers, and telecommunications operators. Because TD-SCDMA was partially incompatible with the mainstream standards WCDMA and CDMA2000, international manufacturers, including indigenous companies, were hesitant to redesign TD-SCDMA equipment. According to a manager working at Huawei's telecom carrier sector, before the large-scale industrialization of China's 3G standard, Huawei was reluctant to deploy R&D spending on the TD-SCDMA system (author interview). The uncertain future of China's indigenous standard restrained the firm's incentive for promoting national interests in the market competition. In addition, Huawei has already placed much emphasis on overseas markets, where products built on the well-established foreign standards have created stable income for the company. The company's ambitions for outward expansion clashed with the state's techno-nationalistic overtones, compelling Huawei to adopt a pragmatic approach toward greater techno-globalism. Therefore, the company had more interests in developing systems based on foreign standards to seize mainstream markets than it had in China's homegrown standard. In particular, Huawei invested heavily in the Europe-backed WCDMA system, which had the largest user base across the world (author interview). The commercial interests transcended the company's nationalistic commitment, which drove Huawei to suspend its R&D project on the TD-SCDMA system.

Huawei's pragmatic strategy was echoed with Chinese policy makers' hesitant attitude toward TD-SCDMA. Wu Jichuan, the minister of the information industry at that time, insisted on the market-oriented, technology-neutral position on the development of China's mobile standard. He believed that "although TD-SCDMA was set to be an international standard, it does not mean it can become the basis for China's 3G network in the future. . . . The deployment of TD-SCDMA has to be determined by market demands and applications."[33] The overarching market logic became a doctrine that determined the state and firms' strategies regarding the standard development. The dispute not only delayed the overall agenda of China's TD-SCDMA development but also undermined Chinese firms' incentive to promote China's indigenous standards.

To promote the industrialization process, the government then took a lead in establishing a domestic industry alliance, with founding members including Datang, Huawei, ZTE, Putian, and four other domestic firms. The Chinese leadership tended to favor the whole TD-SCDMA industry rather than a specific firm like Datang. In July 2003 the Chinese government provided indigenous firms with ¥708 million ($85.4 million) as special funding to support the industrialization of TD-SCDMA.[34] In January 2006, TD-SCDMA was listed as one of China's biggest indigenous technological achievements for the Tenth Five-Year Plan (2001–2005) at the National Scientific Conference. Two months later, TD-SCDMA was officially designated as China's national 3G standard. The Chinese government also deliberately delayed the issuing of 3G licenses until 2009 in an attempt to allow the immature homegrown standard to enjoy adequate time for R&D and commercialization.

The role of the state in nurturing China's sizeable 3G market for indigenous firms was beyond question. As Zhang Guobao, deputy minister of the State Development and Reform Commission, said, "China's mobile telecom market will no longer be a playground for overseas companies in the upcoming 3G age."[35] In turn, Chinese indigenous firms had gained more commercial imperative to develop the homegrown standard when TD-SCDMA increasingly acquired considerable policy importance. Likewise, Huawei started to strengthen its R&D investments on the system. However, the company did not completely draw on its own R&D resources but chose to collaborate with Siemens to form the joint venture Dingqiao Telecommunications in 2005 to focus on the commercialization of TD-SCDMA. By the end of 2006, Huawei and Siemens, two parent companies of Dingqiao, had already invested more than $300 million in TD-SCDMA technologies, which was the largest corporate investment in the homegrown standard at that time.[36]

Although TD-SCDMA was reputed to be the indigenous innovation due to the involvement of Chinese firms in standard setting, the truth was that Chinese ICT companies did not own its core technologies. Meanwhile, collaboration with major global players to establish strategic alliances became a key approach to commercializing TD-SCDMA in the Chinese market. Some critics had doubts about Chinese firms' capability to develop self-reliant R&D, especially when foreign players had become important forces in the national standardization strategy. It is true that Chinese indigenous firms like Huawei continued to wrestle with the contradiction between techno-nationalism and techno-globalism. But "self-reliance" should not necessarily be conflated with autarky. Most Chinese indigenous firms have embraced a globalized R&D network to promote China's globally competitive national standards.

Under the state's standard-setting initiatives, the market share of Chinese indigenous firms, including Huawei, ZTE, and Datang, increased from less than 20 percent in the 2G era to more than 70 percent in the 3G era.[37] The massive investments in TD-SCDMA laid a technological foundation for China to implement a smooth evolution to a 4G TD-LTE system. As China took a major stake in TD-LTE patents, the promotion of the TD-LTE standard improved China's bargaining position in international markets. In contrast with its hesitant attitude toward the TD-SCDMA system, Huawei set TD-LTE as a priority of investment and established an independent R&D team in its own right, with more than four thousand engineers involved. The core competence of Huawei's TD-LTE technology lay in its compatibility with any mobile commercial network, which enabled network operators to converge different modalities and to maximize integration performance. In addition, Huawei provided a complete lineup of TD-LTE terminals, ranging from chipsets to smartphones. Thanks to Huawei's full participation in the TD-LTE technological ecosystem, the company has become a dominant infrastructure and device vendor in the TD-LTE market. Moreover, driven by China's thriving 4G market, Huawei has taken a lead in the overall LTE markets. By 2013 Huawei had accounted for 40 percent of LTE network contracts, with Ericsson following at 34 percent.[38]

In the 4G era, China's domestic telecom operators were more eager to attract global stakeholders and to promote convergence of various standards to change the enclosed ecosystem of TD-SCDMA. Therefore, domestic vendors had to face head-on competition from foreign suppliers in China's 4G market. In some areas of core technologies, foreign giants still occupied dominant positions. For example, Qualcomm has the highest market share for LTE baseband processors in handsets, far exceeding Huawei's shipments in the market. Furthermore, China's patents in the TD-LTE standard were mostly concentrated in peripheral areas of applications, while US and EU firms still played the dominant roles in setting architectural technology standards. To overcome these market and technical constraints, Huawei strove to move from a standard adopter to a standard definer by taking a proactive R&D strategy in 5G technologies. The company began investing in 5G as early as 2009, with more than $600 million invested in 5G technology research. Following the R&D on 5G core technologies, Huawei invested almost $1.4 billion into 5G product development from 2017 to 2018.[39]

In order to end the long-term fragmentation of wireless communications standards and increase the compatibility of global telecommunications networks, a key agenda of creating a unified global standard was set by the global technical governance body for 5G development. In this process, Huawei played a key role in mapping out 5G core technologies through its standard-setting strategies. One milestone was made in November 2016 when the International Wireless Standards Institute 3GPP RAN1 chose Huawei-proposed polar codes as the control channel encoding scheme for the application of 5G. It was Huawei's overwhelming victory over the US-backed LDPC (low-density parity check) program and French-backed Turbo2.0 program. More important, this was also the first time China's telecom technology was adopted as the key standard of the world's next generation of wireless communications systems in the telecom encoding area, which was seen as a "jewel in the crown of wireless communications technologies."[40]

Huawei's standard-setting capability enabled the company to innovate in 5G telecommunications infrastructure and applications in a wide array of products. One of the most prominent contributions Huawei has made to 5G innovation was Huawei's capability to integrate 5G base stations with the most advanced microwave technology. According to Ren Zhengfei, Huawei is the only company in the world to achieve such a technological innovation by combining the most advanced technologies in infrastructure and data transmission.[41] Built on Huawei's 5G proprietary technology, this 5G microwave solution can use superfast microwaves to support ultrawide bandwidth transmission without fiber connection, which significantly saves on high construction costs for optical fiber networks and base station maintenance. This compelling technology not only provides a better solution for wireless communications in remote rural areas but also meets the need for the majority of Western countries where some regions are sparsely populated.

Huawei's success in 5G technologies was more than a technical breakthrough. Rather, it may generate far-reaching political-economic implications for China's repositioning in the global technological system. In contrast with domestic actors' divisions in the deployment of TD-SCDMA, Huawei's innovations in the 5G standards have acquired unified support from Chinese operators and equipment vendors. The China-based IMT-2020 5G Promotion Group, which was founded by the Chinese government in 2013 and made up of more than fifty Chinese homegrown firms and institutions, has become the most important advocate for Huawei's technological proposal. Although domestic divisions still existed due to competing interests in the development of new standards, Chinese corporate players were also increasingly aware of the benefit of forming a united front in achieving China's leadership in the 5G era. The strengthening alliance not only helped Huawei gain ground in global standard wars; it also enhanced China's position in the arena of global technological governance in comparison with the US and EU blocs.

Huawei's success in its standard strategy can be largely attributed to the Chinese state's capacity in creating a "China-only accumulation regime."[42] More important, the company's increasing leverage in the global standard battleground showed an opportunity for domestic firms to alter the path-dependent approach in technological development and to execute the going-out strategy of China's homegrown standards and indigenous innovations. Amid increasing tensions arising from standard wars and inter-state rivalry between the United States and China, Ren Zhengfei posited a vision of techno-globalism in the networked age: "In the area of communications, we have gone through a period where different standards coexisted. That also increased the deployment costs of the networks.... In order to unify communications networks, we have worked hard to come up with a unified global standard. I think the 5G standard serves as a very good foundation for humanity to move toward an intelligent world. Arbitrarily dividing technology into two different camps will only harm the interests of the world.... Personally, I strongly support unified global standards."[43] Although Ren offered a vision toward a unified and cooperative global order in technological development, techno-nationalism and inter-capitalist competition for commercial interests still underpin the ongoing struggle for technological supremacy, which will fundamentally be at odds with Ren's vision of techno-globalism.

CATCH-UP STRATEGY IN SEMICONDUCTOR TECHNOLOGY

Apart from the achievement in standard setting, Huawei also strove to strengthen its self-reliant innovations in hardware technology. Its major breakthrough in integrated circuit (IC) technology—another arena of core technologies China has been pursuing—allowed the company to establish a full industrial chain ranging from chipsets to terminal devices, which significantly reduced its technological dependence on foreign suppliers.

For a long time, China's ICT technology development has been beset by a bottleneck in the field of high-end IC design, leading to the lack of core competitive advantages in electronics hardware production. In light of the strategic significance of the IC sector in high-tech industries, especially in national security, China's national technology policy has placed considerable emphasis on the development of IC technology by listing it as one of the leading industries in national high-tech programs since the late 1980s. However, after several decades China's chip industry still heavily relied on excessive importation. Annual chip imports by China reached more than $200 billion, making it China's largest import in terms of value.[44] Only a few Chinese indigenous firms had the ability to produce advanced chipsets that could meet the demand of the ICT industry. Even for China's own standard TD-SCDMA system, most manufacturers still use the chip design from foreign TNCs, such as Samsung, Philips, and Texas Instruments.

The lack of core technological capability made domestic ICT equipment manufacturers vulnerable to foreign control. The US sanctions on ZTE, for instance, crippled the company's supply chain and main business operations. Arbitrary sanctions from the United States gave rise to China's call for self-sufficiency in core technologies, especially in the development of the semiconductor industry. In fact, the dilemma ZTE encountered was foreseen by Ren Zhengfei many years ago. In a public speech for Huawei's scientists and researchers in 2012, Ren said that chip design as a fundamental R&D project was essentially strategic to achieve the company's self-sufficiency.[45] After the US decision to blacklist Huawei, Ren claimed that the company would not bow to US pressure. Huawei's achievement in developing their own competitive chipset enabled the company to overcome the technology's "Achilles' heel" to support its own products.

Although semiconductor technology is a highly capital-intensive field subject to numerous business risks, Huawei has recognized the importance of mastering essential proprietary technology from scratch. The company attributed such a heightened R&D model as the strategy of "innovation at the pinpoint." According to Ren Zhengfei, "Huawei is not strong enough to catch up in all areas. We have to focus on some key technologies. We put all the eggs in one basket—to invest all the resources in a specific technology and product—hoping that high investment intensity will lead to a breakthrough in the targeted area."[46] Ren further claimed that only through such R&D intensity in the field of sophisticated technology can Huawei get the chance to surpass US companies.

This R&D strategy proved to be very effective in establishing Huawei's independent technological capability. As early as 1991, Huawei already set up an R&D and design center for the application specific integrated circuit (ASIC), becoming one of the few Chinese domestic companies pioneering the independent innovation of IC technology. In 1993 Huawei successfully developed its first digital ASIC. In fact, the majority of China's IC products at that time were primarily restricted to specific-application, commodity memory chips and other low-end products,[47] while Huawei had already started to focus on high-end applications in telecommunications infrastructure and advanced products. For the decade that followed, Huawei made significant technological breakthroughs in advanced chips with high capacity. In October 2004 Huawei established a subsidiary called HiSilicon, which specifically focused on the research and production of high-end chipset products. Along with Huawei's increasing investments in its own smartphone products, in 2006 HiSilicon started to launch independent R&D on the cellular microprocessor for its own system, directly challenging US technological giant Qualcomm. The architecture and performance of its flagship mobile chipset Kirin series has been on par with and even outperformed that of its competitors. Huawei has become one of the very few smartphone manufacturers that has the capability to make its own chipsets for its mobile devices, along with Samsung and Apple. Although Huawei's cellular chipsets at the current stage are primarily used by its own handsets due to the low production rate, other Chinese domestic ICT manufacturers have gradually turned to and adopted Huawei's IC technology. In 2017 HiSilicon was ranked in the global top ten of IC design companies, becoming the largest China-based semiconductor company in the Chinese market in terms of revenue. More important, Huawei's leadership in 5G standard setting was fueled by its sophisticated technological capability in chipset design and innovation. In January 2019 the company launched the world's first 5G base station core chip, Tiangang, and the fastest multimode chipset, Balong 5000. These innovative chipsets have become core technologies ushering in the 5G era.

Huawei's strategy in developing its own IC technology closely cooperated with the state in its endeavor to revitalize China's IC industry. In 2014 the Chinese government issued a National IC Development Guideline and set up a ¥120 billion national IC fund in the form of equity stake ownership to promote the development of Chinese domestic firms.[48] However, a large portion of this fund was invested in state-owned enterprises such as Datang, Spreadtrum, and SMI. To accumulate core technology assets in a short term, these companies used state capital as a source of outward foreign direct investment to acquire foreign companies through overseas mergers and acquisitions. In stark contrast, Huawei insisted on its independent innovation model and technological development processes, including activities in R&D, module design, testing, and manufacturing.

In addition to financial support, the Chinese government created a favorable market environment for domestic firms through a series of protectionist policies. In November 2013, China's National Development and Reform Commission launched an investigation into Qualcomm for its anticompetition practices in China. The investigation ended up with Qualcomm being fined $975 million, the largest penalty in China's corporate history. The regulator also required Qualcomm to lower its royalty rates on patents used in China. Qualcomm's proposed deal for acquiring NXP, a Dutch-based chipmaker, was blocked by the Chinese antitrust regulators due to the concern that the deal would provide an unfair advantage over Chinese indigenous companies. These incidents exemplify Chinese policy makers' significant change from a pro-FDI to a protectionist policy framework in the strategic ICT sector.

As a crucial reminder, it is still too early to determine if Huawei's chipset technology has fully achieved independent innovation capability. In general Huawei has still followed the same technological road as Samsung in chipset manufacturing. Its CPU core is designed based on the ARM architecture platform, and its operating software is running on Google's Android system. This "AA system" constitutes a cornerstone of Huawei's IC design. Therefore, Huawei's design route and applications are still determined by owners of these core technologies. Due to the lack of chipset manufacturing capability in Mainland China, HiSilicon's chipset manufacturing substantially relied on external suppliers like Taiwanese chip company Taiwan Semiconductor Manufacturing Company (TSMC). But given the geopolitical-economic conditions, Huawei has urged some of its suppliers to move production lines to China amid trade war tensions, which would help the company strengthen its control over the supply chain.

Huawei has recognized its limitations in achieving real independent innovation. The company's R&D projects to develop its own core processor and mobile operating system, named HongmengOS, are already under way. According to Ren, "We are working on an operating system of terminal device because of the strategic demand. If they [US companies] suddenly cut off our supply . . . we have to guarantee that our backup system can be used."[49] This strategy has well prepared Huawei for any pressure or blockage. In the wake of the Android ban, Huawei accelerated the schedule to release its own self-developed operating system as a unified platform installed in all of Huawei's consumer devices. Meanwhile, in a letter to staff after the US blacklisting of Huawei, HiSilicon's CEO assured them that the backup products developed by HiSilicon would be able to substitute for critical components banned by the United States.[50]

In addition, Huawei possesses a competitive advantage in its telecommunications infrastructure technology. It is one of the few chipmakers in the world that can develop baseband processor technology, which is an essential core technology in the chipset manufacturing design to support high-speed wireless communications. Huawei also enjoys a cost advantage over other global giants. As the making of semiconductors is a highly profitable industry, the profit margin for transnational capitalists in this field is usually 40 percent or more, which constitutes the largest share of ICT manufacturing profit margin. The presence of Huawei in this monopolized market, on the other hand, would significantly change the market structure as well as the profit-making model in this field. However, it is important to note that the economic scale of Huawei's chipset manufacturing is still far behind that of Qualcomm and many other US and European firms. In recent years, Huawei has been intensifying its investments in HiSilicon and promoting the transnationalization of R&D networks on the global scale in order to diversify its supply chain, especially shifting core suppliers from the United States to China. In the long term, an independent ecosystem and a full value chain might be made part of China's ICT industry when Chinese suppliers achieve self-sufficiency in the supply of key components and core technologies.

CHALLENGES TO THE WEST-DOMINATED INTELLECTUAL PROPERTY RIGHTS REGIME

In the era of digital capitalism, a major route to profitability is to achieve capital accumulation through private appropriation of technology. This also drives owners of technology, usually TNCs, to seek legal protection for intellectual property and to exclude other competitors from using proprietary technologies in the same way. In order to integrate into the global intellectual property rights regime, Huawei, as a latecomer, has been striving to pursue the patent-oriented technological development along with the company's transnationalization. This process has been accompanied by deep-seated conflicts with other TNC's powers as well as inter-state struggles for China's rising status in global technological governance.

Global high-tech giants often invest heavily in patent-based technologies in an attempt to transform intangible techniques and innovations into assets and obtain higher return from licensing royalties. Neoliberal logic further facilitated the process of "accumulation by dispossession" through expropriation of nonproprietary information.[51] During the 1980s IBM led a global campaign pushing for proprietary control over technology and knowledge. The company underwent a dramatic change of policy in developing their software knowledge and techniques by turning open source codes into copyright work. Microsoft also followed such a pattern to establish a monopoly on standards that most PC manufacturers depended on.[52] This model undoubtedly led to "information enclosure," which further consolidated the TNC's control over technology and knowledge.[53]

At the same time, the emphasis on IP protection also changed the evolution of ICT business models. Because telecommunications is a highly standardized industry, owning property rights in specific technology enables the company not only to create a benchmark in the industry but also to generate massive potential profits. For example, Qualcomm does not manufacture ICT equipment by itself but primarily relies on the licensing business model. The company transformed algorithms into specific patents and offered separate licenses for certain patents. Based on this patent-driven business model, Qualcomm reportedly gained about two-thirds of its profit from licensing wireless patents.[54] More important, Qualcomm's business model has gained the US government's outright support. With the US government's intervention, the Qualcomm-backed CDMA system was promoted as a global telecommunications standard, rendering Qualcomm one of the biggest beneficiaries in 3G standard wars. By the early 2000s, Qualcomm had already acquired more than three thousand CDMA-related patents in its portfolio and occupied 90 to 95 percent of global CDMA chipset markets.[55] China's market, in particular, accounted for more than half of Qualcomm's annual revenue and about $13 billion in licensing revenue.[56] One of my interviewees, Huawei's patent attorney, confirmed that almost no Chinese handset manufacturers in the industry could bypass Qualcomm in technology patents (author interview). For instance, Qualcomm charged Huawei and ZTE about 2.5 percent of a device's retail price and higher rates for smaller handset makers.[57] The interviewee explained that nearly 80 percent of Huawei's licensing fees had been paid to Qualcomm before the company made a breakthrough in its self-innovated chipset technology. This profit-extracting model based on the monopoly rents inevitably led to a deeper disparity between patent owners and the remaining companies.

The issue of intellectual property rights has become one of the most important agenda in global economic policy making since the late 1980s. Established corporate powers in alliance with Western governments, in particular with the US government, have pressed for the formation of the US-led global intellectual property rights (IPR) regime. Under this effort, IP protection was no longer a legal issue but was tied to international economic and trade policies. Key strategic ideas relating to intellectual property protection have been further institutionalized by international governance bodies such as the General Agreement on Tariffs and Trade and its successor, the World Trade Organization. Following the logic of the global IPR regime, the Chinese government passed the first patent law in 1985. From the 1990s onward, China has further altered the domestic law and strengthened IPR law enforcement to meet the requirements of the WTO's agreement on trade-related intellectual property rights (TRIPS) under external pressure from its trading partners. However, China and Chinese companies have been under continual attack for the accusation of "IP theft," which was also used as one of the primary excuses by the US government to launch the trade war against China in 2018. Apparently, the globalized principles of IP regulations benefit only those who are at the top of an international hierarchy of the IPR regime and who control the largest intellectual property portfolios.[58]

The mechanism of the global IPR regime has been used as a strategic tool to sustain the political-economic order of neoliberal globalization by dominant powers. This was illustrated in Huawei's first setback in the US market, where the company was caught in Cisco's lawsuit for the so-called IP infringement. As discussed in chapter 3, the primary motive of this lawsuit was due to Cisco's market strategy that aimed to drive Huawei out of the US market. To enforce its comparative advantage in the patent system, Cisco further lobbied the US government to enact more intrusive policies over property rights protection to guarantee and privilege US corporate interests. As Schiller points out, big business usually turns to IPRs to "constitute not defensive but preemptive claims."[59] Such a mechanism not only ensures corporate players' massive commercial interests but also turns the encompassing capitalist logic into part of imperialist rules. As Huawei's patent attorney commented, "Huawei's disadvantage in Western markets had nothing to do with technological or skill levels. It is all about politics and market competition" (author interview).

The capitalist proprietary relationship and US-dominated imperialist rules not only subjects developing nations to a disadvantaged position in the global IPR regime but also generates massive monopoly rents in the form of licensing fees. For example, Huawei has paid over $6 billion in IP royalties since 2001, nearly 80 percent to US firms.[60] As Huawei's rotating chairman Guo Ping stated, these licensing fees were "money paid to bandits for passage" (*mailuqian*) to enter the "international club." But Guo also emphasized that these rules of the "international club" should be rebuilt toward the principle of equality and mutual benefit.[61] It means the global IPR regime can also been transformed into a battleground for ongoing struggles by multiple actors.

In the initial stage of internationalization, Huawei already recognized the importance of IPRs in the business strategy. In 1995 Huawei established its own IP department. At the beginning, the company came to promote the pragmatic approach of "open innovation" by drawing on the R&D experience of well-established technologies. A software developer working at Huawei explained that the company's early R&D process mainly focused on the technique of "reverse engineering" (author interview). This R&D approach was used to break down their rivals' products into specific components to learn how they were built and then rebuild their own compatible products. In this way, key techniques and designs can be reproduced by reducing development time and have less chance of market failure in the intensely competitive global market. This approach allowed Huawei to accumulate patents in a cost-effective way in its initial stage of development. However, at this stage Huawei was primarily occupied in low-end IP activities such as modification and improvement of some particular product performance and features, possessing far less independent IPs and benchmarking innovations in core technologies than their foreign rivals. This follower-and-imitation patent strategy raised rivals' accusation of Huawei's "piracy" activity. Huawei's patent attorney explained that they had to do adequate research on existing patents conducted by rivals and had to be particularly careful in formulating statements of patent filing to avoid duplication (author interview).

Cisco's lawsuit can be seen as a turning point for Huawei's IP management. Frustration in the IP domain compelled Huawei to strengthen its own systematic patent strategy and move away from the reverse engineering approach to high-end robust IP activities to improve qualities of patents. In 2004 the pre-research Standards and Patents Department was set up in all business units to strengthen patent analysis and to focus more on international invention patents, aiming to seize the commanding heights of cutting-edge technology. Huawei's IPR strategy was specifically formulated in such a statement: "Protect and utilize autonomous IPRs, respect others' IPRs, improve corporate core competence, and strongly support global product strategy."[62]

Instead of passive compliance with Western-dominated IPR rules, Huawei started to challenge its competitors in the West. In 2011 Huawei sued Motorola Solutions over intellectual property infringement, attempting to prevent Motorola from disclosing Huawei's confidential proprietary information to Nokia Siemens Networks, which had acquired Motorola's mobile telecommunications unit. This can be viewed as a watershed moment for Huawei, as it was the first time a Chinese enterprise took up arms against US-dominated rules of IPRs and gained more equal power in bargaining and competition. In Europe, Huawei has also been caught in numerous patent legal battles. In order to deal with IP-related lawsuits, the company's IP department had to strengthen patent analysis and prepare for a comprehensive patent portfolio in the pre-research stage. This strategy allowed the company to use its patent portfolio to countercharge its rivals. The patent attorney explained that such patent litigations usually ended up with cross-licensing agreements as a settlement for disputes (author interview). In this sense, IPRs could be used not only as the umbrella of protection in the market competition but also as a means of inter-capitalist collaboration.

At the same time, Huawei also made an effort to link the firms' IPR strategy with the state's technology and innovation policy to gain the Chinese government's support. This attempt was reflected in the speech of Huawei's chairwoman Sun Yafang at the 2006 National Scientific Conference: "We have to promote IPRs as a national strategy for the national development, turning defensive activities into a proactive approach to establish IPRs systems on our own. . . . We have to integrate in the international market club in terms of IPRs. We believe that our national plan for revitalizing our country's science and technology will be realized. IP is the ticket to the international market without which our high-tech products are unable to be sold in the international market."[63]

As a response to Chinese firms' appeal for IP protection at the state level, the Chinese government enacted the Chinese National Patents Development Strategy (2011–2020) in 2011, advancing a specific strategic goal to become an innovation powerhouse through strengthening patent-oriented technology development. This plan included seven strategic industries: biotechnology, alternative energy, clean energy vehicles, energy conservation, high-end equipment manufacturing, broadband infrastructure, and high-end semiconductors. Huawei took a clear lead in China's patent-oriented innovation strategy.

The result of China's efforts in establishing modern IP protection can be directly reflected in the numbers of patents filed. Since 2011 China has become the world's top patent filer, surpassing the United States and Japan. China's ICT corporations, including Huawei and ZTE, have accounted for a large proportion of China's patent filings. Huawei has especially secured a lead in the global IPR regime. Since 2014 Huawei has become the top patent applicant under the Patent Cooperation Treaty system of the World Intellectual Property Organization (WIPO), surpassing other global giants such as Qualcomm, Samsung, Sony, and HP. As of 2017, Huawei had a pool of 74,307 patents in different ICT areas, nearly half of which were filed outside China.[64]

Because standard patents were seen as a pivotal strategy to achieve high-end IP activities, Huawei has also adopted a preemptive approach to participate in the global IPR regime by obtaining important positions in 177 global standardization organizations. Huawei has played an increasingly important role in setting new game rules in the regime and leading key projects of technological development. For example, the company had a more than 6 percent stake in WCDMA patents and owned 25 percent of the 4G patents.[65] Due to the company's successful bidding in 5G standards, Huawei has become the second-largest 5G standards-essential patents (SEP) just behind Samsung, far ahead of other foreign rivals.[66] Huawei's important role in 5G standard setting not only increased the company's bargaining power in pricing but also essentially changed the distribution of power and profits in the IPR-oriented standard regime.

The presence of Chinese firms in the global IPR landscape considerably challenged the US-led international governance structure. But at the same time, it is important to point out that although Chinese firms' participation in the IPR regime complicated the power dynamics, it does not fundamentally change the neoliberal logic and the nature of private property in technology and information. The monopoly of knowledge and technology by private corporate interests, as Ren believed, was still embraced as a fundamental principle for promoting technological progress in global digital capitalism. The mechanism of "accumulation by dispossession" via monopoly over technology and information still stayed intact, and TNCs, regardless of Western or Chinese corporate power, were still the biggest beneficiaries of this game.

Nevertheless, there should be no denying that the disparity between industrialized countries and developing countries is being reduced with the increasing leverage that developing countries exerted in global markets and political systems.[67] The involvement of non-Western players in the global IPR regime further provided third world countries with grounds for democratizing the rule-setting process and achieving what Huawei has desired for a more equitable system under the logic of "techno-globalism."

Conclusion

China successfully developed a distinct technological development trajectory during the Maoist period. However, the dramatic transition to a commercially driven path has completely changed the initiatives, objects, and patterns of the development in the post-Mao era. This strategic change also made Chinese indigenous firms a driving force and a key indicator of national technological capabilities. Huawei was an outgrowth of this transition in the evolution of China's technology policy. To understand Huawei's rise in the global technological landscape, one must take into account the complex relationship between Chinese enterprises and the state. As Huawei's chairwoman Sun Yafang announced, the state created the most favorable environment of innovation for Chinese enterprises.[68] What really lay at the heart of China's desire to "catch up" with the West was the intention of developing China's pathbreaking model of technology development and regaining a significant position in the global technological landscape. To achieve this goal, China has experienced paradoxical policy shifts from dependence on foreign technology transfer to the pursuit of indigenous innovations. Such technology policy shifts combining with the state's interventionist capacity had profound impacts on Huawei's R&D patterns and its technological capability development. The Chinese government's focus on the domestic market-driven growth model in recent years has especially provided more incentives and support for nurturing competitive China-based corporate players.

Huawei's case has broader implications for the shaping of China's technological development in the firm. As Huawei grew from a small private company to a world-class technological force, the key reason for its success lay in its insistence on self-reliant R&D and innovations, which can be viewed as one of the complex legacies inherited from Mao's technological policy. Despite its follower strategy in the early stage of development, Huawei has been striving to explore an alternative path to developing its core competitive advantage in the market competition. Its major breakthrough in self-innovated switching technology was exemplary in demonstrating how the company was able to anchor high-tech R&D activities in the basic demand and practice of China's local telecommunications market. In addition, Huawei's R&D in the areas of high-end ICT technologies such as chipsets and next generation telecommunications standards has achieved compatible levels with its foreign rivals, setting a pioneering example for Chinese ICT enterprises to move away from a labor-intensive stage to an innovation-centered stage. It fully demonstrated that modern high-end technology was no longer the exclusive domain of the West.[69] Meanwhile, Huawei's increasing presence and power in international markets and the arena of technological governance suggested that Chinese technological firms have played an increasingly important role in influencing and even defining global technology. It has also become a crucial step to fulfill China's technological ambitions.

Nevertheless, Huawei's pursuit of self-reliant technological development does not necessarily mean that corporate interests have to closely align with nationalistic developmental goals in its process of transnationalization. Huawei has expressed a strong desire for integration into the globalized market and production system. Its R&D activities were no longer confined in the domestic boundary but extended to broad-scale collaborations and alliances under the principle of techno-globalism. The increasingly transnationalized technology linkages via R&D internationalization actually strengthen its dependence on the transnational capitalist bloc rather than its technological roots in China. This contradiction forced Huawei to adopt more pragmatic policy in choosing its own path of technological development. At the same time, it is important to note that Huawei's technological development trajectory does not fundamentally break with the capitalist logic of accumulation underlying its technological progress and innovation patterns. In this respect, Huawei's technological development trajectory is not yet posited to realize a pathbreaking model.

CHAPTER 5

Ownership, Management, and Labor Discipline

Huawei's innovation capability is reflected not only in its R&D process but also in its structure of ownership and management. Along with escalated transnationalization, Chinese ICT corporations have sought to establish a modern enterprise system through ownership transformation and capitalization. The restructuring of ICT firms' ownership relations, especially with the intensive involvement of financial capital in the industry, has given rise to new forms of capitalist governance toward an equity-based capital structure and reshaped the capital and labor relations at the corporate level. Huawei's practices in its ownership arrangement and corporate governance provide an experience that is quite distinct from those of its domestic and foreign counterparts. It has striven for organizational innovation by establishing an "Employee Shareholding Scheme" (ESS) as a cornerstone of the corporate ownership structure, seeking to create a relatively equitable reward and incentive mechanism. Moreover, unlike many other Chinese ICT companies that were eager to obtain various means of transnational capitalization, Huawei's scheme sought to sustain an independent employee ownership structure, refusing any chance of being controlled by big financial or international ICT capital.

But at the same time, Huawei has been known for its notorious labor control and relentless corporate culture. The company's labor control practices, ranging from recruitment strategies, reward systems, and "soft management skills," provide observable evidence to understand the tensions between capital and labor. By focusing on the interplay of power and control, this chapter combines political-economic analysis of China's structural change with Huawei's corporate analysis and incorporates class analysis to examine the labor conditions, labor control, and labor relations at the corporate level.

The Evolution of Huawei's Employee Shareholding Scheme

Since the 1980s the socialist labor regime has been transformed along with the restructuring of China's economic reform, moving away from state ownership and a socialist welfare system to one driven by market relations and multiple ownership forms.[1] One significant change in ownership forms was the emergence of non-state-owned enterprises as a driving force of the ownership composition reconstruction.[2] As private ownership had not been officially recognized in the early stage of the market reform, collectively owned enterprises flourished in different industrial sectors as a supplement to state ownership. They had developed diverse organizational forms of public ownership such as worker cooperatives and employee-owned corporations, which can be seen as an experiment of indigenous institutional innovation and an essential part of a socialist mixed economy. Starting in the mid-1980s, the ICT sector witnessed the emergence of a large number of collectively owned enterprises, constituting a significant feature of China's ICT industrial reform. Huawei was one of these enterprises encouraged by both the state and local government's policies. In 1987 Shenzhen Municipal Government issued a document encouraging individual technical professionals to establish non-state-owned high-tech enterprises to promote the development of the ICT industry. This policy provided an original incentive for Ren Zhengfei to establish his start-up. In the same year, Ren founded Huawei with a registered capital of ¥21,000. To obtain a legitimate status, the company was originally registered as a collectively owned enterprise affiliated with the Shenzhen Technology Bureau.[3] However, this title was merely a subterfuge to protect the company from its precarious political and legal status. Such an ownership status, which was known as "red hat collectives," became a common arrangement for newly established technology firms in the 1980s. They were actually privately owned and operated but still enjoyed some benefits by wearing a politically correct "red hat." Only with this identity could Huawei be allowed to enter the telecommunications equipment market, in which private capital was still restricted at that time.

However, Huawei suffered from substantial political risks because of its obscure legal definition. Despite policy encouragement, the local government did not provide active support for Huawei's development. Like many other non-state-owned enterprises, Huawei was completely excluded from lending by the state-owned banking system. The company had to rely on reinvested profits and original funders' self-raised monies. In its early years, Huawei had been on the verge of bankruptcy several times. The company was compelled to resort to high-interest (20–30 percent) loans from large SOEs.[4] To rid the company of reliance on external finance, Huawei explored alternatives for diversifying its ownership arrangement. In 1990 Huawei first launched the ESS as a means of internal capitalization. At the beginning, this scheme regulated only that key managers and technical experts could buy the company's shares, and the self-raised capital was primarily reinvested in the company's R&D activities. The original per-share price was ¥1. The low price ensured that employees were able to afford the prices of the company's stock. Moreover, the ESS was used as a means to substitute cash wages with stocks because of the constraints of cash flow in the company's operations. It also allowed the company to spread the risk and retain its professional talent. However, Huawei's experiment in its structure of ownership was viewed as an informal and illegitimate practice at that time, because non-state-owned corporate forms still lacked both external legitimacy and social approval by the state.

At the same time, China's enterprise reformation has been extended to the urban SOE sector since the late 1980s. Instead of radical privatization of public ownership, the initial urban enterprise reform adopted a gradual approach by sustaining the continuity of socialist transition and mirrored much of the rural reform.[5] Inspired by the success of the rural contract responsibility system, the urban enterprise reform introduced a "profit responsibility system" into the state sector.[6] Guided by this principle, corporate governance was evaluated by various performance targets, such as targets for sales, market share, profitability, and capital accumulation. During the 1986–1992 reform period, the ICT industry, including the sectors of integrated circuits, computers, telecommunications equipment, and software, became a trial site of the urban enterprise reform.[7] The establishment of incentive mechanisms and managerial autonomy was widely adopted by non-state-owned enterprises that were eager to establish the Anglo-American models of modern enterprises.

Beginning in the mid-1990s, the enterprise reform experienced a second wave of institutional changes through capitalistic reorganization. One of the central issues was to implement internal restructuring through corporatization under the "share-ownership scheme." The early trial experiments were initiated by local governments at the privatization of collectively owned enterprises.[8] This process of corporatization created new corporate forms, including limited-liability shareholding corporations, limited-liability firms, employee shareholding companies, and private firms. In 1993 the central government first determined that a modern enterprise system had to "clarify property rights, designate authorities and responsibilities, separate government and enterprise functions, and establish scientific management,"[9] officially identifying principles of post-socialist enterprise reformation. In the following year, the country's Corporation Law came into force, laying down a fundamental legal framework for corporatization. The law set up the standards and principles of mainstream corporate organizational forms in line with Western-style corporate governance. The newly adopted elements of a "modern enterprise system," to some extent, "became synonyms of modernity and economic progress, symbols of legitimacy and prestige in China."[10] This policy directly led to an essential change of Huawei's ownership status. In 1997, just three years after the enactment of the Corporation Law, Huawei finally took off its collective red hat and registered as a limited liability company.

However, Huawei's practice in its employee shareholding ownership was still considered an informal structure. The scheme was merely an internal practice without legal registration at any relevant government department. It means the status of Huawei's employees who were also the company's shareholders was not legally protected by relevant laws or regulations. It also raised widespread controversies concerning the nature of the company's ownership structure, making the accusation that Huawei's shareholding structure intended to institutionalize private property rights and completely deviated from the principle of socialism. In 1997 the central leadership assigned a group of scholars and officials to conduct fieldwork research on Huawei's operations. The result of the research unexpectedly won the central leadership's endorsement for Huawei's ownership experiment.[11] In the same year, Huawei's experience was written into the 15th National Congress of the Communist Party of China.[12] The Congress report specifically declared that "the emerging form of joint stock cooperative venture which was characterized by the association of laborers in labor and the association of laborers in capital" should be viewed as a form of the "new collective economy," and it should constitute an important component of a socialist market economy.[13] According to the definition, such a new form of the collective economy was first built on the base of workers' collective work and mutual cooperation for shared interests. Meanwhile, it also encouraged workers to buy shares of corporations and enjoy the ownership of corporate assets. Under this ownership arrangement, workers played the role not only of labor but also of the owner of the enterprise in the form of shareholders. Moreover, the report stressed that the shareholding system could be used under both capitalism and socialism, but the key principle lay in who held the controlling shares. This definition essentially distinguished Chinese firms' experience from the Anglo-American mechanism.

The policy endorsement fundamentally legitimated Huawei's ownership status. In 1997 the company's ESS was overhauled by extending the scale of the shareholding to benefit more nonexecutive employees. The standard of share distribution was based on an employee's positions, contributions, comprehensive capability, and future development potential. As Huawei's rapidly growing businesses since the mid-1990s helped the company overcome the financial difficulty in the initial stage, the ESS was no longer primarily used for self-funding but served as an important incentive mechanism.

In 2001 Huawei passed the ESS restructuring plan by introducing the concept of "virtual restricted shares" based on the output-related principle. Under this arrangement, employee shareholders can receive dividends based on corporate performance, but their stocks cannot be transferred or disposed; and if they leave Huawei, they have to sell their stocks back to the company for redistribution or to be voided. It means Huawei workers do not possess the company's property rights except the profit-sharing benefit. To encourage employees' capital injection, Huawei coordinated with Shenzhen's local commercial banks to set up an "individual business loan" program. This financial program allowed Huawei workers to obtain low-interest loans from banks to purchase the company's stocks, while Huawei served as a guarantor on the loans. However, given the potential financial risk to the banks, this program was eventually banned by the central government. Despite this restriction, Huawei workers were able to allocate their high dividends to reinvest increasing shares every year.

As American scholars Christopher Balding and Donald Clarke write in the article "Who Owns Huawei?," "Huawei" is "an umbrella term" that covers multiple entities.[14] Huawei Technologies is a single-shareholder limited-liability company that is owned by Huawei Holding. Huawei Holding comprises two shareholders: the entity called Huawei Investment and Holding Company Trade Union Committee and Ren Zhengfei. Different from the public nature of trade unions in China, Huawei's labor union committee was established largely out of legal convenience, because employee ownership was not legally recognized in China in the early stage and only certain kinds of entities can be registered as owners of a private company (author interview). As a former Huawei executive who had worked at Huawei for more than twenty years and had participated in the design of the ESS said, Huawei's ownership structure was innovative and flexible, able to experiment in different institutional arrangements and legal situations (author interview). The ESS involved nearly ninety-seven thousand employees as of January 2019, accounting for almost 60 percent of its global workforce.[15] According to Ren, no external institution, government department, or the military department owns the company shares or intervenes in the ESS structure.[16] But in the current stage, only Chinese employees are allowed to participate in the shareholding plan, which means Huawei is still a 100 percent Chinese-owned company despite its highly transnationalized operations.

The Distinctness and Limitation of the ESS

Huawei's ESS design is by no means a new practice. Emerging in the 1950s in the United States, employee ownership was originally designed as a "third way" alternative to capitalism and socialism by turning workers into capitalists. After the collapse of the fixed-wage-and-benefit system in the postwar capitalist system, employee equity was often offered as a means of compensation complementary to a flexible wage system. Today employee ownership has become a popular "share-ownership scheme," allowing workers to participate in profit sharing through stock ownership or stock options. Especially in technology companies, this ownership structure is often used to enhance company performance by allying interests of employees and shareholders in risky markets. In essence, employee ownership represents a new paradigm of the economic organizational form that moves beyond the traditional Marxist binary conceptions of worker and capitalist. Under the employee ownership arrangement, workers who are entitled by their direct ownership of corporate equity are turned into part of the "new capitalists." Huawei's innovative ownership design is also characterized by this nature, but at the same time it has both distinct features and limitations in its practices.

CAPITALIZATION OF KNOWLEDGE

Different from other Chinese low-end ICT manufacturing firms that are entrenched in the downstream of global production cluster, Huawei identifies itself as part of a high-end "knowledge-based economy," with a belief in the principle of the "capitalization of knowledge." This means knowledge is not only a primary means and resource of production but can also be translated into capital and surplus value. Under this assumption, knowledge workers who can produce a surplus value of knowledge are perceived to have the most important labor power. Based on this assumption, Huawei's ownership structure is designed to fulfill the value of knowledge labor. Laborers therefore have become both the owners of capital and the recipients and beneficiaries of corporate capital returns. Thanks to Huawei's generous dividend distribution scheme, Huawei employees can get much higher cash dividends than their fixed salaries.

However, the adoption of employee ownership, even at its best with a broadening capital ownership base, would not fundamentally change the capitalist production relations. In fact, Huawei's workers do not completely possess proprietary rights of corporate equity; instead they primarily hold profit-sharing opportunities. The ownership scheme is still subject to the conditions of employment contracts under which the company plays a decisive role in determining the mechanism of stock allocation and dividend distribution. The capitalist class relation between capital and labor stays intact, which constitutes the antagonistic character of capitalist accumulation. Moreover, it is clear that corporate equity shares under the ESS are not equally distributed. At Huawei the difference in stock allocation may relate to one's seniority and job performance. New hires usually do not enjoy equity share grants. They are required to "stay around" at the company until full ownership of the shares is vested. Senior employees who are allocated more shares can enjoy much greater profit return from the company. The ESS has become a key factor in the income inequality at Huawei.

DECENTRALIZED OWNERSHIP STRUCTURE

Despite the difference in equity allocation, Huawei ownership structure is highly decentralized compared with many other ICT companies. Many joint-stock companies tend to concentrate corporate stock option grants in the hands of executives and allocate only a small portion of surplus profits as shareholder returns. For example, the stock option scheme of Baidu was granted to only a few senior executives and key technical experts who joined Baidu from its inception. At Tencent the ratio of employee shareholding was 17 percent in 2013. From 2009 to 2011, Tencent launched millions of employee stock options to award some selected "excellent employees," but this part of options accounted for only 0.55 percent of its circulating shares.[17] On the other hand, Huawei's ESS ensured a broader base of ownership structure, with the majority of Chinese employees enjoying stock ownership. Unlike other Chinese ICT capitalists, who appropriated the largest shareholding, Huawei's Ren Zhengfei held only 1.14 percent of the company's total stocks in 2019, while the remaining shares were distributed among Huawei's Chinese employees across different layers.[18]

In today's ICT industry, the widening income gaps have become a growing phenomenon. Huge portions of surplus profits were actually appropriated by high-ranking executives or senior managers. The financial speculation in the industry further created the myth of "new riches" among the new group of IT entrepreneurs. According to the Forbes' China Rich List in 2019, leaders from some well-known high-tech company, such as Alibaba, Tencent, Baidu, Jingdong, and Xiaomi, were ranked on the top of the list.[19] Capitalists' wealth and income fluctuate with the market, largely influenced by their firms' performance and growth opportunities.[20] This market-driven system of corporate governance further consolidated the capitalistic logic of management and income inequality. Although Huawei's ESS was also based on the performance-oriented premise, the company attempted to constitute a relatively equitable system of redistribution. Besides the high ratio of employee shareholding, Huawei also allocated a large portion of corporate annual earnings to pay employees in the forms of dividends, bonuses, and benefits. It is reported that the company's total net profit over the last twenty years was considerably smaller than the total amounts paid out to its employees.[21] Such an ownership structure effectively prevents the company from the concentration of capital monopolized by big capitalists. Corporate wealth and profits became common goods that were primarily shared by internal workers.

A SELF-SUSTAINING MODEL

Under the complex corporate shareholding regime, the question concerning "who is controlling for whose benefit" should be considered a central issue to unfold the power relations underlying the ownership structure and governance system. Huawei's ESS intended to shift the corporate control from external shareholders to internal shareholders by insisting on its self-sustaining model of development. This feature of ownership structure greatly differs from that of public companies where interests of internal workers are hijacked by external shareholders, especially by big financial capitalists. With the increasing injections of "deterritorialized" capital, particularly the inroad of financial and venture capital into the ICT sector, the capitalist logic of financialization has become a determining feature in reshaping

ICT companies' ownership structure and governance. Under such logic, the valuation of a firm is determined not simply by its products or technological innovation but by its speculation on future profitability. Venture capitalists or outside investors whose interests are based on a firm's premium profit return play increasingly important roles in corporate ownership structure and corporate governance. It subjects the management of the firm to the principle of "shareholder value" to pursue the maximization of shareholders' gains and profits. It also concentrates major responsibility of corporate control in the hands of only a few major shareholders. The ownership structure and governance of many companies have gradually been controlled by the emerging network of TCCs, which are primarily comprised of capital owners, corporate executives, and international financiers. These transnational capitalists often take a concrete shape in the organizational form of a board of directors at the firm level.[22]

Despite the Chinese government's restrictions on foreign ownership, most Chinese ICT companies still sought to adopt a new equity structure with Chinese characteristics, known as variable interest entities (VIEs), to attract foreign capital financing and to complete offshore listings. This complicated ownership composition helped foreign investors to find inroads into China's ICT industry and take control of the corporate shareholding system through indirect foreign ownership. In fact, most leading China-based ICT companies are not exactly Chinese owned. For example, the biggest single shareholder of Tencent is the South African multinational media group Naspers. Alibaba's principal shareholdings were held by Japan's SoftBank Corp and Yahoo, which far outweighed the shareholding by its founder, Jack Ma. Capital relations became a bond that tied various shareholders together to maintain and run the networks of TCCs.

Huawei, however, refused the involvement of external financing control in its corporate ownership and governance. Ren claimed that Huawei would not go public in the future, because he realized that Western capital markets were "greedy" in nature, which may eventually undermine Huawei's long-term self-development.[23] According to Huawei's 2011 audit report, the company's external financing, all taking the form of bank loans, accounted for less than 15 percent of cash flow. The remainder was from the self-owned cash flow from operation and internal financing.[24] In an overarching trend of financialization and capitalization occurring in the global ICT industry, Huawei's ownership structure is distinct from and even contradictory to global common practices. To the largest extent, this self-sustaining mechanism successfully protected employees' interests from the control of global speculative capital and enabled the company to focus on the competitive advantage in technological innovation rather than merely on capitalist tools of accumulation.

Speculations on involvement of the Chinese government and military in Huawei's ownership and corporate governance have been a crucial point of contention.[25] According to an interview with a former vice president of Huawei's business unit, the company has been insisting on its independence from any state and military control in its ownership structure and business operations (author interview). Contrary to the suspicions about Huawei's exclusive ties with the Chinese military, Huawei has actually been excluded from the military supply chains because of its private ownership status. The interviewee claimed that although the Chinese government consistently put pressure on Huawei, Ren rejected all of the offers from state-owned organizations that intended to buy shares in the company. Ren's business strategy was able to ensure the independent structure of the employee ownership.

MANAGEMENT STRUCTURE

It is important to note that ownership is not only a means of allocation of property rights, but it also embodies different forms of social relations. Under the bedrock standard of "one share, one vote," the controlling shareholders make the basic decisions of what, how, and where to produce goods and undertake the key capitalist roles—appropriating and distributing the surplus to serve shareholders' interests.[26] Nonexecutive employees are excluded from the decision-making circle. The power of management is unequally distributed based on equity relations.

Employee ownership nevertheless provides a partial vision of democratic management through redistribution of power and control. The very existence of employee ownership creates a mechanism for worker control and for their participation in decision making at the firm level. Huawei's ESS also attempted to go along with practices of democratic management. Huawei's labor union, which is not a true trade union but an organization comprising all employee shareholders, represents the highest authority of corporate management. Members of the union have equal voting rights. They vote every five years to pick 115 representatives, who then select 17 members for the board of directors. Employees can also nominate their preferred candidates on the ballots, with elections held at roughly four hundred voting sites around the world.[27] In this way, Huawei employees can delegate management functions to directors of their own choosing. They are also empowered with certain governance rights to implement their control over the decision-making process.

Huawei's management innovation also took place at the leadership level, where Huawei intended to avoid domination of individual leaders within the company. A system of rotating and acting CEOs was adopted in the company starting in 2012. In this system the three deputy chairs rotate into the top executive role for a tenure of six months and together with another four standing committee members form a board of seven. Ren Zhengfei has maintained his role as chair to act as a mentor for the rotating CEOs. He has retained authority on major decisions such as corporate development strategies and corporate culture building, but he has fully empowered workers when the decision-making process comes to R&D, human resources, benefit allocation, and other areas. Although Ren may still be viewed as a "heroic leader" in the company, thanks to his significant influence in leadership, he has attempted to challenge the concentration of power by introducing such an innovative leadership model. This managerial innovation has delivered a collective decision-making process and a platform where the ideas of democracy and centralized decision making are balanced. It also has ensured that Huawei's collective and sustainable interests will be served under the shared leadership model.

Managerial Style: A Contradictory Mixture

Huawei's management can be seen as a contradictory mixture, comprising both socialist residues and Western-style management in its practice. On the one hand, Huawei inherited part of the legacies of pre-reform socialist enterprise management—that is, the values, attitudes, and behavioral norms deriving from a set of ideals and practices of "socialist democratic management." These inherited legacies can be better seen as a product of a socialist regime that actively sought a mechanism to achieve politicization of the workplace. But on the other hand, the company also enshrined Western management structures and strategies to promote the doctrine of a modern enterprise. Huawei's managerial experience in combining traditions of socialist practices and Western corporate management represents the most distinctive features of Chinese enterprises in transition.[28]

In addition to organizational innovations, Huawei is also renowned for its distinct corporate culture, which is informed with "Chinese characteristics" by incorporating the essence of socialist practices of management. This distinct feature has been largely influenced by Ren's leadership. As a representative figure among the first generation of private entrepreneurs in the reform era, Ren has fostered some key reconstructed characters and legacies of the Chinese traditional national bourgeoisie. What distinguishes this generation of private entrepreneurs from other capitalists is their highly politicized consciousness and ideological loyalty to the Chinese party-state. Although Huawei has consistently denied its connections with the military, Ren's experience of military service in his early career nevertheless has shaped his ideological orientations and political identities, which in turn has exerted great influence on Huawei's military-style management. Moreover, Maoist thought has had lingering influence on Ren's leadership tactics, which allows him to employ a business version of Mao style in cultivating corporate culture and ideology to ensure employees' compliance with the company's management approach, culture, and core organizational practices. Ren once said, "The unification of an organization must be built on the basis of the construction of ideology and culture. An organization is a structure system, and culture power and ideology power are the biggest powers."[29] This thought constitutes a key feature of Huawei's corporate management style.

Drawing from the Maoist practice of self-criticism, Ren has instituted regular "democratic meetings" in which lower-level employees are mobilized to criticize mid- and upper-level executives. The company's online forum Xinsheng Community allows employees to participate in public discussion and self-criticism. Such a Mao-style mass movement was applied to break the hierarchical structure entrenched in the firm. In addition, drawing on Maoist ideas about combining "knowledge with practice," Ren also emphasizes the combination of practical education and participation in labor. For example, in 1998 Ren launched a rotating campaign, requiring all technicians, especially those with higher education degrees, to participate in shop-floor production. In his speech, Ren said, "Our current management, in fact, is to promote the Party's exemplary working style of the 50s and 60s when Chairman Mao required that technicians had to align with workers and peasants and combine with productive practice. Now Huawei's engineers with PhD or Master degrees should become 'workers and peasants' on the production line."[30] Huawei also has adopted progressive terminology to "revolutionize" employees in a business context, with which moral and political incentives have been established as the primary corporate values. For example, Ren uses the archetypal Communist hero-soldier Lei Feng and the cadre Jiao Yulu as symbols to promote the spirit of selfless hard work and dedication. Employees have even been organized to sing revolutionary songs as part of the company's ideological education.

One of the critical steps in institutionalizing Huawei's organizational practices was marked by the formation of the Huawei Basic Law in the

1990s, which intended to imitate the far-reaching "Angang Constitution" in Huawei's management.³¹ The Maoist "Angang Constitution," a democratic mass-line-style managerial revolution against Soviet "one-mass bossism" and Western-style Taylorism, pioneered a distinct Chinese model of industrial democracy. Its core elements, known as "two participations, one reform and three combinations," were appropriated in Huawei's management practices. Ren accentuated workers' "right to management" in planning, production, and decision making. For example, during the drafting process of the Huawei Basic Law, Huawei held a company-wide campaign to debate elements of Huawei's corporate culture. Workers were encouraged to participate in the debate, and their opinions were incorporated into the written rules. As a result of this large-scale participation, the Huawei Basic Law, with 103 articles, was finally completed in 1997. The Huawei Basic Law has an important symbolic character in signaling the company's fundamental values and offering guidance for day-to-day practices. Workers' participation in formulating these written rules has formed an internal source of legitimacy and further consolidated shared value orientation among top executives, management teams, and employees.

Although the enactment of the Huawei Basic Law incarnated an ideal of "democratic management" that Ren hoped to attain, it is important to point out that Ren's paternal style of management, which was also a residual managerial character of pre-reform socialist enterprises, still permeated Huawei's practices of management. This contradiction constituted a distinct feature of Huawei's managerial approach.

As observed by Wang Jing, the usage of "corporatized Maospeak" is the most striking approach to constructing corporate culture in some leading ICT firms.³² This managerial strategy still works in China's business context because of its deep ideological origins and socialist legacies. Noticeably, it clearly indicates "the continuity between Mao's China and corporate China."³³ The underlying value of Huawei's corporate culture and corporate structure embodies the ideals of socialist economic democracy. In practice, it also incorporates the work ethics of socialist enterprises in the Mao era and articulates individual self-identification with collective interests by motivating workers' moral attitudes. This distinct managerial method plays an important role in molding the company into a cohesive entity.

Apart from socialist residues, Huawei also made an effort to incorporate Western managerial styles and methods through which the myth of a "modern enterprise system" was reproduced. With the company's accelerated process of internationalization, in 1997 Ren Zhengfei decided to introduce Western managerial experience in corporate restructuring after his visit to the United

States. He commented that the management restructuring process was painful, but Huawei had to "cut the feet to fit in the American shoes [*xuezushilv*] to modernize the company's management."³⁴ Beginning in 1998, Huawei hired IBM Consulting and spent over ¥1 billion to implement new managerial systems at different corporate levels. Another pivotal human resource system was developed in cooperation with the Hayes Group—a US-based management consulting firm—from 1997 onward. It included standardized models for job design, reward systems, assessment and appraisal, performance management, and employees' qualifications, selection, and retention practices. A former Huawei human resource manager explained that the company's restructuring efforts were meant to rectify "the previous unorthodox structure" and adapt to a global growth model by bringing in Westernized experience (author interview).

Underlying the managerial restructuring process was Huawei's ambition to catch up with Western counterparts and to become a well-recognized global player. However, it should be remembered that the pursuit of building the Western-style modern enterprise system is often accompanied by a decoupling from socialist practices of management and indigenous organizational innovation. Such contradictory practices not only undermine Huawei's ongoing efforts in searching innovative measures of management but also lead to a standardized and rigid corporate managerial system.

Labor Practices

The analysis of a firm's ownership pattern not only reveals the vast corporate structure but also provides an insight into the relationship between capital and labor. To capture the complicated process of class restructuring and labor relations in a transnationalized production system, the following section analyzes Huawei's labor practices, including its procurement practices, training systems, hierarchical job structure, divisive salary regime, and "soft management" skills.

Running in tandem with the corporate restructuring, employment relations in China have undergone a significant shift from socialist social contract to the "market-oriented, voluntaristic and individualistic 'labor contract.'"³⁵ On the one hand, the state-sector workers' "iron rice bowls" (guaranteed lifetime employment) were smashed, replaced with a commodified employment relationship under the capitalist labor market; permanent lifetime employment in the pre-reform socialist welfare system gave way to market-based contractual and temporary employment; and the equal eight-grade wage system was replaced with performance-related pay based on the principle of economic efficiency. The corporate restructuring in the SOE sector led to massive layoffs of redundant labor. On the other hand, the emerging non-state sector has become a key force for labor absorption. Especially with China's deeper participation in the international division of labor, the formation of the FDI-driven and export-oriented ICT industry has reshaped the country's employment structure.[36] Globalization created interdependence on the part of capital, but it also integrated workers into the global productive system. In this sense, it is important to take into account the transnational dimension in examining the characters of Chinese ICT labor.

At the same time, increasing stratification in China's ICT workforce continued to underlie the ongoing class restructuring. The soaring ICT professional labor such as R&D and technical workers that are situated in the high-end segment of the workforce presents different characters of Chinese ICT workers. Yet the social formation and changing conditions of this segment of skilled Chinese ICT labor remain under-explained in extant literature. The case of Huawei provides an insight into this dimension at the enterprise level.

LABOR PROCUREMENT

As non-state-owned enterprises were positioned outside the formal state-run labor allocation system in the initial stage of market reform, Huawei initially had difficulties in developing labor procurement channels. In Huawei's early start-up days, the company had only five employees.[37] The lack of procurement of technical and managerial workers became a crucial challenge to Huawei's operations. In addition, the situation of a private enterprise was far from promising in the early 1990s. Especially under the state's FDI-friendly policy, foreign-invested firms became not only the major source of job creation for low-skilled labor but also the most sought-after choice for top talent in the labor market due to their high pay and full welfare packages.[38] Some renowned high-tech TNCs, such as Siemens, Motorola, IBM, and Microsoft, were the most desired employers for graduates from prestigious Chinese universities. During the same period, China's high-tech labor market faced the "brain drain crisis," because the best-performing Chinese science and engineering graduates flocked to high-tech companies and leading research laboratories in the United States.

In contrast, Huawei was in a low tier in the job market compared to SOEs and foreign-invented firms. This compelled Ren Zhengfei to turn to personalized recruitment channels for hiring professional workers in the initial stage of development. Nevertheless, Huawei's strategic decision to build its in-house technological capability later attracted some skilled engineers who were eager to look for new challenges and excitement. During my interviews, several engineers expressed that at Huawei they had more autonomy in R&D activities and obtained more fulfillment from developing indigenous innovative technology. An engineer who switched his job from a foreign high-tech company to Huawei explained that Chinese employees were often excluded from the mastering of core proprietary technologies and were allowed to take only some peripheral R&D activities in foreign-invested companies. He further commented that Huawei's job, in contrast, seemed more interesting to him, because his values could be better realized as a skilled engineer by fully engaging in the company's technological development (author interview). Technical workers at different levels can be empowered to make decisions without intervention from the top managerial circle. In this situation, labor is not a necessarily alienated form of work but possesses the subjectivity of self-determination and self-achievement.

In order to procure the most suitable employees who could fit into the company's "hard work" culture, Huawei set up a series of norms in its standardized recruiting practices. Huawei preferred to hire employees with humble family backgrounds, such as from rural or urban laid-off workers' families (author interview). Workers with such backgrounds were perceived to be more diligent and disciplined. They were assumed to have strong incentives to change their material conditions through hard work. These virtues were posited to be congruent with Huawei's corporate culture, which placed priority on the spirit of diligence in its quasi-military management. In addition, Huawei preferred to recruit graduates from interior areas at its early stage of development. Some recognized universities in this region, such as Huazhong University of Science and Technology in Wuhan, the University of Electronic Science and Technology of China in Chengdu, and Xidian University in Xi'an, became the major channels to find skilled talent. Due to Huawei's rapid expansion since the late 1990s, Huawei has adopted a "sweeping recruitment strategy" to hunt for graduates across China. From 1998 to 2002, more than ten thousand university graduates were employed by Huawei. According to an informal survey conducted by the Ministry of Education, over 20 percent of science and telecom engineering graduates from China's top twenty universities were hired by Huawei during this period. And over 80 percent of these new graduates were appointed to R&D positions.[39] Such a sweeping strategy not only enabled Huawei to lure talent away from other competitors but also constituted the company's R&D-based, ICT-skilled workforce.

Since 2002, Huawei's procurement channels have focused more on the existing labor market to hire experienced workers in order to increase "average labor productivity." An interviewee told me that the majority of his colleagues were actually procured from competitor companies such as Ericsson, Siemens, ZTE, and Foxconn (author interview). Besides R&D talent, Huawei also placed more emphasis on recruiting experienced employees in the fields of marketing, technical services, human resources, and finance.

With Huawei's deepening engagement with transnationalization of the R&D network, the company shifted its focus to the procurement of high-end talent on the global scale. Since the 2000s, Huawei has strengthened recruitment of advanced and experienced scientists and researchers working in basic scientific research. They are not involved in practical R&D activities but are mainly responsible for exploring forward-looking research and cutting-edge technologies in multiple domains such as 5G standards, chip architecture, big data, and platform systems. Despite low capital return on their scientific research in the short term, Ren has still insisted on consistent investment in high-end talent in the field of basic scientific research, which was incorporated as one of the significant strategies to achieve the company's "sustainable development." In 2015 nearly 45 percent of employees were engaged in R&D, which is significantly higher than that of many other tech companies in China. In terms of the workforce's education level, more than

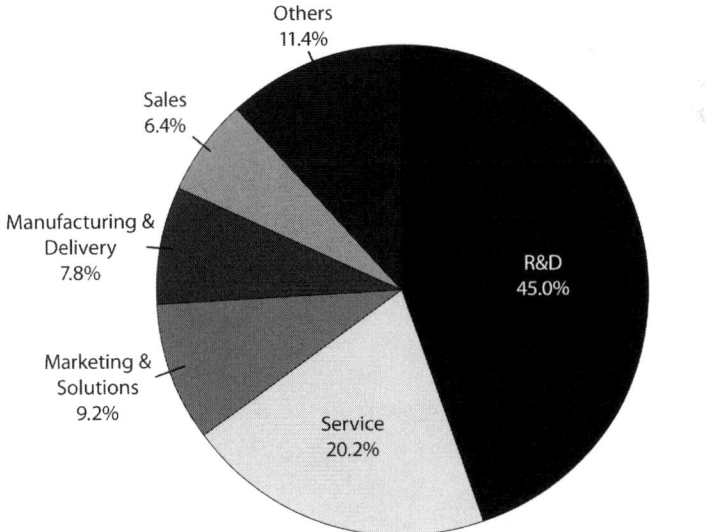

Figure 5.1. Huawei Labor Composition
Source: Huawei 2015 Sustainability Report

85 percent of its employees had at least a bachelor's degree, and over 60 percent of them had a master's or PhD degree.[40]

TRAINING METHODS

In order to create disciplined and proficient workers, Huawei developed the so-called New Employee Cultivation program. All new recruits were required to receive one to six months' internal tailored training at its in-house training center—the Shenzhen-based Huawei University. The training primarily involved cultural education, technical training, and production shop floor practices. Ren Zhengfei mentioned that the Huawei University functioned in ways that were different from the formal education at Chinese universities, combining "training with practical experience." Ren used the military metaphor to emphasize the importance of cultivating an "elite combat force" before they were sent to the "battlefront."[41] The training process often started with a military-style boot camp that was designed to instill the company's core values and culture and develop employees' spirit of cooperation, loyalty, conformity, and solidarity. An interviewee recalled that all trainees had to get up at 5:30 a.m. to do morning exercises and then continued a long day of technical and professional training classes from 8:30 a.m. to 11:00 p.m. Before the classes they were often organized to sing revolutionary songs and read the company's propaganda materials. After professional training, all engineers were sent to the production shop floor to learn from production line workers manufacturing processes such as assembly and testing. These training methods served to cultivate new recruits with the spirit of collectivism and facilitate the combination of technical skills and production practices. Many Huawei employees mentioned in the interviews that most new recruits were completely "brainwashed" by Huawei's training and formed very strong identification with Huawei's hard work culture from the beginning. Besides intensive training, Huawei also adopted a mentoring scheme through which each new hire was assigned to an experienced employee in the first three months. Mentors were responsible for helping new hires adapt to Huawei's corporate culture and provide advisory support in their work and life.

SALARY REGIME AND REWARD SYSTEM

Huawei has been well known for its generosity to employees in terms of the company's salary regime. In the early 1990s, when Huawei's business took off, its employees' salaries were already equivalent to that of many other foreign-invested competitors. An interviewee commented that one of the greatest contributions Huawei made in the 1990s was to increase the overall levels of Chinese ICT skilled workers' salaries in the domestic industry (author interview). The high-salary policy has been further institutionalized in the Huawei Basic Law as one of the key characters of Huawei's human resources strategies. In 2013 Huawei increased the salary package of its entry-level employees by an average of 30 percent. Meanwhile, starting salaries for new graduates increased from ¥6,000 to ¥9,000 for undergraduate students and from ¥8000 to ¥10,000 for those with postgraduate degrees. The company reportedly spent ¥1 billion on this salary increase.[42] The average of Huawei employees' annual income, including their basic salaries, bonuses, and stock dividends, is substantially higher than the market average.

Although Huawei's highly competitive pay package significantly distinguishes the company in talent hiring wars in the domestic ICT industry, a huge wage gap exists within the firm's reward system. The company adopted a strict evaluation system to determine employees' income and rewards based on its strong performance-driven policy. Ren highlighted that the standard of income distribution should hinge on individual contribution, responsibility, capability, and attitude, complying the principle of "efficiency first then equity."[43] This principle of distribution is reflected in a variety of labor control devices such as the company's salary structure, reward and punishment mechanism, and evaluation grading system.

In general, Huawei employees' income comprises base salary, annual bonus, and stock dividends. With increasing years of employment and growing corporate profits, the proportion of bonus and stock dividends would be far greater than that of base salary. In 1998 Huawei implemented the position-based reward scheme based on Western human resource techniques, with each employee's role and performance scored and graded in the job assessments. Performance pressure is also internalized as a factor of labor discipline. Huawei's employees are ranked from Grade 8 to 22 according to their positions, education, technical levels, performance, and working experience; each grade is further divided into three different levels (A, B, C). The lowest-ranked three thousand workers (below Grade 13), such as factory production line workers, operators, and warehouse workers, are excluded from the company's ownership arrangement, the ESS. New entry-level employees with a bachelor's or master's degree are ranked Grade 13. Experienced employees usually start from Grade 15. Ren and other chairs are ranked Grade 22A at the top. In addition, a general proportion of performance evaluation grading is implemented based on the strict result-oriented standards.[44] Only those who are ranked above 50 percent (performance rating levels A and B) are eligible to receive dividends.⁴⁵ Those who are ranked at the lowest level twice are likely to be dismissed.

Huawei's performance-related management techniques created a mechanism of strict discipline. It subjected labor to corporate control and disciplinary apparatus through which workers became individualized, objectified, and differentiated. Such a coercive discipline mechanism functioned to establish a standardized norm to extract compliance from the workforce. The development of "advanced" methodologies in the company's human resources management actually sought to strengthen the machinery of capital control and to legitimize the harsh labor regime.

Moreover, the performance-related and result-oriented reward system led to erosion of job security and welfare provision. In addition to the grading evaluation scheme, labor control was exercised through some invisible coercive approaches. For example, the company's ESS, which was previously designed as a relatively equal means of income distribution for the majority of employees, has increasingly been tied to the productivity- and efficiency-oriented values. Because of the rapid expansion of Huawei's workforce in recent years, Huawei's employee stock distribution has been shrinking. In 2014 the company made an adjustment in its ESS, regulating that new Chinese hires were no longer eligible to obtain stocks in their first three years. This policy forced them to stay at the company as long as possible in order to obtain the shares offering. Although the new ESS policy was used as an incentive by Huawei to retain talent and reduce turnover, it is effectively a form of invisible coercion and a means to increase surplus-value production by exploiting entry-level graduates and new hires. In an interview, a new employee complained that new hires like him were the most "exploited" in the company. They had to work harder than veteran workers and sacrifice their own short-term benefits to obtain stocks. The ESS was no longer a guarantee of employees' welfare but a "golden handcuff" to bind employees together and to test their loyalty to the company. Moreover, the ESS tended to consolidate and even widen the wealth gaps. According to the stock options structure, 30 percent of employee shares were granted to "excellent" and "loyal" employees who were at the top level, approximately 40 percent to medium-level employees, and merely 10–20 percent to selected lower-level employees.⁴⁶

At Huawei the hierarchical job structures are also reflected in its culture of "staff ID numbers" (*gonghao*). It means those people with longtime working experience at Huawei, whose ID numbers were also at the top of the list, usually enjoyed much higher salaries and more privileges than others. It resulted in an unequal system of power and wealth distribution. Some senior managers and technical engineers who have been working at Huawei for more than ten years can earn more than one million yuan a year because of the high dividends of their accumulated stocks (author interview). These veteran employees who earned surplus wages became the "aristocratic" workers in the hierarchical labor structure. But new recruits mainly relied on base salary for their incomes. The mismatch between veteran and new employees has been further institutionalized by the divisive reward system.

The deepening inequality generated the need for Huawei to carry out a deep reform of its distribution policy. To solve this problem, Huawei started to implement a large-scale salary adjustment to optimize its distribution structure. On the one hand, Huawei boosted the base salaries of grassroots workers considerably instead of offering equity packages. On the other hand, veteran employees' stocks would be diluted and extra shares would be redistributed to lower-level employees. This approach was intended to reduce the salary gap between veterans and grassroots employees by striking a balance between efficiency and equity.

SOFT MANAGEMENT SKILLS

Unlike the way many other Chinese manufacturing factories relied depersonalized management in the discipline of low-skilled workers, Huawei tended to use soft and social forms of coercion to exercise its labor control. Huawei kept emphasizing the combination of collectivism and individual entrepreneurship spirit to engage and mobilize employees. It used the ESS to bind individual interests with the company's collective interests, embracing the idea that Huawei belonged to every worker and that the development of the company was determined by workers' contribution and commitment. The socialist moral ethos of dedication and hard work was reappropriated as a core value of corporate culture in order to inspire workers' subjectivity in making collective efforts. The corporate culture also highlighted competitive individual performance in the organization, a mechanism that is usually employed by modern capitalist enterprises to transform workers into individualized, self-managed, and self-directed "entrepreneurial employees."[47] For example, Huawei is well known for its "wolf spirit," a core value proposed in the company's initial stage of development. It relentlessly emphasized employees' spirit of self-sacrifice and self-motivation in the work and promoted the principle of "survival of the fittest" in the fierce market competition. This aggressive work culture compelled workers to invest a lot of time in their work to fulfill both collective and individual interests.

Huawei's "dedication" culture was employed as a means to justify the high intensity of work and the lengthening of working hours. There is considerable anecdotal evidence of Huawei's hard work culture in its everyday labor practices. In the early stage of Huawei's development, its workplace was known for its "mattress culture." At Huawei every engineer had a folded mattress under their desk. They often kept mattresses to sleep off their overtime hours in offices to maximize their productivity. "Mattress culture" was not only a symbol of Huawei's hard work spirit but also an indicator of workers' intense workload and pressure. Although the company claimed that "employees worked overtime voluntarily," overtime working actually has become a norm at Huawei, which is well known by the so-called 996 culture of working from 9:00 a.m. to 9:00 p.m., six days a week. The frequency of overtime was even considered an essential part of performance evaluation. Many workers said working a twelve-hour day was normal and the average weekly working time often exceeded sixty hours (author interview). One interviewee claimed that he had to be on call throughout the night and on weekends. He explained that at Huawei overtime work was "non-compulsory." Employees could barely get paid for overtime hours unless one's supervisor approved his or her application for compensation. The unpaid extra work time was turned into surplus value and profit for the company. Additionally, there was no annual paid vacation at Huawei. Employees who wanted vacation days were required to work every last Saturday of the month, which was seen as the "official overtime working day."

What was worse, the extremely heavy workload seriously damaged workers' physical and mental health. In 2006 Hu Xinyu, a twenty-five-year-old engineer at Huawei headquarters in Shenzhen, died from exhaustion. Before his death he had worked every day from 9:00 a.m. till 3:00 a.m. for nearly two weeks.[48] From 2007 to 2008, several Huawei employees committed suicide, yet all of these tragedies were described as "unnatural deaths" and concealed by the company's public relations department. This evidence was indicative of the cruel working conditions China's tech workers faced. As a consequence, Huawei adopted some overtime management measures for "stress relief," attempting to help staff alleviate stress and improve their physical and mental health. For example, workers' overtime work was monitored through an IT platform. Any abnormal overtime work would be recorded and reported to managerial staff. Health education and psychological counseling activities were carried out to promote the idea of work-life balance and healthy living and work. However, such changes in the "soft management style" had little effect in changing the deep-rooted hard work corporate culture and the mechanism of surplus value production. Employees who were dissatisfied with working conditions usually chose to leave their jobs. There was high labor turnover among new graduates, especially doctoral staff, in their first five years of employment at Huawei. According to the company's survey, the accumulative turnover rate of Huawei's doctoral staff from 2014 to 2018 was as high as 21.8 percent.[49] Only a small proportion of new graduates can eventually survive the company's hard work culture and become the backbone of R&D staff. As an interviewee commented, these workers were not the strongest talent in terms of their technical capability, but they were the fittest ones to endure hardship. In turn, veteran employees who benefited from the company's high capital returns usually had more identification with the company's hard work culture.

As discussed above, Huawei's managerial practices were largely influenced by Ren's paternal authority despite the ideals of "socialist democratic management" the company has been pursuing. To further advocate the "dedication" culture, Ren Zhengfei launched a campaign in 2010 calling for employees to sign "agreements of dedicated workers" (*fendouzhexieyi*). Ren classified three categories of workers: ordinary workers, general dedicated workers, and outstanding dedicated workers. Employees who wanted to obtain the high reward of bonuses and stock dividends had to sign such an agreement, declaring that they voluntarily gave up paid vacations and overtime pay to work harder. An interviewee who was working at an overseas branch at that time told me that almost all of the employees in different departments were "forced" to sign the agreements, or they would be labeled as "general workers" and disqualified for annual bonus, equity, and opportunity of promotion in the future. Ren Zhengfei explained that this campaign was designed as a scheme of redistribution with an attempt to guarantee material rewards for "outstanding dedicated workers." While China's regulations on payment of overtime and paid vacation have been widely publicized in recent years, Huawei's practices were calculated to evade these regulations through nontransparent methods in order to impose unfair conditions on workers. This measure not only deprived workers of basic rights but also intensified the conflicts between management and workers. It raised widespread discontent among Huawei employees, who disputed this managerial measure as "a covert act of exploitation." To some extent, it also contradicted the fundamental principle of the Huawei Basic Law, which claimed to protect workers' rights and benefits in the company's management.

Despite Huawei's massive effort to align labor's interests with corporate interests, measures to control or suppress workers' rights were also employed to guarantee the conditions of capitalist accumulation. This even involved the violation of the labor law to overcome the limits posed by the state. In December 2007, just before the country's new Labor Contract Law came into effect, Huawei implemented a large-scale layoff program. This program urged all veteran employees who had worked more than eight years in the company, including Ren Zhengfei, to hand in "voluntary resignations" and then re-sign new employment contracts on one- to three-year fixed-term agreements. This layoff program, which was presented as a "corporate restructuring scheme," in fact would preempt the Labor Contract Law and replace permanent employment with casual labor relations.[50] Huawei nevertheless explained that this "voluntary resignation scheme" was meant to dismantle the aristocracy-oriented "staff ID culture" by rearranging the ranks of senior employees' positions and salaries. As a result, 6,687 senior employees who submitted their resignations obtained compensation packages of ¥20,000 to ¥160,000 according to their length of service, and 99.9 percent of them were eventually rehired by Huawei.[51] Although Huawei claimed to break managerial elites' entrenched interests and hierarchical structure existing in the management system, the approach was highly controversial. It endeavored to create a sense of insecurity by breaking veteran workers' permanent employment contracts. Such a fear of job insecurity can be translated into workers' self-disciplinary value, which further subjects labor to more arbitrary and stringent control.

REPRODUCTION OF CAPITALIST LABOR RELATIONS

As part of its "carrot-and-stick" managerial strategy, Huawei provides a convenient working and living environment for employees as part of its corporate welfare. The company's Shenzhen headquarters, unlike other typical Chinese ICT manufacturing factories, such as nearby Foxconn, resembles Silicon Valley–style campuses with acres of R&D facilities and recreational amenities. Employees can rent apartments on campus at very low prices. However, this situation also results in a blurred boundary between work and social life. Some interviewees have complained that there is almost no life outside their work. Located in the outskirts of Shenzhen, the neighborhood of Huawei's campus is more like an urban village (*chengzhongcun*). It usually takes more than one hour to get to the Shenzhen city center. An interviewee mentioned that Ren Zhengfei even refused the local government's proposal for extending subway lines to Huawei campus because he attempted to create an environment that is relatively isolated from the outside world (author interview). Huawei's internal office environment was also isolated. Some

R&D offices even have no windows, which made engineers feel extremely depressed. In this environment, engineers were compelled to concentrate on and dedicate themselves to work regardless of if it is day or night. In this way, the corporate disciplinary apparatus penetrated into workers' social life and into the circle of reproduction, which significantly dismantled their work-life balance.

At the same time, Huawei employees had to face increasing pressure due to the housing affordability crisis in Shenzhen. The continuous flood of financial capital into the city in search of property assets sparked a housing bubble, leading to a big surge in the property market. The Longgang District, a major industrial district of Shenzhen, which is also home to Huawei, witnessed the expansion of a real estate bubble in which industrial estates were being converted into more profitable residential properties. This speculation-led trend hollows out the city's pillar industries, compelling many high-tech companies and leading manufacturers to relocate their headquarters to lower-cost districts. Likewise, Huawei moved its global consumer business arm to Dongguan to reconstruct its manufacturing facilities. The city's middle-class professionals, like Huawei employees, had to face soaring costs of living, which forced them to leave the city. According to official figures, the number of Huawei employees in the Shenzhen headquarters slid by 10.5 percent in 2015.[52] A Huawei engineer who has worked at Huawei for five years said his family faced incredible difficulties in settling down in Shenzhen despite his monthly income tripling the average income there (author interview). During my fieldwork at Huawei headquarters, an interviewee showed me the construction sites of commercial housing estates around the neighborhoods of Huawei's campus. The construction development showcased the area's potential to become a convenient and attractive living environment for middle-class residents, but it also led to greater segregation within the district, with new and expensive gated communities on one side and poorer communities for Foxconn industrial workers on the other. At the same time, the quest of the middle class for an urban lifestyle, which is primarily embodied in the possession of private housing property, is coupled with their precarious work and life status. The dilemma Huawei workers faced is typical among Chinese middle-class professionals as a whole. In comparison with Chinese industrial workers, there is no doubt that Chinese technical workers occupy more privileged economic status and enjoy better social reproduction opportunities. Nevertheless, as part of the Chinese emerging middle class, they are also subsumed in the global capitalist system particularly under the ideology of cosmopolitan consumerism and the concentration of speculative capital. The exploitative relationships they face come not only from direct extraction of their labor power in the production but also from the appropriation of their life materials in the circle of reproduction.

LABOR SUBJECTIVITY

Huawei's structured disciplinary mechanism does not necessarily mean the alienation of workers in their consciousness and subjectivity. Many of my interviewees expressed their strong pride in Huawei's achievements and being a "Huaweier." They also believed Huawei represented China's national pride in the global ICT industry. Some veteran workers in their thirties and forties were especially willing to internalize Huawei's practices and culture, because their collective memories were still imprinted with the country's socialist experience. Even though the hard work culture at Huawei seems crucial, they said most Huawei workers were far from being atomized and apathetic about their work; rather, they have fostered a strong consciousness of being "masters" of their enterprise, which was also a crucial base of socialist residues. However, divisive attitudes toward Huawei's corporate culture have been formed among workers. In recent years there has been a gap between Huawei's corporate culture and young generations of workers who have grown up in China's transition era. The ideologies of nationalism and collectivism have less appeal for this group of younger employees.

The strained labor control has also raised some workers' resistance. For example, when the campaign of "agreement of dedicated workers" was deployed, some reluctant employees voiced their discontent through different channels, including the company's internal online community and some influential websites. A Huawei employee founded the organization Underground Resistance Fighter, calling for widespread resistance against exploitation in Chinese ICT companies. The organizer published a "Manifesto of a Fighter" on the Tianya website—one of most popular and influential online communities in China—to criticize Huawei's crucial managerial practices and claim to defend workers' basic rights. This petition was widely circulated among Huawei's different departments.

Complaints against the harsh working culture in Chinese high-tech firms has spread and escalated into widespread protests. The campaign "996.ICU" was launched on the online code-sharing community GitHub in March 2019. In this campaign, Chinese tech workers have drawn up a blacklist of the high-tech companies that have a harsh overtime work culture. Among these companies, Huawei was put on the top of the list along with other Chinese tech giants such as Alibaba, Tencent, and JD.com. Just like their blue-collar counterparts, including Foxconn's workers, Chinese tech workers are subject to the same capitalist logic of exploitation. Yet it is important to note that such a mechanism of exploitation is disguised by the high-pay reward system as well as multiple ways of soft management skills, such as the capitalists' advocacy of work ethic for dedication and the spirit of entrepreneurship. The 996.ICU campaign, along with other forms of protests, showed new possibilities for the formation of digital labor's subjectivity and agency to resist the exploitative production relations in digital capitalism.

Transnational Labor Regime

The globalization of production not only provides the basis for the formation of the transnational capitalist class but also constitutes a large pool of transnational labor. However, in the contemporary stage of globalization, transnational mobility of labor is not as fluent as that of capital flow due to the nation-state-embedded regulations and control. This labor control leads to fragmentation and heterogeneity of the global working class in its formation and structure. But physical mobility across territorial boundaries is not the only criteria to define the nature of transnational labor. To some extent, Huawei is a prototypical company for analyzing heterogonous compositions of transnational labor.

One important indicator of Huawei's transnationality is its highly multinational workforce. Along with Huawei's global expansion, the company's global workforces, which are composed of Chinese expatriate workers and local employees in host countries, grew significantly. They operated across more than 300 Huawei branches in more than 170 countries and regions, with a localization rate of over 70 percent for nonmanagerial employees and 18.7 percent for middle and senior managers.[53] These global workers, whether geographically fixed or flexible, are subordinated to the transnationalized labor regime under new ways of exploitation. Within this regime, centralized labor management has become a pivotal mechanism for strengthening control over the decentralization of global production and geographically diffused labor.

CHINESE EXPATRIATE WORKERS

Within Huawei's transnationalized workforce structure, Chinese expatriate workers played a critical role in facilitating the company's global expansion. Every Huawei employee has an equal chance to be sent to overseas subsidiaries. Because the company's internationalization started in underdeveloped countries, Chinese workers had to overcome extremely tough environments and challenging working conditions to explore new markets. Some veteran employees were purely inspired by the company's "hardship" culture. During my interviews, I heard many Chinese expatriate workers' stories. What impressed me most was the story of an engineer who had stayed in Africa for eight years. He described his extraordinary experience:

> We often faced life-threatening conditions when working in Africa. We had experienced a terrorist attack in which one of our colleagues had been seriously injured. The majority of Chinese employees had suffered malaria or many other diseases. The working conditions were also challenging. In many cases we had to go to the remote areas on foot to install and maintain base stations. . . . Because of longtime expatriation, we were unable to take care of our family. There was a high divorce rate among expatriate workers. It is hard to imagine what difficulties we have gone through no matter in our work or in our personal life. (author interview)

Chinese workers' dedication to hardship was the prerequisite of Huawei's success in its global expansion. To inspire more Chinese employees to work overseas, especially in underdeveloped regions, Huawei offered generous compensation and benefit packages for overseas employees. In addition to base salary, annual bonus, and stocks, a Chinese expatriate worker can receive a "hardship allowance," a "living-away-from-home allowance," and a food allowance. The amounts of allowance are determined by the conditions of host countries. For example, workers living and working in African countries can receive as much as seventy dollars per day for allowance, which is much higher than that of employees working in developed countries. One interviewee said that material reward was the key factor that motivated the majority of employees to work overseas in the initial stage of internationalization. Nevertheless, at the current stage the new generations of employees generally had no incentives to endure hardship in tough conditions. Ren recognized that this has become an obstacle and a challenge to the company's expansion. Therefore, Ren has advocated for "enhancing frontline employees' welfare" and ensuring massive rewards for employees in underdeveloped regions.[54] In addition, Huawei tended to tie employees' expatriate experience with their career development. Employees who had overseas working experience, especially in underdeveloped markets, had more opportunities of promotion. The company also sent groups of senior cadres to regional markets for training and appointed employees from the "front line" to managerial positions.

It is important to recall that China-based TNCs' approach to accessing China's qualified and diligent labor is the key factor that made these TNCs competitive in international markets. Many interviewees who had overseas working experience agreed that Chinese workers were more compliant with the company's tenets and labor discipline than their foreign coworkers. At Huawei's overseas branches, the lives of Chinese workers were generally segregated from those of local workers in their own compound, equipped with security guards, canteens, and entertainment spaces. Most of them lived in company-based industrial dormitories, which resembled a typical "collective" way of living of Chinese industrial workers. These practices, framed as the "dormitory labor regime,"[55] were reproduced by Chinese firms abroad to strengthen control over transnational labor.

LOCALIZATION

Since the mid-2000s, Huawei has accelerated the pace of localization under the strategy of "internationalization through localization." For example, Huawei's operations in India have the highest rate of localization. Over 98 percent of employees at India-based subsidiaries are local workers, with the majority of them working at R&D positions.[56] In the Asia-Pacific area, 70 percent of employees are non-Chinese. In developed countries, natives are employed at high-level managerial positions to carry out PR strategies. Yet in underdeveloped countries, the localization rate of employment is much lower. A former Huawei marketing manager who had worked in Africa and the Middle East explained that Chinese workers usually occupy technical or managerial positions that are vital for local subsidiaries' operation, while local staff usually act as administrators to support Chinese managers and engineers (author interview). This has led to the company's hierarchical employment structure between Chinese employees and local workers. At the bottom of the hierarchy are local temporary/outsourced workers who work in Huawei's subcontracting units and undertake major manufacturing and construction work. They are either casual workers or on fixed-term contracts, working in precarious conditions and receiving much lower wages and allowances than permanent workers. The casualization of the employment system, which is an outgrowth of the neoliberalized labor regime, has been adopted by Chinese TNCs to reduce labor costs and to achieve flexible capital accumulation.

INTERNATIONAL MANAGEMENT

The decentralization of production and workforce networks gave rise to a centralized management process. Huawei's control over its transnationalized workforce is actually built upon such a centralized management mechanism that has unified standards, structures, and processes across all of Huawei's global operations. The centralized corporate control has somewhat deprived global workers of local empowerment and autonomy. A Huawei service manager working at the North African subsidiary explained that Huawei's managerial practices at overseas subsidiaries basically duplicate those of its domestic models (author interview). From regional managers to grassroots employees, all employees at different levels have to keep communicating with the headquarters every day and implement policy and strategy issued by the headquarters.

In terms of reward structure, Huawei's foreign workers were previously excluded from the company's employee ownership scheme. This divisive reward structure not only undermined foreign workers' incentive but also increased the income gap within the transnational labor structure. To solve this problem, Huawei reformed its profit-sharing plan by rolling out the Time-Based Unit Plan (TUP) in 2013. This long-term incentive plan was designed to provide foreign employees with share compensation similar to that of Chinese employees. Foreign employees can receive large amounts in dividends and bonuses every five years. This plan was also adopted as a strategy of "integration into internationalized management" by Huawei in order to reduce the gap between Chinese employees and foreign workers. However, foreign workers who are rewarded by the TUP actually don't have the same ownership and voting rights as Chinese employees. This means Huawei's unique employee ownership and governance structure based on domestic practices is far from being realized across its global operations.

Moreover, Huawei has also faced the challenge of identification among foreign workers. To overcome such an obstacle in transnational management and obtain global recognition, Huawei has increasingly changed its nationalistic image toward the "customer-centric" value that is based on the universal language of market logic to integrate transnational labor into its corporate culture. To advocate the company's corporate social responsibility, Huawei has set up a number of training centers in underdeveloped countries for professional and technical training. These training programs provide local workers with engineering skills in the field of telecommunications as well as a wide range of training in project management and "soft skills." This strategy of international management aims to transfer skills to the local workforce and to strengthen the company's unified standards of management and culture.

TENSIONS BETWEEN CHINESE MANAGEMENT AND FOREIGN WORKERS

Despite Huawei's massive efforts in constructing a unified corporate culture across the world, foreign workers' views on Huawei's practices are mixed and layered. I used Glassdoor and Indeed, websites that offer an inside look at jobs and companies, to analyze thousands of job reviews by Huawei employees, especially by foreign employees working outside China. Some people appreciated the company's innovative culture and the opportunities for keeping up with trends in technological advancement, while a large number of reviews complained about Huawei's crucial hard work culture. These reviews foreground the tensions between Huawei's centralized management and localization.

One of the most salient conflicts arising from Chinese capital's localization lay in the gap between the work ethics that Chinese managers require and local workers' resistance.[57] Huawei's hard work culture, which was understood by interviewees as the spirit of devotion to work and a willingness of self-sacrifices, was repeatedly emphasized by these managers as the fundamental principle of "work ethics." Local workers, on the other hand, viewed these requirements as cruel methods of "exploitation." The complaints about overtime work and an "imbalance between work and life" were also common among non-Chinese workers. Such a gap existing in the labor process has further strengthened the class and racial tensions between Chinese capital and local workforces. Especially in some countries, racial stereotypes were institutionalized in the management. In my interviews with Huawei's managers working in Africa and Latin America, they all complained about local workers' "backward" work ethics and indolence. They held up their own hard work as standards for demanding similar work styles from their local coworkers, but this method of management usually intensified tensions and raised resistance from those workers.

In some countries, foreign workers' struggles have escalated to labor strikes. For example, in 2011 workers at Huawei's Algerian subsidiary went on strike over the company's poor working conditions, calling for higher wages and a collective bargaining agreement. In 2014 Huawei's Indonesian labor union launched two strikes against Huawei's unfair treatment of Indonesian workers. The union claimed that temporary workers accounted for 70 percent of Huawei's entire workforce in Indonesia. A lot of Huawei's outsourced workers have been contracted several times and still haven't been offered full-time positions. They have called for the conversion of casual contracts into full-time employment.[58]

Although it is too early to predict that the global working class has developed a subjective consciousness of itself or a shared cultural identity to form transnational agency, the incipient labor activism and increasing militancy among transnational workers has significantly increased their bargaining power, which may disrupt China's capital accumulation process and "reverse the mounting class power of capital against labor."[59] The tension between Chinese capital and transnational labor may generate profound effects on Chinese capital's behavior on the ground.

Conclusion

Huawei's experience provides a typical yet distinct case for examining the transformation of the Chinese TNC's ownership structure and labor practices. The company's employee shareholding scheme, which was originally designed as a self-funding measure, has developed into a form of collective ownership. Although this ownership arrangement is far from an ideal model, it can still be viewed as a meaningful experiment in breaking down the monopoly of big capitalists in the property ownership structure. Under this structure, workers consist of primary shareholders and recipients of corporate surplus profits; capital is highly decentralized; and financial capitalists are excluded from the firm's ownership system and corporate control. These characteristics of the ESS entail a relatively democratic system of management and corporate governance.

However, in reality Huawei's management has still involved some relentless practices and coercive modes of labor control. The inculcation of the corporate hard work culture is implemented in the company's labor process through a variety of disciplinary apparatus. Although Huawei ensures substantial share earnings for workers, the antagonism between capital and labor has not yet been mitigated under the so-called employee ownership. Moreover, Huawei's ownership structure has generated very complicated impacts on its labor practices. On the one hand, the high-reward mechanism has become a key incentive for workers' dedication to their jobs. Under the ownership arrangement, workers also enjoy a certain level of autonomy and power in management. But on the other hand, the alignment of corporate interests and individual interests has been used as a means to legitimize the exploitative production relations and to extract more surplus value from labor.

What distinguishes Huawei from many other ICT firms also lies in its distinct mechanism of ideological construction and politicized corporate culture. Such a mechanism is particularly reflected in Ren's use of "corporatized" Mao's thoughts in management, which is not merely taken at its face value. It is reminiscent of some managerial experience of socialist enterprises in the Mao era. It is argued that Ren represents the old generation of Chinese corporate leaders who possess some key characters of the Chinese national bourgeoisie. These characters have enabled the company to develop alternative approaches to Western-style management. But at the same time, Huawei's structured management is characterized by paternalism and a strong style of leadership with which employees have absolute loyalty to the company's supreme commander—the founding father, Ren Zhengfei.

The transnationalization of Chinese capital has proceeded in conjunction with a transnational labor regime. Those workers who are incorporated into the circuit of global capital accumulation are increasingly subject to the hierarchical, precarious, and exploitative capital-labor arrangement. Huawei's practices in constructing and disciplining its workforce foreground the conflicts between Chinese transnational capital and labor. At stake are the growing divisions within the transnational labor, which are primarily reflected as the gaps between Chinese workers and foreign workers, between technical professionals and manufacturing workers, and between full-time workers and casual/outsourced workers. Nevertheless, the ongoing struggles of transnational workers, which are contingent upon their national and local experience, might pose a daunting challenge to China-based transnational capital and complicate the tensions between Chinese capital and transnational labor.

Conclusion

In the context of China's rise to global power, the growth of China-based ICT corporations has gained new attention and relevance. The fundamental question underlying the rise of Chinese ICT firms finds roots in a broader set of issues—that is, how to reorient the direction of China's high-technology industry growth and to reposition China in the global system. The development of China's ICT industry has been facing the deep-rooted internal predicaments characterized by heavy dependence on foreign capital and on low-end ICT manufacturing capacity, or the Foxconn model.[1] One of China's efforts at industrial restructuring rests on the growth of Chinese indigenous high-tech companies and their development capability. At the same time, the growing presence of Chinese ICT corporate power in global markets indicates a new trend of China's path toward "outward-bound transnational capitalism."[2] In this context, a competing mode of development—the BAT model, led by the trio of China's internet giants Baidu, Alibaba, and Tencent—has increasingly gained leverage in China's national economies and has been at the forefront of China's innovation-led growth. However, this model, which can be seen as an emulation of the Silicon Valley experience, converges into part of the universal model of globalized digital capitalism. Is there a genuine Chinese model that shows traces of the country's local trajectories of ICT development and provides some normative values for its future development? This book has provided new evidence to extend the debate with regard to the Chinese model of digital economy development by focusing on the case of Huawei.

The Huawei story is not isolated in addressing one particular company's history and influence within national, regional, and geopolitical-economic contexts. Rather, the case allows us to understand the legacies of China's socialist industrialization in the past in order to reveal the paradoxical nature of the country's development strategy of the present and to elucidate the potential of the Chinese model, or a sustainable mode of development, in the future. This concluding chapter discusses the important trends and implications deriving from Huawei's experience and the challenges that Chinese high-tech firms must tackle in forging their own paths of development.

Distinct Experience and Tendencies of Chinese ICT Enterprises' Development

Huawei was born in the late 1980s when China sought to aggressively launch its great "digital leap forward" in the post-Mao era. This period witnessed a drastic shift from the Maoist policies of industrialization to a civilian, commercial-driven pattern of growth. The resulting high profit margin in the ICT equipment business further provided strong incentives for indigenous manufacturers to enter the highly competitive market. Nevertheless, the "trading market for technology" strategy for China's industrial restructuring led to the encroachment of the domestic market by foreign vendors and trapped China in systematic dependence on foreign capital and technologies.

Since the early 1990s, China's ICT sector has been explicitly embraced as the priority of the state's neoliberal-oriented developmental strategy and the beachhead of China's reintegration into transnational capitalism. Despite rapid expansion of China's information and communication networks during the most explosive phase, China's domestic ICT industry is still locked into undesirable patterns of growth: foreign investment has continued to dominate the ICT manufacturing and export sectors; indigenous firms have relied heavily on unskilled-labor-intensive production such as assembly and processing activities; structural imbalance between oversupply of production capacities and shortage of domestic demand aggregated the crisis of capital accumulation; and the digital divide between urban and rural areas has become increasingly acute under the city-centered development scheme, which has further depressed the Chinese rural market and purchasing power. These structural problems have largely constrained the development of Chinese indigenous firms in their home markets. In particular, market unevenness has reinforced an unfavorable environment in which Huawei found itself squeezed between state-owned enterprises and foreign competitors. This sheer disadvantage forced Huawei to escape from the Chinese domestic market and start the process of internationalization. The imperative of Chinese ICT firms' initial internationalization was not precisely driven by the aggressive motive of exporting surplus capital from home market to new territories as Western multinationals did but was instead a means of looking for the new space of survival and capital accumulation in overseas markets.

At the same time, the Chinese leadership was aware of the structural disparity brought by the FDI-driven regime. Instead of being captured by interests of foreign capital, the Chinese party-state possessed the autonomy and capacity to seek reorientation of China's ICT developmental path and to increase the country's competence in indigenous technology. As Lin Chun argues, post-Mao China still inherits some outstanding advantages from the Maoist regime, which amount to a "super model of a socialist developmental state."[3] These advantages include a strong state capacity, which is defined here as the capacity to implement the country's priority policies, to mobilize nationwide resources and social participation, to control strategic industries, and to keep ideologies of social and redistributive justice alive.[4] The powerful state capacity has made the cooperation of indigenous business more likely, which has led to a strong state-capital alliance to carry out strategic developmental plans. Furthermore, the failures of neoliberal market policies have resulted in massive pressure on the Chinese government to seek more state intervention in the new stage of reform. In particular, even in the liberalized ICT manufacturing industry, the Chinese state has made ongoing struggles against the overriding logic of neoliberal capitalism, aiming to strengthen its state machinery in order to coordinate diverse interests of national champions and make the emergence of Chinese globally competitive ICT firms viable. The complicated role the Chinese state played in the making of transnational ICT corporations is manifest throughout the evolution of the country's ICT development.

First of all, in parallel with market liberalization policies, a techno-nationalistic strategy continued to underpin China's dual-track developmental model. Since the late 1980s, China has embarked on a set of state-led technology programs to guarantee core technology development and to create an environment conducive to innovation for corporate players. China's major technical breakthroughs in the realm of ICTs, such as the country's first indigenous central switching, fiber-optic telecommunications technology, and mobile network technologies, precisely benefited from the state-supported programs like 863 Plans with the collaboration of indigenous high-tech firms. Particularly, Huawei was promoted as the backbone enterprise to facilitate the state's strategic goals and to take a lead in the forefront of China's cutting-edge technology research and development. Instead of a pure market-driven model, the combination of Chinese corporate players' R&D participation and the state's techno-nationalistic initiatives explored a "multi-driver model" of technology development and innovation system.[5] This model allowed national R&D projects to generate greater technological spillover effects and transform them into higher production capacity at the enterprise level.

Second, Huawei's experience illuminates the Chinese government's effort to create particular sizes of indigenous firms in the ICT industry, which is also part of the state's big business strategy. In the early to mid-1980s, the Chinese government had proposed building state enterprises into vertically integrated and international competitive giant companies at the national level. In response to this national scheme, in 1986 Li Tieying announced the extension of enterprise reforms into the electronics industry. Although the big business strategy primarily involved large state-owned enterprises, Huawei's increasing influence in the domestic high-tech industry endowed the company with the status of "national champion" and more preferable policies from the central and local governments. As observed by Peter Nolan, Huawei's development after the mid-1990s was crucially related to government support.[6] From the late 1990s into the 2000s, Huawei started to join the global level playing field and spearhead the state's going-out strategy.

Despite Huawei's remarkable success, it should be noted that many other Chinese indigenous ICT firms generally have not yet matched the economies of scale or technology capability that Huawei has achieved. More important, after the 2008 global crisis, the drastic decline in foreign investment and the slump in ICT product exports bankrupted a large number of Chinese ICT manufacturers and exporters. The crisis propelled the Chinese state to launch a set of economic readjustment policies to boost domestic demand, hoping to reduce Chinese firms' reliance on external markets and change the imbalance between overcapacity and underconsumption.[7] These domestic market-driven initiatives included directing state and corporate investment into rural markets, a vast and uncharted frontier for ICTs goods, to transfer the overcapacity in saturated urban markets. Following this strategy, a few Chinese internet giants, such as Alibaba and JD.com, have taken some aggressive measures to tap into rural markets. By the same token, it could be expected that the state's readjustment programs would motivate Huawei to revive the rural market–driven strategy that had helped the company achieve its initial success in the mid-1990s.

In addition, other selective import-substitution measures, such as the adoption of indigenous 3G/4G wireless standards and government procurement policies, were expected to generate huge domestic demand as well as a domestically accumulated regime for indigenous companies. Especially in the aftermath of the Snowden revelation, the Chinese government planned to gradually remove foreign technologies from banks, the military, state-owned enterprises, and key government agencies, replacing them with homegrown technologies at all layers, including infrastructure hardware, networking equipment, servers, and operating systems. This move indicates that the Chinese state would take a more energetic role in moderating the presence of foreign companies and preserving domestic markets for indigenous high-tech firms. This policy shift also came as a sign that Chinese indigenous companies like Huawei, which had lagged far behind foreign multinationals, became more competitive to join the fray in the Chinese domestic market and gradually regained market status through their foreign rivals. From being a laggard "escaping" from the home market, to an international market-driven multinational, and currently to a heavyweight "national champion" rivaling foreign giants in both domestic and overseas markets, the course of Huawei's development has been marked by a detour moving from "inside-out" to "outside-in" paths. Its distinctive features of growth also illustrate how the state's policy struggle and inter-capitalist market competition shaped domestic corporate players' development and how Chinese indigenous firms have the capacity to cope with market dynamics and policy changes.

Meanwhile, accompanying the state's domestic demand-driven policy, the Chinese leadership endeavored to redress the development course toward an innovation-driven growth pattern. It is not surprising to see that most Chinese indigenous ICTs firms still stay away from the core competitive areas, engaging in less-specialized activities and downstream niche markets and following modularized production.[8] Nevertheless, Huawei's technology development model might provide a distinct experience of industrial upgrade for the Chinese state to readjust its industrial policy. It also sets a pioneering example for latecomer firms on how to move from the labor-intensive stage to the innovation-centered stage. As analyzed in chapter 4, Huawei has been pursuing its core competitive advantages by insisting on the centrality of research and development and the innovation-driven growth strategy. Huawei's technical progress in the areas of high-end technologies, such as chipsets and new-generation telecommunications technologies, shows us its capability in pushing forward China's technology frontier.

In the early 2000s, China's ICT industry came to a hugely important turning point. By recognizing the country's disadvantaged position in the global

ICT sector, the Chinese state geared up to pursue its own indigenous and proprietary technologies central to the country's national competitiveness.[9] Since 2006, indigenous innovation has been formally designated as one of the government's strategic priorities.[10] In the 18th National Congress of the CPC of 2012, the Chinese leadership proposed "speeding up the creation of a new growth model . . . and increasing motivation for pursuing innovation-driven development."[11] The congress report stressed the need to promote integration of IT application and industrialization as the new approach to the "Chinese-style path of development." In response to the appeal of domestic internet entrepreneurs who clamored for massive policy support, in 2015 Chinese premier Li Keqiang proposed the "Internet Plus" action plan in his "Government Work Report," advocating the priority of the internet and other information technology in building a new technology-driven economic engine. Furthermore, this internet-based developmental scheme was posited to trigger a "new Industrial Revolution," or "Internet 4.0," by using informatization to propel industrialization. It also signaled the centralized government's policy support for the internet-led BAT model. In parallel with the Internet Plus action plan, China's ambitions of industrial upgrading were further buttressed in its MIC2025 strategy, a plan unveiled in 2015 to lay out the road map for the country's industrial modernization. Under the principles of indigenous innovation and self-sufficiency, MIC2025 was designed to nurture China-based global high-tech giants that can catch up with global rivals in the newest technologies. Although the Chinese government has been playing down MIC2025 policy amid the US-China trade tensions, the plan, along with other state-driven policies, indicates the Chinese state's initiative in forging a new model of economic development. In the state-orchestrated industrial restructuring, ICT-enabled technologies, including big data, cloud computing, and the Internet of Things, would become the forefronts of new technological trends and renewed sites of capital accumulation. Moreover, the applications of these emerging technologies are also posited to modernize traditional industries and to generate a new wave of ICT infrastructure expansion in the near future.

When facing growing geopolitical-economic tensions, the Chinese leadership has increasingly turned the policy focus to what it terms "civil-military fusion" (CMF). This strategy hoped to achieve the goal of modernizing China's military through informatization, demonstrating the country's drive to techno-military independence. As a mainstay policy of China's industrial restructuring, CMF was further integrated into the overall design of China's ICT development through top-level planning, including MIC2025, Internet

Plus, a "Next Generation Artificial Intelligence Development Plan," and a "National Guideline for the Development and Promotion of the IC Industry." Different from the Maoist military-dominated industrialization as well as the trickle-down effect from the military to civilian sectors, CMF intended to integrate the commercial and military functions of core technologies, with a particular effort to assimilate indigenous innovations and to leverage the private sector in strengthening China's defense industrial base. China's leadership also encouraged the country's technology leaders to translate the significant progress it has made in some core technologies such as artificial intelligence (AI), quantum computing, robotics, and smart manufacturing into a military advantage.[12] Under this plan, some backbone enterprises were promoted to lead the CMF. For instance, in October 2017 JD.com signed a strategic cooperation agreement with the PLA's Air Force Logistics Department in order to assist in the creation of an intelligent logistics system. Hailed as an "innovative specimen of CMF," this partnership represents the enhanced role that private internet companies have played in the state's industrial restructuring plan.[13]

Among the beneficiaries of China's pro-internet policies are certainly those newly emerging internet giants such as Alibaba, Baidu, Tencent, and JD.com. The BAT, for instance, were identified as first members of China's AI national teams to lead the country's "open innovation platforms" in the different areas of AI technologies, with Baidu focusing on self-driving technology, Alibaba on smart cities,[14] and Tencent on health care. Huawei, however, tended to obscure its role in the most recent state-led initiatives amid growing criticism of the company's links to the Chinese government and military.

Unlike many other Chinese high-tech firms that have a reputation for simply copying or "indigenizing" Western designs and innovations, Huawei has been endeavoring to turn itself from a technology follower to an innovation leader. In recent years, the company's core business areas, such as its basic telecommunications equipment business, are confronting considerable challenges. It is clear that the traditional telecommunications equipment manufacturing industry has been caught in the "sunset stage," characterized by lower profit margins, increasingly saturated markets, and adherence to standardized technologies. Under the pressure, the company made a push to transform its mobile-handset business from a manufacturer of cheap phones to a global brand that can compete with Apple, Samsung, and other top players in the industry. Meanwhile, it ramped up R&D in chipset and other core proprietary technologies to reduce its reliance on foreign technology.

Although Huawei downplayed its role in China's national strategy of AI development, the company has been placing tremendous strategic R&D resources in its AI solutions, at the core of which is the innovation and development of AI chipsets with cutting-edge capability. In an interview, Ren Zhengfei projected the future of China's AI-enabled society; in his words: "China's AI such as self-driving technologies can start with tractors.... We will not compete with the West in the same track. [For example,] we can build the driverless tractors that can perform time-consuming tasks [to increase agricultural productivity]."[15] Ren's vision sheds light on a distinct model of China's technological development, which is set to support the country's digital transformations. Meanwhile, Huawei's efforts in strengthening its own intellectual property regime and standard-setting activity have enabled the company to acquire a leading position in international governance. In short, Huawei's experience not only reflects the potential of Chinese indigenous companies in the high-tech development but also provides important policy lessons for the Chinese state to build independent and sustainable innovation capacities.

The case of Huawei also demonstrates the interaction of local development and the centralized statist policy initiative. Because of the legacy of the decentralization of state authority, China's development still relies heavily on its local-oriented, bottom-up approach.[16] This has led to a multilayered mechanism of capital accumulation, or "local state corporatism,"[17] in which local governments and institutions play more active roles in nurturing indigenous companies. For example, industrial policy decisions made by Shenzhen Municipal Government not only catalyzed Huawei's creation but also directly impacted the company's funding strategies and internal organizational structure. The decentralized telecom policy that endowed local telecom operators with decision-making autonomy also assisted Huawei in obtaining market shares in marginal markets, especially at county and village levels. Such a local, bottom-up mechanism based on the interaction of local states and business, created distinct patterns of Chinese ICT companies' development.

Uncertainties: Geoeconomic and Geopolitical Challenges

The contradictory nature and tendencies of China's ICT development have shaped the historical contour and internal accumulation of Chinese ICT firms. At the same time, Huawei's external accumulation also generates profound understanding of the transnationalization of Chinese corporate power. For one thing, Huawei's outward expansion is touted as one of the most successful cases of China's going-out strategy. The company has not only established itself as a global industrial leader but has also provided an illustration of a Chinese firm's significant step in the ascent of "corporate China" to the international business stage. For another thing, Huawei's transnationalization has also encountered many obstacles and uncertainties. As a primary target of Washington's new "technology cold war" against China, the Huawei case to the fullest extent highlighted inter-capitalist and interstate tensions engendered by capitalist globalization. To understand such dynamics and tensions, it is crucial to embed the enterprise strategy with regional and international political-economic processes to assess the global rise of China's ICT corporations.

REPOSITION IN THE GEOECONOMIC ORDER

One significant global impact in relation to the rise of Chinese transnational ICT corporations is the country's changing geoeconomic position in global production networks and in the regional economic system. Although China's ICT developmental trajectory shared some similar experiences with that of the Asian "developmental states," it is problematic to treat the Chinese experience as another example of the "East Asian miracle." As discussed earlier, the rapid economic growth of East Asia was far from a miracle merely shaped by these countries' endogenous conditions. In fact, they were consciously cultivated by the United States as part of its anti-Communist strategy during the Cold War period. This geopolitical condition has led to Asia's "twin dependence," both economic and geopolitical, on the US-led capitalist powers. On the hand, China's distinct path of industrialization in the Maoist period laid an independent industrial foundation and the legacies of socialist self-reliance for China's spectacular growth in the reform era.[18]

When Cold War tensions started to ease in the 1980s, Chinese policy makers expressed their desire to integrate into transnational capitalism. The country's initial move to jump-start economic growth was to participate in the "flying geese model" of East Asia's regional production networks, specializing in exporting low-value-added goods to the Western world. However, it came as no surprise that China's aggressive promotion of information and communication technologies, along with its active participation in global ICT production networks, has not necessarily improved China's geoeconomic position. China's export-led economic growth, which is based on the exploitation of domestic labor and underconsumption of the domestic population, actually has become a precondition to sustain the United States' mounting appetite for low-cost manufactured imports.[19] In addition, tremendous trade surplus generated by China's growing low-cost exports has made China the world's largest foreign-exchange reserve. Like many other exporters, China invested most of its savings in US Treasury bonds, emerging as the largest creditor to the United States to finance US domestic consumption.[20] This unbalanced relationship exposed the unsustainability and vulnerability of China's export-oriented economic growth.

Apart from reliance on the US consumer market, China also heavily depended on the imports of high-end technology products from industrialized countries, especially from the United States. China's trade liberalization policy has created a market that is of great importance for globally dominant US high-tech firms. Between 1990 and 1998, US exports of communications equipment to China increased more than ninefold.[21] US policy makers put intense pressure on the Chinese side to make concessions in the ICT sector upon China's entry into the World Trade Organization. The White House even claimed that access to the potentially vast Chinese market for ICT products and services was "vital to maintaining US global leadership in information technology."[22] Obviously, China's role in global digital capitalism was in line with the US interests to sustain global production network and the US-led political economic order. But for China, the country's "disadvantaged" geoeconomic position not only limited its own technological development and industrial diversification but also locked Chinese ICT companies into the country's current structure in global value chains.[23]

China's ICT industrial restructuring initiative, therefore, involved the industrial upgrade at the national level and included a policy shift from the "attracting-in" to "going-out" strategy to reposition its role in the global political-economic system. Under the selective import-substitution policy, Chinese indigenous firms, especially private ICT companies, have played increasingly important roles in China's exports structure. Meanwhile, Chinese leaders have acted out of a conviction that China-based indigenous backbone enterprises must move from simple exporting activities to in-depth engagement in the globalized circuit of accumulation. Chinese firms' "going-global" process witnessed more qualitative expansionary activities, such as outbound foreign direct investment, cross-border acquisitions and mergers, cross-border financial investment, and the set-up of global assembly lines, joint ventures, and global R&D centers.

Huawei's initial internationalization fully took advantage of China's geoeconomic position by exporting its low-cost ICT products to neighboring countries in order to gain a foothold in the region. Following this geoeconomic strategy, Huawei became an export-driven company and quickly acquired large market share in many developing countries by providing high-end products close to Western quality at competitive prices.[24] In addition to the export-driven strategy, Huawei has placed increasing weight on brand building and technology acquisitions as rationales of deepening internationalization. Its business spans the whole chain of the industry, taking control from the R&D of core technologies to equipment manufacturing and from marketing to after-sales maintenance service. Huawei and other thriving China-based ICT firms are reshaping the distribution of profits along the global value chain, the upstream of which has primarily been controlled by Western multinationals. The increasing influence that Chinese ICT firms have gained in global markets has also endowed them with growing bargaining power vis-à-vis transnational capital and Western governments. In short, Huawei's experience has created a greater inspiration for other Chinese high-tech firms to find innovative ways of development and to win a competitive position in the global economy rather than reliance on their existing cost-effective manufacturing capabilities. More important, it has drawn wider policy implications for the Chinese government to improve its geoeconomic position and reshape the balance of power in the global economic order.

GEOPOLITICAL IMPLICATIONS

The rise of Chinese ICT firms is renovating the landscape of the global ICT sector and altering China's position in the global production network. At the same time, China's ambitious going-out strategy has generated some significant geopolitical implications. If attracting-in was used to facilitate China's reinsertion into global capitalism and to jump-start the country's digital revolution in the post-Mao period, the going-out strategy, in contrast, was likely tied to the Chinese state's geopolitical efforts for an assertion of greater political and economic power.[25]

The combination of foreign direct investment and economic assistance in developing nations has been used as a new approach of China's economic diplomacy to project its power in the global South. At the same time, China's growing outward foreign direct investment by China-based transnational corporations can be better seen as an attempted strategy to gain relative geopolitical autonomy from the United States. The Chinese government has gradually retreated from US government debt and redirected its surplus capital to the global South in order to diversify the country's OFDI. This indicates China's efforts in increasing its leverage outside the orbit of the US influence and cultivating a new form of South-South relations. The Chinese government's drive to push forward the going-out policy served to align with Chinese corporate players' extraterritorial strategies and to embrace the China-based transnational capitalist class's interests as an integral component of China's national interests. In turn, the global expansion of China-based capital can be posited as an extension as well as an expression of China's geopolitical-economic initiatives. Take Huawei's trajectory of internationalization, for example: the company's global expansion has been closely entangled with China's foreign policy to serve the country's geopolitical interests. The company also received relevant state support, such as preferential loans from the state policy banks, to finance its global operations. This case fully illustrates the mutual relations between the state and China-based capital in forging the regime of corporate China.

However, China's increasing weight and active engagement in the global South have also elicited widespread controversy. Chinese firms' expansion into developing nations was always accompanied with Western criticism against China's "new colonialism." But in fact, as argued by Deborah Brautigam, many of the fears about China's rise are misinformed.[26] China's going-out initiative has no intention of colonizing other countries, dictating the politics or economy of local countries, bringing destruction to local culture, or depriving them of development opportunities. Although China's current engagement in the global South is primarily driven by economic interests and realpolitik, there is no doubt that the legacies of Mao's Third World internationalism have continued to evolve and exert influence on China's diplomatic strategies with developing nations. The long history of China's involvement in developing nations' struggle for national autonomy and development gave the country legitimacy and credibility for building the South-South relationship.[27] These historical factors and linkages made many developing countries more willing to accept the Chinese model as an alternative to the Washington Consensus.[28]

In essence, the patterns of Chinese firms' engagement in developing countries are still different from those of Western multinationals. First, Chinese investment and economic assistance has not always come with political conditionality, allowing developing countries to be free to find their own pathway for development. Second, contrary to Western capital pursuing the doctrine of "profit maximization," Chinese capital's engagement in the global South is characterized by the logic of "encompassing accumulation," which is based on strategic, long-term, and result-oriented involvement.[29] The presence of Chinese ICT firms in developing countries is exemplary of such a pattern of capital accumulation, which goes beyond the imperative of profit maximization and economic efficiency. The growing engagement of these firms has not only prevented developing nations from reliance on Western companies' provisions of telecom infrastructure and technologies but has also considerably contributed to underdeveloped countries' social development. Third, unlike the United States' mighty military presence across the world, China's military power used to be contained within the country's boundary and its immediate neighborhood. But the Chinese defense strategy tends to redefine the boundaries of China's national security by extending its military presence overseas along with Chinese capital's growing outward expansion.[30] For instance, China's first overseas military base, established in Africa's Djiboutian in 2017, represents the country's initiative in gaining greater geostrategic influence in this area. There is no doubt that the acceleration of Chinese capital's outward expansion will increasingly generate the need for greater military protection to secure Chinese-funded projects and infrastructure. This strategic shift will inevitably clash with US overseas interests and lead to heightened geopolitical tensions in the future.

However, Chinese capitalists' engagement in developing countries is far from the story of "love without borders." As a matter of fact, Chinese capital's forays into developing nations were motivated more by pragmatic imperatives such as securing a steady supply of strategic resources and exporting domestic overcapacity to overseas markets than by the pure solidarity rationale of the past. The infrastructure loans provided by the Chinese government were not merely a form of financial assistance to underdeveloped countries but a means used by Chinese ICT firms to secure long-term construction contracts from local governments. Although the Chinese government as well as Chinese firms appreciated this approach of trading loans for markets to a win-win model of engagement in the global South, it is important to point out that this approach will usher underdeveloped nations into new cycles of debts that might deepen their reliance on the debt-driven growth model.

Moreover, what was less noticed is that China's going-out initiative coincided with some developing countries' opening-up process. China-based capital actually constituted part of the forces of neoliberal globalization that brought exploitation, polarization, and environmental destruction to local communities. In this vein, the Chinese transnational capitalist class acted in ways similar to those of their Western counterparts. The rigorous labor regime built by Chinese transnational corporations, which is characterized by low-wage exploitation, precarious employment, poor working conditions, and hierarchical organizational structure, is precipitating class conflicts between

Chinese capitalists and local workers. Increasing social upheavals against Chinese capital's involvement has started to ferment, which may develop into widespread anti-Chinese sentiment across some nations.[31] Such conflicts may raise a great deal of uncertainties and risks for Chinese capital's expansion in the global South.

Not surprisingly, Huawei has increasingly shifted away from its image of a Chinese national brand to a market-oriented multinational enterprise and has denounced its linkage to the Chinese military in order to accommodate international markets in its newly globalized stage of development. Especially in European and North American markets, Huawei has tended to seek cooperation and coalition with multiple actors in different ways, such as establishing joint R&D centers, signing global procurement agreements with global leading vendors, and even cooperating with its competitors in many respects. Huawei has also actively participated in a number of international standardization organizations to strengthen its position in international governance. However, the company's efforts have received completely different results in different markets. In Europe, Huawei has made deep inroads in multiple business domains, including the supply of telecom equipment, network infrastructure construction, data services, and consumer electronics hardware. Apart from its role as a telecommunications equipment supplier, Huawei has been treated as a preferred investor by many European countries that have attempted to rely on surging Chinese outward investment to boost the EU economy and to renew their economic interests in the ICT industry. But under pressure from the United States, Europe has been torn over its approach to Chinese ICT giants, especially to Huawei's 5G technologies. In May 2019 more than thirty countries reached an agreement at the Prague Summit to apply more stringent security for 5G deployment, a move aimed at setting hurdles on Huawei's expansion in the 5G markets. It is expected that the struggles in global technological governance will constitute one of the most important forms of geopolitical competition along with the global rise of China's ICT corporate power and the resulting counterattack on China.

Huawei's entry into the United States was fraught with complicated issues and conflicts. Huawei was blocked at the door of the US market from inception. For one thing, in view of the pivotal role of ICTs in economic growth and national defense, the US side had fears of Chinese ICT firms' expansion into its core telecom businesses. For US policy makers, China's increasing weight in the global economy appears at the expense of the relative weight of US political-economic powers in a zero-sum competition for global influence.[32] In particular, there is also a prevailing concern that Huawei's widespread ICT applications and infrastructure construction across the world will eventually post a direct threat to the US control of global network infrastructure and its own national security system. For another thing, Huawei's businesses are in direct competition with American giants in multiple ICT business domains. For example, Huawei has challenged Cisco's dominant position in the business networking market. In the burgeoning consumer electronics markets, Huawei has increasingly encroached on Apple's turf with an unprecedented rate of market expansion. Moreover, Huawei's emerging chipset business has grown rapidly, posing a threat to Qualcomm's position in the high-end chipset market. In the race to 5G, the company's leadership in the next-generation mobile communication technologies has given China an edge in the rivalry, prompting the United States' broader crackdown on Chinese companies. In these profitable, high-value-added markets, Huawei is emerging as one of the most formidable rivals to undercut US multinationals' profits and interests. To outflank Chinese corporations' expansionary initiative, the US government has played an important role in setting the rules of games to drive Chinese competitors out of its home market. This also explains why the US government overstated China's rise and national security concern to justify its protectionist policy.[33] Moreover, the ongoing worldwide political shifts toward protectionism would eventually lead to "multinationals in retreat,"[34] which has compelled global companies to localize their operations into regional or national units.

The new technological cold war recalls China's experience in developing its own nuclear weapon program during the 1960s when China was facing geopolitical isolation. This historical experience offered a legacy as well as an important lesson for Huawei to independently develop its own "nuclear weapon," a backup technology system that can break away from its reliance on foreign core technologies. Meanwhile, the harsh crackdown by the United States is likely to spur the company's efforts to develop a fully independent supply chain and alternative markets under the Chinese state's support. The enormous market dynamics of emerging-market countries and new frontiers of businesses are producing seemingly unlimited opportunities for Chinese high-tech firms to offset their disadvantaged positions in the global North.

BELT AND ROAD: A NEW GEOPOLITICAL-ECONOMIC INITIATIVE

China's escalating conflicts with core powers are tempting it to seek new geopolitical strategies and alliances with other developing nations that are aspiring to move out of the US orbit of influence and to challenge the US-led global capitalist order. China's BRI can be seen as a real example of such a geopolitical-economic strategy. This initiative was planned to reconstitute a new regional development pattern, with an attempt to counter the post-2008 US rebalance strategy to the Asia-Pacific region. Exterritorial telecommunications networks, in particular, were designated as one of the most crucial infrastructure construction plans to promote intraregional trade and connectivity and to export China's infrastructure know-how. As part of the BRI, the Chinese government tended to strengthen intercontinental backbone networks, also known as the "fiber-optic Silk Road," linking Europe to Asia and facilitating international data traffic within this region.[35] Chinese ICT giants, including Huawei and ZTE, have become the key investors and actors in such a new strategy. Apart from commercial incentives driven by Chinese ICT corporations, at the core of this new road is the geopolitical goal of constructing independent network sovereignty as a counter-hegemonic offensive.

As Yuezhi Zhao observes, "The Snowden-triggered implosion of the US imperial information surveillance state has created a hegemonic crisis" to the US legitimacy in global governance.[36] In the post-Snowden era, Russia and China evidently have shared a desire to construct alternative communication routes to the US-controlled surveillance network. Chinese ICT firms are posited to play more important roles in pushing forward the realignment of extraterritorial communications systems. However, the division, as well as the geopolitical tensions, among developing nations might prevent the formation of a coherent counter-hegemonic alliance, which would pose challenges to the BRICS (Brazil, Russia, India, China, and South Africa) bloc's initiative in forging an alternative communications system. For example, the flop of the BRICS cable project, an initiative devised to connect all of BRICS member countries (which stalled in 2015), is illustrative of the potential, follies, and contradictions of such a counter-hegemonic initiative.[37]

It should be emphasized, however, that the fiber-optic Silk Road is more than a strategy of exporting domestic excessive capacity. In fact, the reconstituted Silk Road tended to incorporate the goal of China's industrial restructuring with the state's geopolitical strategy to redress internal imbalance and to inspire new growth impetus. As Chinese critical scholar Wang Hui argues, the BRI is bound to coordinate both internal and external opening and both east and west opening in China's new regional development policy.[38] Given the geographical advantage of China's central and western region in the BRI, the demand for cross-border network connectivity linking Belt and Road countries and China's inland interior region will generate a new strategic growth pole for indigenous ICT firms. Moreover, it will encourage both the government and firms' investment in infrastructure construction and promote industrial relocation from the coastal region to the western interior or to markets along the Belt and Road. The prospect underlying China's fiber-optic Silk Road strategy not only indicates a new direction of China's ICT development and industrial upgrade but also presents a new approach of regional development and a favorable geopolitical environment for the growth of China-based ICT firms.

Self-Reliant Mode of Development

This book delineates a China-based ICT firm's trajectory of development and a realistic picture of China's ICT industry, including its strengths, weakness, and potential. A central question running through this story is, Can China provide an alternative approach to ICT development? Though the answer is still uncertain, given the paradoxical nature of China's post-Mao market reform and the complicated characters of its reintegration into global capitalism, the case of Huawei, or the "Huawei model," might demonstrate some potential dynamics and great impacts of Chinese ICT firms on the global political economy system.

First, China's quest for an alternative model of development is characterized by the tensions between integration and autonomy.[39] At the heart of China's distinct experience of industrial development was its self-reliant path toward industrialization and modernization. In the 1980s, Ren Zhengfei had already gone further than government officials to challenge the doctrine of China's neoliberal-oriented technological development and "trading markets for technology" policy. He questioned the government's technology transfer schemas, warning about the consequences of relinquishing the country's technology autonomy and industrial self-protection. As noted by Armand Mattelart, the schemas of technology transfers were far from a simple process of transferring skills, knowledge, technologies, or methods of manufacturing; rather, they conveyed "transplantations of power structures" and linear industrialization strategies.[40] Instead of reliance on foreign trade and transfers, a self-reliant mode of development can be envisioned by the mobilization of local resources to satisfy local needs. In practice, Huawei firmly adhered to such a doctrine on its own terms by committing to independent research and development. From its first self-invented digital switch that satisfied fundamental needs of the Chinese local market, especially China's neglected rural market to its high-end chip-making technology, the achievements Huawei has made fully illustrate the capacity of Chinese indigenous high-tech companies in creating an independent path of development and coming up with creative solutions to satisfy local needs.

Of course, self-reliance does not mean autarky or exclusion of external cooperation. It also emphasizes the capacity to absorb new techniques and adapt them for generation of local technology. Huawei's innovation activities were not implemented in a closed internal circuit; rather, the company was open to hybrid forms of research and development. Drawing on its "learning-by-doing" practices, Huawei quickly built up core competence by acquiring knowledge and capability from rivals and collaborators. At the same time, the company insisted on its own autonomous trajectory of development and took a measure of command over core proprietary technologies. This approach enabled the company to rapidly move from the position of a late follower to an industrial leader that plays a significant role in influencing and defining global technology.

More important, this approach implies broader cooperation for "collective self-reliance" at different levels. For example, the genesis of Huawei's first self-invented digital switch owed much to technical assistance from China's military research institutions and inland manufacturing factories that were part of the Maoist legacies of military R&D capabilities. In addition, Huawei's involvement in the development of the indigenous standard, along with other of China's technology developers, telecommunications operators, and equipment manufacturers, can be seen as part of the endeavor of collective self-reliance. While the interests of different actors are hardly unified in such a national project, the national self-reliance strategy is still vital to overcome domestic divisions and to promote national development. Amid rising unilateralism and protectionism, especially amid the unprecedented trade war tensions with the United States, President Xi Jinping has further revived the Maoist call for self-reliance in China's development.[41] This historical experience will surely strengthen China's pursuit of technological sovereignty, assuring a genuinely unique Chinese path toward its long-term restructuring.

Collective self-reliance is not just confined to a national strategy. Instead, the new trend of collective self-reliance tends to extend collaboration to broader South-South cooperation. Although there remain wide divisions within global Southern countries, the emergent powers' consensus on pushing the move "from a liberal-unilateral to a developmental multipolar" discourse created the cornerstones of South-South cooperation and the conditions for forging counter-hegemonic forces.[42] In this sense, the alignment of collective self-reliant efforts may become a strategy to construct a more equitable global information and technology order.

Another one of the important lessons deriving from Huawei's self-reliant development is its innovative design of the ownership structure and independent financial system, which distinguishes itself from that of other conventional transnational corporations. In the context of globalization, the contradiction between integration and self-reliance has been quite pronounced. Since the late 1990s, many Chinese ICT firms have also plugged into global financial networks to speed up corporatization and capitalization. The influx of short-run, speculative capital into the high-tech sector not only engendered Chinese ICT firms' dependence on transnational financial capital and external stakeholders, but it also increased their vulnerabilities in global ICT markets. In comparison, Huawei's experiment in its distinct employee-shareholding ownership structure provides an innovative measure to solve the problem of structural dependence and to unravel the contradiction between integration and self-reliance to some extent. Its collective ownership structure has enabled the company to resist the control of transnational financial capital and external capitalist groups and to create a relatively independent corporate structure to implement self-management.

The increasing global operations and transnationalization of capital ownership have made the nationality of multinationals less irrelevant, leading to the formation of the "stateless" corporate identity. The corporate nationality of Chinese ICT multinationals remains an enigma in light of their intricate ownership and corporate structure.[43] Although major China-based internet giants such as Tencent, Baidu, and Alibaba are highly dependent on the Chinese domestic market for revenue and profit, they are barely considered purely independent "Chinese companies" because of their extensive ties with transnational capital.[44] Rather than falling into the reification of the "corporate identity," we should bear in mind that the corporate identity is actually an expression of transnational capitalist class interests.

According to William I. Robinson, the spread of large corporations from the third world resulted in an accelerated transnational integration of local capitalists into the ranks of the transnational capitalist class.[45] These emergent capitalist groups tended to converge on certain economic and political interests along with shared values of global corporate responsibility, which constituted the underpinning of their class identity. However, it is also important to note that the formation of the TCC identity does not prevent particular national and regional contingents tied to specific histories, norms, and values. Such a contradiction between preserving a distinct national identity and forging a globalized corporate identity is also manifest in Huawei's experience. Even while Huawei's business and assets became increasingly globalized, its corporate culture and managerial methods continued to be shaped by particular Chinese cultural practices and experience inherited from pre-reform socialist enterprise management. These practices include the socialist work ethic, the use of ideological education, organized political control, and the institutional culture of authority. In addition, the nationalistic sentiment that combined the development of the enterprise with the fate of the country was used as an inspiring ideology to mobilize workers. As a representative member of the Chinese national bourgeoisie emerging from the post-Mao market reform, Ren Zhengfei has tended to preserve such distinct legacies and cultural practices to consolidate his experiment of management and growth path. His declaration to construct autonomous corporate culture and identity contributes to the formation of a globally competitive corporation "with Chinese characteristics."

However, there is also a deep contradiction embedded in Huawei's managerial practices. Paradoxically, while Ren emphasized the importance of Chinese socialist management practices in the early stage of Huawei's development, he was open to bringing Western managerial doctrines into the company's management with an aim to build up a modern, formal corporate management system. This incentive is due in part to Chinese entrepreneurs' common belief, or the mythmaking, that equates Western-style experience with modernization. In the ongoing process of transnationalization, the contradiction between Westernization and indigenization in corporate management will become one of the most striking characteristics of corporate China.

As analyzed in the previous chapter, Huawei's innovative ownership arrangement was designed to create a fairer system of redistribution for employees through its profit-sharing bonus plan. The desired strategy also sought to create a democratic mechanism by encouraging workers' participation in management to protect their basic rights. This organizational innovation at the firm level played an important role in constructing Huawei's core competence, which is highly reliant on its R&D and quality labor resources. It contrasts sharply with many other Chinese manufacturing firms' growth strategy hinging on the competitive advantages of hiring low-cost, cheap labor. Despite these advantages, there are also some critical flaws underlying Huawei's ownership arrangement and management. Though Huawei workers can enjoy pretty high salary and material rewards, the ownership design and rigid corporate culture led to brutal labor exploitation. While Huawei's Chinese workers are ostensibly the shareholders of the company, they actually do not "own" the company except for the material incentive. The tale of a handful of Huawei senior employees becoming millionaires has obscured the huge income gap between executives and lower-paid workers. Hierarchy and disparities still exist in Huawei's labor practices. The collective redistribution scheme combining corporate revenue growth with individual gain tended to extract more labor surplus value from their work. The "hard work" culture expressed in its "wolf spirit" actually brought a great deal of labor issues, such as long working hours, high work stress, and poor work-life balance. Moreover, its transnational labor practices exposed deep conflicts between Chinese managers and local workers, which has become one of the thorny problems for Huawei's internationalization. In short, although Huawei has taken some extraordinary measures in advancing workers' benefits and incentive mechanism, its labor practices and ownership arrangement have still failed to solve the fundamental antagonism between capitalists and labor. However, it is important to bear in mind that the experiment of Huawei's ownership structure and management still provides some important lessons as to how to construct a more democratic corporate system and revive the socialist management experience in contemporary corporate China.

An Open-Ended Contour in the Future

This book has examined the nascent and expanding phenomenon of the rise of Chinese transnational ICT corporations through the case of Huawei. At issue is not the specific business strategies that forge Chinese globally competitive firms, nor is it simply a matter of China's growing corporate power in the context of the country's rise. What does need to be emphasized is the internal dynamics of China's ICT development and the geopolitical-economic implications of its corporate globalization strategy. For one thing, Huawei's path to becoming a global industrial leader allows us to reflect on the trajectory and tendencies of China's growth schemas that are historically contingent on the process of the country's integration into global digital capitalism. This process is also in concert with China's paradoxical dynamics of technological development, a process blending the developmental paradigms of techno-nationalism and neoliberalism.[46] Such internal dynamics have pushed China to a crossroads: it is facing a deepening process of capitalist development on the one hand and the paradigmatic reorientation toward a more sustainable path of growth on the other.[47] The possibility of breaking free from the deep-rooted predicament of capitalist mechanism actually lies in local alternatives and indigenous agencies.[48]

The Huawei model sheds light on certain distinguishing features that contribute to dynamic advantages of China's transnational ICT corporations and a pathbreaking model of development. At the core of China's competitive advantages is its ability to insist on self-reliant, open-minded, innovation-oriented development strategies. The successful experience of renovating the socialist collective legacies is also proven in Huawei's story, which may provoke other Chinese firms to seek more desirable options of development and the revival of indigenous experience.

Huawei's story is not only highly relevant as a reference of China's domestic developmental trajectory; it also raises legitimate questions about China's evolving position in the global system. In the past several decades, China has turned itself into a new space and growth center of the global capitalist system. The conjunction of the two poles of market growth—China's expanding domestic markets and the momentum of ICTs' development—has especially been perceived as one of the most important antidotes to the ongoing global economic crisis. Nevertheless, the Chinese state's FDI-dependent policy and the "race to the bottom" industrial strategy have impoverished the domestic market and native entrepreneurship and entrenched the country in a relatively disadvantaged position in the global system. To a certain extent, however, it is also such a disadvantaged status and "backwardness" situation that provoked China's quest for its corporate globalization strategy. A parallel movement to China's domestic industrial restructuring was the extension of Chinese economic influence on the global scale. While many Chinese high-tech companies have gained the scale of multinationals, few have been able to climb up the technology ladder, to transfer a business model from a low-cost market to an advanced market, and to compete via innovation rather than with cheap manufactured goods and speculative capital investment.[49] Huawei's unique path of internationalization, which can be distinguished from those of state-owned national champions and private internet enterprises with foreign linkage, presents a possible solution for Chinese corporate players to climb up the global value chain and the potential to reposition themselves in the global industry. It also indicates a means of springboarding into a stronger and more independent role within the transnational political economy.

The other side of the coin is that the unprecedented expansion of China-based ICT capital has generated growing geopolitical-economic conflicts. The Huawei case strongly reflects the contradiction between technological sovereignty and the expansionary logic of capital accumulation in capitalist globalization. On the one hand, the US confrontation over China's ICT companies is escalating, precipitating global digital capitalism into the geopolitical rivalry between the two superpowers. On the other hand, Chinese ICT companies' engagement in the global South generates mixed geopolitical-economic implications. Facilitated by the Chinese state's going-out initiative,

Chinese ICT giants are becoming a significant source of FDI in many developing countries. To be sure, their foreign investment and aid reduce these developing countries' dependence on Western powers and improve their technology infrastructure. The involvement of Chinese firms in the global South also presents the potential model of South-South cooperation that is built on the legacies of international solidarity and mutual geopolitical-economic benefits in the current context. This process will change the operating rules of the multinational game and the dynamics of power relations in unexpected ways with the rise of China's corporate power. We should bear in mind, however, that Chinese firms' expansion is still driven by the same capitalist logic of accumulation as that of Western corporate powers. We can hardly say an anti-neoliberal ideology has been articulated in the development of corporate China. Therefore, whether the advent of corporate China constitutes an alternative, anti-capitalist model of development remains an open-ended question. However, it is noteworthy to point out that the strong tradition and historical legacies of China's socialist approaches continue to cast a long shadow in its future transformations. The Chinese state's initiative of repositioning itself in the global political-economic system, an effort that is articulated with the ongoing transnational politics for pursuing a multipolar order, might contribute to the radical realignment of global power relations.

Notes

Introduction

1. Dan Schiller, *How to Think about Information* (Urbana: University of Illinois Press, 2007).

2. Friedrich Wu, *The Globalization of Corporate China*, vol. 13 (Seattle: National Bureau of Asian Research, 2005).

3. Schiller, *How to Think about Information*; Dan Schiller, *Digital Depression: Information Technology and Economic Crisis* (Urbana: University of Illinois Press, 2014).

4. Schiller, *How to Think about Information*, 197.

5. Yu Hong, *Labor, Class Formation, and China's Informationized Policy of Economic Development* (Lanham, MD: Lexington Books, 2011).

6. Lutao Ning, *China's Rise in the World ICT Industry: Industrial Strategies and the Catch-Up Development Model* (New York: Routledge, 2009), 103.

7. Giovanni Arrighi, *The Long Twentieth Century: Money, Power, and the Origins of Our Times* (New York: Verso Books, 1994).

8. Rhys Jenkins, *Transnational Corporations and Uneven: The Internationalization of Capital and the Third World Development and Underdevelopment* (New York: Routledge, 1987), 4.

9. Dan Schiller, "Geopolitical-Economic Conflict and Network Infrastructures," *Chinese Journal of Communication* 4, no. 1 (2011): 90–107; Dwayne. R. Winseck and R. M. Pike, *Communication and Empire: Media, Markets, and Globalization, 1860–1930* (Durham, NC: Duke University Press, 2007).

10. Winseck and Pike, *Communication and Empire*.
11. Schiller, "Geopolitical-Economic Conflict."
12. Winseck and Pike, *Communication and Empire*.
13. Jill Hills, *The Struggle for Control of Global Communication* (Urbana: University of Illinois Press, 2002), 6.
14. Jonathan Reed Winkler, *Nexus: Strategic Communications and American Security in World War* (Cambridge, MA: Harvard University Press, 2008).
15. Armand Mattelart, *Mapping World Communication: War, Progress, Culture* (Minneapolis: University of Minnesota Press, 1994), 63–64.
16. Leo Panitch and Sam Gindin, *The Making of Global Capitalism* (London: Verso Books, 2012), 112.
17. Schiller, *Digital Depression*, 59.
18. Schiller, "Geopolitical-Economic Conflict," 93.
19. Mattelart, *Mapping World Communication*.
20. Ibid., 70.
21. Peter Nolan, *China and the Global Economy: National Champions, Industrial Policy and the Big Business Revolution* (Houndmills, Basingstoke, UK: Palgrave Macmillan, 2001), 137.
22. Schiller, *Digital Capitalism*, 46–50.
23. Dwayne Winseck, "The Political Economies of Media and the Transformation of the Global Media Industries," in *The Political Economies of Media: The Transformation of the Global Media Industries*, ed. Dwayne Winseck and Dal Jong Yin (New York: Bloomsbury, 2012), 14–15.
24. Dwayne Winseck, "The Geopolitical Economy of the Global Internet Infrastructure," *Journal of Information Policy* 7 (2017): 228–67.
25. Nolan, *China and the Global Economy*; Peter Nolan, *Transforming China: Globalization, Transition and Development* (London: Anthem Press, 2004).
26. Yini He, "Top 10 Internet Companies in the World.," *China Daily*, November 11, 2015, http://www.chinadaily.com.cn/business/2015-12/11/content_22686526.htm.
27. Joel Backaler, *China Goes West: Everything You Need to Know about Chinese Companies Going Global* (Houndmills, Basingstoke, UK: Palgrave Macmillan, 2016); Ping Deng, "What Determines Performance of Cross-Border M&As by Chinese Companies? An Absorptive Capacity Perspective," *Thunderbird International Business Review* 52, no. 6 (2010): 509–24; Arthur Yeung et al., *The Globalization of Chinese Companies: Strategies for Conquering International Markets* (Singapore: John Wiley & Sons, 2011).
28. Sunny Li Sun, "Internationalization Strategy of MNEs from Emerging Economies: The Case of Huawei," *Multinational Business Review* 17, no. 2 (2009): 129–56; Tian Tao, David D. Cremer, and Wu Chunbo, *Huawei: Leadership, Culture and Connectivity* (Los Angeles: Sage, 2016); Donglin Wu and Fang Zhao, "Entry Modes for International Markets: Case Study of Huawei, a Chinese Technology

Enterprise," *International Review of Business Research Papers* 3, no. 1 (2007): 183–96.

29. Ilan Alon and John R. McIntyre, *Globalization of Chinese Enterprises* (Basingstoke, Hampshire, UK: Palgrave Macmillan, 2008); Peter J. Buckley et al., "The Determinants of Chinese Outward Foreign Direct Investment," *Journal of International Business Studies* 38, no. 4 (2007): 499–518; Ping Deng, "Outward Investment by Chinese MNCs: Motivations and Implications," *Business Horizons* 47, no. 3 (2004): 8–16.

30. Yu Hong, *Networking China: The Digital Transformation of the Chinese Economy* (Urbana: University of Illinois Press, 2017).

31. Immanuel M. Wallerstein, *The Modern World-System I: Capitalist Agriculture and the Origins of the European World-Economy in the Sixteenth Century* (New York: Academic Press, 1974).

32. Winseck and Pike, *Communication and Empire*, 8.

33. Michael Hardt and Antonio Negri, *Empire* (Cambridge, MA: Harvard University Press, 2000).

34. Alex Callinicos, *Imperialism and Global Political Economy* (Cambridge, UK: Polity, 2009); David Harvey, *The New Imperialism* (Oxford: Oxford University Press, 2003); Ellen M. Wood, *Empire of Capital* (London: Verso Books, 2005).

35. Callinicos, *Imperialism and Global Political Economy*.

36. Schiller, "Geopolitical-Economic Conflict."

37. Harvey, *New Imperialism*; Wood, *Empire of Capital*.

38. Harvey, *New Imperialism*.

39. Ibid., 185.

40. William. I. Robinson, *A Theory of Global Capitalism: Production, Class, and State in a Transnational World* (Baltimore: Johns Hopkins University Press, 2004); William I. Robinson, *Latin America and Global Capitalism: A Critical Globalization Perspective* (Baltimore: Johns Hopkins University Press, 2008).

41. Leslie Sklair, *Sociology of the Global System* (Baltimore: Johns Hopkins University Press, 1995); Leslie Sklair, *The Transnational Capitalist Class* (Oxford: Wiley-Blackwell Publishing, 2001); Leslie Sklair, *Capitalism and Its Alternatives* (Oxford: Oxford University Press, 2002).

42. Jerry Harris, *The Dialectics of Globalization: Economic and Political Conflict in a Transnational World* (Newcastle, UK: Cambridge Scholars Press, 2006); Jerry Harris, "Outward Bound: Transnational Capitalism in China," *Race and Class* 54, no. 1 (2012): 13–32.

43. Carol Upadhya, "A New Transnational Capitalist Class? Capital Flows, Business Networks, and Entrepreneurs in the Indian Software Industry," *Economic and Political Weekly* 39, no. 68 (2004): 5141–51.

44. Jason Struna, "Toward a Theory of Global Proletarian Fractions," in *The Nation in the Global Era of Conflict and Transformation*, ed. J. Harris (Boston: Brill, 2009), 120–50.

45. Enda Brophy, "System Error: Labour Precarity and Collective Organizing at Microsoft," *Canadian Journal of Communication* 31, no. 3 (2006): 619–38; Nick Dyer-Witheford and Greig S. de Peuter, "'EA Spouse' and the Crisis of Video Game Labour: Enjoyment, Exclusion, Exploitation, and Exodus," *Canadian Journal of Communication* 31, no. 3 (2006): 599–617; Christian Fuchs, *Digital Labour and Karl Marx* (New York: Routledge, Taylor & Francis Group, 2014); Hong, *Labor, Class Formation, and China's Informationized Policy*.

46. Armand Mattelart, *Transnationals and the Third World: The Struggle for Culture* (Santa Barbara, CA: Praeger, 1985).

47. Biao Xiang, "Introduction: Return and the Reordering of Transnational Mobility in Asia," in *Return: Nationalizing Transnational Mobility in Asia*, ed. Biao Xiang, Brenda S. A. Yeoh, Mika Toyota (Durham, NC: Duke University Press, 2013), 1–20.

48. Ibid., 5.

49. David Harvey, *Brief History of Neoliberalism* (Oxford: Oxford University Press, 2007); Martin Hart-Landsberg and Paul Burkett, *China and Socialism* (New Delhi: Aakar Books, 2005).

50. Harris, "Outward Bound"; Beverly J. Silver and Lu Zhang, "China as an Emerging Epicenter of World Labor Unrest," in *China and the Transformation of Global Capitalism*, ed. Ho-fung Hung, 174–87 (Baltimore: Johns Hopkins University Press, 2009); Ho-fung Hung, *The China Boom: Why China Will Not Rule the World* (New York: Columbia University Press, 2015).

51. Hung, *China Boom*, 5.

52. Chalmers Johnson, *MITI and the Japanese Miracle: The Growth of Industrial Policy: 1925–1975* (Stanford, CA: Stanford University Press, 1982).

53. Lin Chun, *The Transformation of Chinese Socialism* (Durham, NC: Duke University Press, 2006).

54. Dallas Smythe, "After Bicycles, What?," in *Counterclockwise: Perspectives on Communication*, ed. Thomas Guback, 230–44 (Boulder, CO: Westview, 1994).

55. Yuezhi Zhao, "After Mobile Phones, What? Re-Embedding the Social in China's 'Digital Revolution,'" *International Journal of Communication* 1, no. 1 (2007): 92–120.

56. Hongzhe Wang, "Machine for a Long Revolution: Computer as the Nexus of Technology and Class Politics in China, 1955–1984," Chinese University of Hong Kong, 2014.

57. Ning, *China's Rise in the World ICT Industry*.

58. Adam Segal, *Digital Dragon: High-Technology Enterprises in China* (Ithaca, NY: Cornell University Press, 2003).

59. Ibid.

60. Schiller, *How to Think about Information*.

61. Dan Schiller, "Power under Pressure: Digital Capitalism in Crisis," *International Journal of Communication* 5 (2011): 933.

62. Schiller, *Digital Depression*, 142–47.

63. Hong, *Networking China*.

64. Zhao, "After Mobile Phones, What?"; Yuezhi Zhao, "China's Pursuits of Indigenous Innovations in Information Technology Developments: Hopes, Follies, and Uncertainties," *Chinese Journal of Communication* 3, no. 3 (2010): 266–89.

65. Ibid.

66. Yuezhi Zhao, *Communication in China: Political Economy, Power, and Conflict* (Lanham, MD: Rowman & Littlefield, 2008), 342.

67. Hong, *Labor, Class Formation, and China's Informationized Policy*; Jack Linchuan Qiu, *Goodbye iSlave: A Manifesto for Digital Abolition* (Urbana: University of Illinois Press, 2016); Yutao Sun and Seamus Grimes, *China and Global Value Chains: Globalization and the Information and Communications Technology Sector* (New York: Routledge, 2018).

68. Nick Dyer-Witheford, *Cyber-Marx: Cycles and Circuits of Struggle in High-Technology Capitalism* (Urbana: University of Illinois Press, 1999); Catherine McKercher and Vincent Mosco, *Knowledge Workers in the Information Society* (Lanham, MD: Lexington Books, 2007); Hardt and Negri, *Empire*.

69. Hong, *Labor, Class Formation, and China's Informationized Policy*, 18.

70. Foxconn (officially known as Hon Hai Precision Industry Co., Ltd.) is one of the world's largest contract electronics manufacturers; its customers include some of the world's best-known high-tech companies, such as Apple, Dell, Hewlett-Packard, Samsung, and Microsoft. The company was renowned for a series of worker suicides in 2010, revealing the poor working conditions and depersonalized management in the factory. The "Foxconn Model" is representative of the Chinese economy as the "world factory," characterized by the exploitation of China's cheap labor and the export-led, foreign capital–dependent model of development.

71. Hong, *Networking China*; Min Tang, *Tencent: The Political Economy of China's Surging Internet Giant* (New York: Routledge, 2019).

72. The Belt and Road Initiative (BRI) was proposed by the Chinese government in 2013 to reorient the country's global development strategy. This initiative mainly focuses on infrastructure development and investments in nearly seventy countries in Asia, Europe, and Africa, aiming to enhance the regional connectivity and to accelerate economic growth across the BRI countries.

Chapter 1. Huawei's Domestic Accumulation: A Path Intertwining with China's ICT Development

1. Jerry Harris, *The Dialectics of Globalization* (Newcastle, UK: Cambridge Scholars Press, 2006).

2. Maurice Meisner, *Mao's China and After: A History of the People's Republic*, 3rd ed. (New York: Free Press, 1999), 273.

3. Eric Harwit, *China's Telecommunications Revolution* (New York: Oxford University Press, 2008), 30.

4. MEI, *Yearbook of Electronic Industry, 1986* (Beijing: China Electronics Industry Press, 1986).

5. Lutao Ning, *China's Rise in the World ICT Industry: Industrial Strategies and the Catch-Up Development Model* (New York: Routledge, 2009), 49.

6. MEI, *Yearbook of Electronic Industry, 1986*.

7. Harwit, *China's Telecommunications Revolution*.

8. Ibid.

9. Data from National Bureau of Statistics of China.

10. *Dangdai zhongguo de youdian shiye* [Contemporary China's Posts and Telecommunications Facilities] (Beijing: Renmin Youdian Chuban She, 1983), 286.

11. Ibid.

12. Harwit, *China's Telecommunications Revolution*, 162–63.

13. Meisner, *Mao's China and After*, 211.

14. Barry Naughton, "The Third Front: Defence Industrialization in the Chinese Interior," *China Quarterly* 115 (1988): 351–86.

15. Ning, *China's Rise in the World ICT Industry*.

16. Ibid.

17. Manfredo Macioti, "Scientists Go Barefoot: Successor January 1971," *Survival* 13, no. 7 (1971): 232–38.

18. MEI, *Yearbook of Electronic Industry, 1986*.

19. Lin Chun, *The Transformation of Chinese Socialism* (Durham, NC: Duke University Press, 2006).

20. Dallas Smythe, "After Bicycles, What?," in *Counterclockwise: Perspectives on Communication*, ed. Thomas Guback, 230–44 (Boulder, CO: Westview, 1994).

21. Meisner, *Mao's China and After*.

22. Ibid.

23. Ibid., 212.

24. Joshua Eisenman, *Red China's Green Revolution: Technological Innovation, Institutional Change, and Economic Development under the Commune* (New York: Columbia University Press, 2018); Hongzhe Wang, "Machine for a Long Revolution: Computer as the Nexus of Technology and Class Politics in China 1955–1984," Chinese University of Hong Kong, 2014.

25. Eisenman, *Red China's Green Revolution*.

26. Tiejun Wen, *Eight Crises: Lessons from China 1949–2009* (Beijing: Oriental Publishing, 2013).

27. Tean Chen, "Rooted in the Chinese Market: Nortel Network Leads the Way Out," *People's Daily*, December 11, 2003, http://www.people.com.cn/GB/guoji/14549/2240636.html.

28. China Telecom, "The Historical Events of China's Telecommunications Development 1970–1979," http://www.chinatelecom.com.cn/news/06/hh60n/60nlsjc/t20090911_53999.html.

29. Ibid.

30. Ibid.

31. Dan Schiller, *Networks and the Age of Nixon* (Beijing: Beijing University Press, 2018).

32. Dan Schiller, *Digital Depression: Information Technology and Economic Crisis* (Urbana: University of Illinois Press, 2014), 74.

33. Dan Schiller, "The Geopolitics of Information in the Era of Digital Capitalism," lecture, Peking University Global Fellowship Program, October 24, 2016.

34. Chris Bramall, *Chinese Economic Development* (New York: Routledge, 2008); Meisner, *Mao's China and After*.

35. *People's Daily*, December 5, 1977; editorial on the "Electronic Industry: The Level of the Electronics Industry Is a Hallmark of Modernization," as cited in Jon Sigurdson, *Technology and Science in the People's Republic of China: An Introduction* (Oxford: Pergamon, 1980).

36. MEI, *Yearbook of Electronic Industry, 1986*.

37. "Looking for Breakthroughs—Wen Minsheng's Reform in the Post and Telecommunications System," http://www.cnii.com.cn/20080623/ca579840.htm.

38. Yuezhi Zhao, "Communication, Crisis, & Global Power Shifts: An Introduction," *International Journal of Communication* [online] 8 (January 15, 2014): 26.

39. Yuezhi Zhao, "After Mobile Phones, What?" Re-Embedding the Social in China's 'Digital Revolution,'" *International Journal of Communication* 1, no. 1 (2007): 92–120.

40. MEI, *Yearbook of Electronic Industry, 1986*.

41. Bramall, *Chinese Economic Development*, 410.

42. Zhao, "After Mobile Phones, What?"

43. Naughton, "Third Front."

44. Ning, *China's Rise in the World ICT Industry*, 59.

45. Ibid., 62.

46. Barry Naughton, *The Chinese Economy: Transitions and Growth* (Cambridge: MIT Press, 2007), 280.

47. S. Cao, *China's Shift of Military Production towards a Civilian Orientation* (Beijing: China Economics Publisher, 1994), as cited in Ning, "China's Rise in the World ICT Industry."

48. Harwit, *China's Telecommunications Revolution*, 118.

49. Maurice Meisner, *The Deng Xiaoping Era* (New York: Hill and Wang, 1996), 283.

50. MEI, *Yearbook of the Electronic Industry, 1988* (Beijing: Electronic Industry Press, 1988).

51. Yu Hong, *Labor, Class Formation, and China's Informationized Policy of Economic Development* (Lanham, MD: Lexington Books, 2011), 35.

52. Martin Hart-Landsberg, *Capitalist Globalization: Consequences, Resistance, and Alternatives*, (New York: NYU Press, 2013), 34.

Notes to Chapter 1

53. MEI, *Yearbook of the Electronic Industry, 1994* (Beijing: Electronics Industry Press, 1994).

54. Hong, *Labor, Class Formation, and China's Informationized Policy*, 37.

55. *Dangdai Zhongguo Dianzi Gongye* [Contemporary China's Electronics Industry] (Beijing: Chinese Academy of Social Sciences Press, 1987).

56. Ibid.

57. MEI, *Yearbook of the Electronic Industry, 1996* (Beijing: Electronic Industry Press, 1996).

58. A port is a physical interface through which information transfers in or out. The price of the telecommunications equipment is measured by the cost per port.

59. HAX was the name of the PBX produced by Hung Nien Electronics. Huawei was the sales representative of this product in Mainland China.

60. MEI, *Annual Yearbook, 1986*.

61. Yu Hong, Francois Bar, and An Zheng, "Chinese Telecommunications on the Threshold of Convergence: Contexts, Possibilities, and Limitations of Forging a Domestic Demand-Based Growth Model," *Telecommunications Policy* 36, nos. 10–11 (2012): 914–28.

62. Min Zhong, "The History of China's Digital Switch," *Telecommunications Industry Newspaper*, September 11, 2002, http://tech.sina.com.cn/it/t/2002-09-11/1020137952.shtml.

63. Harwit, *China's Telecommunications Revolution*.

64. Zixiang Alex Tan, "Product Cycle Theory and Telecommunications Industry—Foreign Direct Investment, Government Policy, and Indigenous Manufacturing in China," *Telecommunications Policy* 26, no. 1 (2002): 17–30.

65. Harwit, *China's Telecommunications Revolution*, 118.

66. Dongsheng Cheng and Lili Liu, *The Truth of Huawei* (Beijing: Contemporary China Press, 2003), 25.

67. Yuezhi Zhao, "'Universal Service' and China's Telecommunications Miracle: Discourses, Practices, and Post-WTO Accession Challenges," *Info* 9, nos. 2/3 (2007): 108–121.

68. MEI, *Yearbook of the Electronic Industry, 1994*.

69. Harwit, *China's Telecommunications Revolution*, 163.

70. Yu Hong, "Repurposing Telecoms for Capital in China," *Asian Survey* 53, no. 2 (2013): 333.

71. Yukun Wang, *Dance with Globalization: Overseas Expansion of Chinese Enterprises* (Beijing: Beijing Normal University Press, 2006), 19–21.

72. Harwit, *China's Telecommunications Revolution*.

73. Zhengfei Ren, "The Current Situations and Our Tasks" (December 26, 1995). This was a speech in a meeting of Huawei's marketing department.

74. Harwit, *China's Telecommunications Revolution*, 128.

75. Ibid.

76. MII, *China Electronics Industry Yearbook, 2001* (Beijing: Electronic Industry Press, 2001).

77. Ibid.

78. Ding Lu and Chee K. Wong, *China's Telecommunications Market: Entering a New Competitive Age* (Cheltenham: Edward Elgar Publishing, 2003), 4.

79. Ibid.

80. MII, *China Electronics Industry Yearbook, 2001*.

81. MII, *China Electronics Industry Yearbook, 2000* (Beijing: Electronic Industry Press, 2000).

82. Lu and Wong, *China's Telecommunications Market*, 81.

83. Tan, "Product Cycle Theory," 25.

84. Zhao, "Caught in the Web: The Public Interest and the Battle for Control of China's Information Superhighway," *Info* 2, no. 1 (2000): 41–65.

85. MII, *China Electronics Industry Yearbook, 2001*.

86. Tan, "Product Cycle Theory."

87. Dan Slater, "Emerson Acquires China'[s] Huawei Subsidiary in Historic Deal," *FinanceAsia*, October 23, 2001, https://www.financeasia.com/article/emerson-acquires-china-huawei-subsidiary-in-historic-deal/34135.

88. Xiaofeng Liu and Ji An, "International Telecom Giants Struggle to Seize China's Telecom Market," *Economics Daily*, December 18, 2001, http://www.china.com.cn/chinese/EC-c/87691.htm.

89. Hui Dai, "Huawei's Long March.," *Huawei Xinsheng Community*, April 18, 2018.

90. Ibid.

91. Hongyan Chen and Xu Wang, "A Serious Judgement Given to the Smuggling Case of Nokia Telecommunication Equipment in Xiamen," *China News Service*, September 13, 2001, http://www.people.com.cn/GB/shehui/44/20010913/559800.html.

92. Dai, "Huawei's Long March."

93. Ibid.

94. Luyi Zhang, "CDMA Development in China," *China Business*, July 1, 2001, http://www.people.com.cn/GB/it/49/4695/20010601/479744.html.

95. Zhou Mi and Sheng Yin, *ZTE: The Strategies of Comprehensively Reducing Enterprise Risk*. (Beijing: Contemporary China Press, 2005), as cited in Hong, Bar, and Zheng, "Chinese Telecommunications," 918.

96. "ZTE Company History," n.d., http://wwwen.zte.com.cn/pub/en/about/corporate_information/history.

97. Chuantao Li, "Five Telecom Equipment Vendors Divided Up China Telecom's CDMA Bidding," September 22, 2008, http://www.c114.com.cn/topic/615/a346751.html.

98. Ibid.

99. Hong, Bar, and Zheng, "Chinese Telecommunications."
100. Ibid.
101. Ibid.
102. The term "Internet of Things" (IoT) refers to the system of interrelated computing devices, mechanical and digital machines, and objects that are connected to the internet.
103. Schiller, *Digital Depression*, 87.
104. Edward Snowden, a former National Security Agency (NSA) contractor, revealed thousands of top-secret government documents of the US mass surveillance programs in 2013.
105. Ibid.
106. "Huawei 2018 Annual Report."
107. Li, Guodong, "The Report on China's Smart Phone: Chinese Brands Account for 65.7 Percent," August 27, 2019, http://news.zol.com.cn/725/7254224.html.
108. Hong, *Labor, Class Formation, and China's Informationized Policy*, 80.

Chapter 2. Going Global: Outward Expansion into the Global South

1. Joel Backaler, *China Goes West: Everything You Need to Know about Chinese Companies Going Global* (Houndmills, Basingstoke, UK: Palgrave Macmillan, 2016); Ping Deng, "What Determines Performance of Cross-Border M&As by Chinese Companies? An Absorptive Capacity Perspective," *Thunderbird International Business Review* 52, no. 6 (2010): 509–24; Arthur Yeung, Katherine Xin, Waldemar Pfoertsch, and Shengjun Liu, *The Globalization of Chinese Companies: Strategies for Conquering International Markets* (Singapore: John Wiley & Sons, 2011).

2. Friedrich Wu, *The Globalization of Corporate China*, vol. 13 (Seattle: National Bureau of Asian Research, 2005).

3. Xiaohua Yang and Clyde Stoltenberg, "Growth of Made-in-China Multinationals: An Institutional and Historical Perspective," in *Globalization of Chinese Enterprises*, ed. Ilan Alon and John McIntyre, 61–76 (Basingstoke, Hampshire, UK: Palgrave Macmillan, 2008).

4. Deborah Brautigam, "China's Foreign Aid in Africa: What Do We Know?," in *China into Africa: Trade, Aid, and Influence*, ed. R. I. Rotberg (Washington, DC: Brookings Institution Press, 2008), 203.

5. Ansheng Li, "China's New Policy toward Africa," in *China into Africa: Trade, Aid and Influence*, ed. R. I. Rotberg (Washington, DC: Brookings Institution Press, 2008), 22.

6. MEI, *Yearbook of the Electronic Industry, 1988* (Beijing: Electronic Industry Press, 1988).

7. MEI, *Yearbook of Electronic Industry, 1986* (Beijing: Electronic Industry Press, 1986).

8. MEI, *Yearbook of the Electronic Industry, 1994* (Beijing: Electronic Industry Press, 1994).

9. MIIT, *The Yearbook of China's Information Industry 2011* (Beijing: Electronic Industry Press, 2011).

10. WTO, "International Trade Statistics 2014," 2014, https://www.wto.org/english/res_e/statis_e/its2014_e/its14_highlights2_e.pdf.

11. MIIT, *Yearbook of China's Information Industry 2011*.

12. Ibid.

13. Richard P. Appelbaum and Gary Gereffi, "Power and Profits in the Apparel Commodity Chain," in *Global Production: The Apparel Industry in the Pacific Rim*, ed. Edna Bonacich, Lucie Cheng, Norma Chinchilla, Nora Hamilton, and Paul Ong (Philadelphia: Temple University Press, 1994), 43.

14. Ho-fung Hung, "America's Head Servant? The PRC's Dilemma in the Global Crisis," *New Left Review* 60, no. 6 (2009): 5–25.

15. Zhihua Yin, "The MII Minister Wang Xidong Raised 7 Points for 2005 Industrial Industry Work," *Telecommunication World*, 2005, http://tech.sina.com.cn/t/2005-01-12/1351502058.shtml.

16. MOC, *Report on Development of China's Outward Investment and Economic Cooperation* (Beijing: MOC, 2015).

17. Xinhua, "Chinese Direct Investment in US Drops amid Policy Shifts," *China Daily*, April 11, 2018, https://www.chinadailyhk.com/articles/20/62/247/1523429696267.html.

18. Evelyn Chen, "Chinese Investment in the US Drops 90% amid Political Pressure," June 20, 2018, https://www.cnbc.com/2018/06/20/chinese-investment-in-the-us-drops-90-percent-amid-political-pressure.html.

19. MOFCOM, "MOFCOM Department of Outward Investment and Economic Cooperation Comments on China's Outward Investment Cooperation in 2017," January 18, 2018, http://english.mofcom.gov.cn/article/newsrelease/policyreleasing/201801/20180102706193.shtml.

20. Ibid.

21. Thilo Hanemann and Mikko Huotari, "Chinese FDI in Europe in 2017: Rapid Recovery after Initial Slowdown," April 17, 2018, https://www.merics.org/en/papers-on-china/chinese-fdi-in-europe.

22. John. H. Dunning, *Multinational Enterprises and the Global Economy* (New York: Addison Wesley, 1993); Rajneesh Narula and John H. Dunning, "Industrial Development, Globalization, and Multinational Enterprises: New Realities for Developing Countries," *Oxford Development Studies* 28, no. 2: 141–67.

23. MOC, *Report on Development of China's Outward Investment and Economic Cooperation* (Beijing: MOC, 2014).

24. J. Lu, *"Walking-Out" Strategy and the Rise of Chinese Multinational Corporations* (Beijing: Capital University of Economics and Business Press, 2012), 227.

25. Lutao Ning, *China's Rise in the World ICT Industry: Industrial Strategies and the Catch-Up Development Model* (New York: Routledge, 2009), 114.

26. MOC, *Report on Development*, 2014.

27. MOC, *Report on Development of China's Outward Investment and Economic Cooperation* (Beijing: MOC, 2017), 4.

28. MOC, *Report on Development of China's Outward Investment and Economic Cooperation* (Beijing: MOC, 2016), 9, http://images.mofcom.gov.cn/fec/201711/20171114083528539.pdf.

29. J.P. Morgan, "The Investment Landscape for Chinese ADRs," June 2014, https://www.jpmorgan.com/jpmpdf/1320676276731.pdf.

30. MOC, *Report on Development*, 2016.

31. MOC, *Report on Development*, 2015.

32. MOC, *Report on Development*, 2014.

33. Ibid., 100.

34. "Top 10 Smartphone Vendors in Q1 2018," https://www.telecomlead.com/telecom-statistics/10-smartphone-vendors-in-q1–2018–83864, May 2, 2018.

35. Hong Shen, "Building a Digital Silk Road? Situating the Internet in China's Belt and Road Initiative," *International Journal of Communication* 12, no. 19 (2018).

36. "Huawei 2017 Annual Report," 2018, https://www.huawei.com/en/press-events/annual-report/2017. Huawei's 2017 global sales was converted from Chinese Yuan Renminbi to US dollars using the exchange rate of 2017.

37. Paul R. Krugman, "Increasing Returns, Monopolistic Competition, and International Trade," *Journal of International Economics* 9, no. 4 (1979): 469–79.

38. Zhengfei Ren, "Cross the Pacific Bravely and Proudly," January 18, 2001, no.113 http://app.huawei.com/paper/newspaper/newsPaperPage.do?method=showSelNewsInfo&cateId=3561&pageId=4101&infoId=7203&sortId=1.

39. ZTE, "The 'ZTE' Model of Firm Internationalization," *ZTE New Communications*, no. 5 (2006), https://www.zte.com.cn/china/about/magazine/zte-technologies/2006/5/cn_420/148910.html.

40. Huawei, "Huawei: The Path of Breakthrough in Core Technologies," July 28, 2003, http://pr.huawei.com/cn/news/media-coverage/hw-091885-news.htm.

41. Zhengfei Ren, "Walking across the Boundary of Asia and Europe," May 8, 1997, http://www.iceo.com.cn/zazhi/2003/1021/187040.shtml.

42. Ibid.

43. "State Councilor Wu Yi Visited Huawei," *Huawei People*, August 15, 1998, no. 72, http://app.huawei.com/paper/newspaper/newsPaperPage.do?method=showSelNewsInfo&cateId=3662&pageId=4224&infoId=7471&sortId=1.

44. Yunshi Mao and Jiancheng Wang, *Guangdong 500 Business Enterprises: Growth and Restructuring* (Beijing: Tsinghua University Press, 2005), 243.

45. Jerry Harris, "Outward Bound: Transnational Capitalism in China," *Race and Class* 54, no. 1 (2012): 27.

46. China's Development Research of State Council, "Analysis on Internationalization Strategies of Six Industries," December 16, 2006, http://fjgyw.fjinfo.gov.cn/DRCNet.Channel.Web.

47. Zhengfei Ren, "Huawei's Winter," *Huawei People*, March 2001, http://www.iceo.com.cn/renwu/46/2012/1002/258231.shtml.

48. Zhengfei Ren, "Tiandao Chouqin," *Huawei People*, July 21, 2006, no. 178, http://app.huawei.com/paper/newspaper/newsPaperPage.do?method=showSelNewsInfo&infoId=18845&commentLanguage=1&isCopy=0&isDownload=0&sortId=1&cateId=8467.

49. Ren, "Cross the Pacific Bravely."

50. Yuezhi Zhao, "China's Pursuits of Indigenous Innovations in Information Technology Developments: Hopes, Follies, and Uncertainties," *Chinese Journal of Communication* 3, no. 3 (2010): 278.

51. Anquan Jiang, Jirong Yuan, and Miao Yin, "African Telecom Industry Develops Rapidly amid Cooperation," *People's Daily*, July 27, 2012, http://world.people.com.cn/n/2012/0627/c1002-18388021.html.

52. Qifa Yan et al., "The Condition and Development Trend of African Telecom Industry," *West Asia and Africa*, no. 6 (2009): 59–65.

53. Ibid., 61.

54. Ching Kwan Lee, "The Spectre of Global China," *New Left Review*, no. 89 (2014): 29–65.

55. Xiaofang Ma, "The Ten-Year Venture of Huawei and ZTE in Africa," *China Business News*, May 10, 2007, http://tech.sina.com.cn/t/2007-05-10/03411499435.shtml.

56. "Huawei 2007 Annual Report," 2008, https://www.huawei.com/ucmf/groups/public/documents/annual_report/092585.pdf.

57. Yalin Hao and Jianmin Li, "Minister of Commerce: China Will Expand Cooperation with African Countries in the Field of Telecom," *Xinhua News Agency*, December 10, 2004, http://www.people.com.cn/GB/shizheng/1027/3047540.html.

58. "China's African Policy," January 2006, http://en.people.cn/200601/12/eng20060112_234894.html.

59. Shu Tan, "CDB Promotes China Enterprises' "Going Abroad.," *International Financing*, December 9, 2010, http://www.ifmbj.com.cn/meiyuezazhi/jigou--8226-quyu/201012/09-628.html.

60. "China in Africa: A Strategic Overview," Executive Research Associates Ltd., October 2009, 77, https://www.ide.go.jp/library/English/Data/Africa_file/Manualreport/pdf/china_all.pdf.

61. Iginio Gagliardone and Sam Geall, "China in Africa's Media and Telecommunications: Cooperation, Connectivity and Control," Norwegian Peacebuilding Resource Centre, April 2014, 3.

62. Ibid., 186.

63. Ibid., 187.

64. R. Evan Ellis, *China on the Ground in Latin America: Challenges for the Chinese and Impacts on the Region* (New York: Palgrave Macmillan, 2014), 104.

65. Ibid.

66. "From Manufacturer to Innovator, Huawei Upgrades Brand Image in Brazil," *China Daily*, May 6, 2015, http://www.chinadaily.com.cn/business/tech/2015-05/06/content_20633790.htm.

67. Ellis, *China on the Ground in Latin America*.

68. "From Manufacturer to Innovator."

69. Ellis, *China on the Ground in Latin America*.

70. Ibid., 109.

71. R. Evan Ellis, "Chinese Soft Power in Latin America: A Case Study," *Joint Forces Quarterly* 60, no. 8 (2011): 88.

72. Lee, "Spectre of Global China."

73. Ibid., 34.

74. Ibid., 34–35.

75. Jevans Nyabiage, "Kenya Says It Supports Chinese Tech Giant Huawei Regardless of US Policy," *South China Morning Post*, July 25, 2019, https://www.scmp.com/news/china/diplomacy/article/3020074/kenya-says-it-supports-chinese-tech-giant-huawei-regardless-us.

76. William I. Robinson, *Global Capitalism and the Crisis of Humanity* (New York: Cambridge University Press, 2014), 28.

77. Baoliang Chen, "China's Telecom Companies Invest US$15 Billion in Africa to Build 'Eight Vertical and Eight Horizontal' Network," *21st Century Business Herald*, June 8, 2016, http://epaper.21jingji.com/html/2016-06/08/content_41293.htm.

78. "Chinese Firm Hopes to Wire Continent with Same Strategy That Boosted Internet Access across China," *Global Times*, March 13, 2017, http://www.globaltimes.cn/content/1037500.shtml.

79. Lian Jian, "The Development Issues in Ethiop and the Role of Chinese Telecommunication Equipment Vendors," January 14, 2014, http://www.guancha.cn/JianLian/2014_01_14_199665.shtml.

80. Barney Warf, "Uneven Geographies of the African Internet: Growth, Change, and Implications," *African Geographical Review* 29, no. 2 (2010): 41–66.

81. Dwayne Winseck, "The Political Economies of Media and the Transformation of the Global Media Industries," in *The Political Economies of Media: The Transformation of the Global Media Industries*, ed. Dwayne Winseck and Dal Yong Jin, 3–48 (New York: Bloomsbury Academic, 2011).

82. "The 4th Asia-Pacific Submarine Networks Forum Successfully Held in Shenzhen," Huawei.com, August 30, 2018, https://www.huawei.com/en/press-events/news/2018/8/4th-asia-pacific-submarine-networks-forum.

83. "Huawei Marine Contracts to Build Cameroon-Brazil Cable System," *Ocean News* (blog), July 3, 2017, https://www.oceannews.com/news/communication/huawei-marine-contracts-to-build-cameroon-brazil-cable-system.

84. Nicole Starosielski, *The Undersea Network* (Durham, NC: Duke University Press, 2015), 30.

85. Sijia Jiang, "China's Huawei to Sell Undersea Cable Business, Buyer's Exchange Filing Shows," *Reuters*, June 3, 2019, https://www.reuters.com/article/us-huawei-tech-usa-cable/chinas-huawei-to-sell-undersea-cable-business-buyers-exchange-filing-shows-idUSKCN1T40BS.

86. Wenran Jiang, "China's Emerging Strategic Partnerships in Africa," in *China into Africa: Trade, Aid, and Influence*, ed. Robert I. Rotberg (Washington, DC: Brookings Institution Press, 2008), 62.

87. Jedrzej George Frynas and Manuel Paulo, "A New Scramble for African Oil? Historical, Political, and Business Perspectives," *African Affairs* 106, no. 423 (2007): 229–51; Tukumbi Lumumba-Kasongo, "China-Africa Relations: A Neo-Imperialism or a Neo-Colonialism? A Reflection," *African and Asian Studies* 10, nos. 2–3 (2011): 234–66; David Zweig and Bi Jianhai, "China's Global Hunt for Energy," *Foreign Affairs* (2005): 25–38.

88. Barry Sautman and Yan Hairong, "Friends and Interests: China's Distinctive Links with Africa," *African Studies Review* 50, no. 3 (2007): 78.

89. Jiang, "China's Emerging Strategic Partnerships," 61.

90. Lee, "Spectre of Global China."

91. Barry Sautman and Hairong Yan, "Trade, Investment, Power, and the China-in-Africa Discourse," *Asia-Pacific Journal* 52, no. 3 (2009), https://apjjf.org/-Barry-Sautman/3278/article.html.

92. Iginio Gagliardone, "China and the Building of Africa's Information Societies," AsiaGlobal Online, Asia Global Institute, University of Hong Kong, April 26, 2018, https://www.asiaglobalonline.hku.hk/china-africa-information-society.

93. Brautigam, "China's Foreign Aid in Africa"; Brautigam, *Dragon's Gift*.

94. Huawei, "Huawei 2014 Sustainability Report," 2014, http://www-file.huawei.com/~/media/CORPORATE/PDF/Press-Center/media-kit/2014Huaweisustainabilityreporten.pdf.

95. Chen, "China's Telecom Companies."

Chapter 3. March into the Global North: Opportunity or Peril?

1. Adam Segal, Cobus Van Staden, Elsa B. Kania, Samm Sacks, and Elliott Zaagman, "Is an Iron Curtain Falling Across Tech?," *Foreign Policy*, February 4, 2019, https://foreignpolicy.com/2019/02/04/is-an-iron-curtain-falling-across-tech.

2. Jing Xie, "Global Telecom Industry Was Stranded," *International Financial News*, April 8, 2002, http://www.people.com.cn/GB/it/50/145/20020408/704353.html.

3. Yangfeng Cao and Xin Li, "Huawei: Conquering Europe," *Business Review* 5 (2014): 126–39.

4. Dan Schiller, *Digital Depression: Information Technology and Economic Crisis* (Urbana: University of Illinois Press, 2014).

5. Ibid., 87.

6. "Huawei Topped the Global IP Access Market with Continuous Growth in DSL Market Share," Huawei, January 11, 2008, http://pr.huawei.com/cn/news/hw-089939-news.htm.

7. Zedong Mao, *On Contradiction* (Beijing: People's Publishing House, 1975); Zhengfei Ren, "Ren's Public Speech at Huawei's UK Office," London, July 13, 2007, http://xinsheng.huawei.com/cn/index.php?app=forum&mod=Detail&act=index&id=2874429.

8. "Vodafone's Approval Should Help Huawei in More Markets," *Gartner*, November 28, 2005, https://www.gartner.com/doc/487094/vodafones-approval-help-huawei-markets.

9. "Huawei 2007," Huawei, 2007, https://www.huawei.com/ucmf/groups/public/documents/annual_report/092585.pdf, 9.

10. "Huawei Claims That the European Market Share Increased to 10%," cww.net.cn, August 24, 2009, http://www.cww.net.cn/manufacture/html/2009/8/24/2009824115443009.htm.

11. William I. Robinson, *A Theory of Global Capitalism: Production, Class, and State in a Transnational World* (Baltimore: Johns Hopkins University Press, 2004).

12. "Huawei's Place in the EU's Research and Innovation Landscape," Huawei Europe, February 2013, https://www.huawei.eu/sites/default/files/huawei_rd_brochure_en_feb2012_0.pdf.

13. "Huawei Launches New European Research Institute to Gear Up European Digitization Progress and Achieve Win-Win Outcomes," Huawei, May 7, 2015, https://huawei.eu/media-centre/press-releases/huawei-launches-new-european-research-institute-gear-european.

14. "Huawei's Place in the EU's Research and Innovation Landscape."

15. The Digital Agenda for Europe (DAE) is one of the flagship initiatives under the Europe 2020 strategy, aiming to boost Europe's digital economy by 2020.

16. "Huawei's Place in the EU's Research and Innovation Landscape."

17. "China Invests More in Europe Than in US," February 26, 2013, http://www.china.org.cn/business/2013-02/26/content_28058590.htm.

18. Eric Pfanner, "Chinese Telecom Firm Finds Warmer Welcome in Europe," *New York Times*, October 10, 2012, https://www.nytimes.com/2012/10/12/business/global/huawei-chinese-telecom-company-finds-warmer-welcome-in-europe.html.

19. Archibald Preuschat, "Huawei Says Europe Is 'Like a Second Home Market,'" *Wall Street Journal*, July 17, 2015, https://blogs.wsj.com/digits/2015/07/17/huawei-says-europe-is-like-a-second-home-market.

20. Sam Schechner, "Huawei Founder: Company Aims to Be Viewed as 'European,'" *Wall Street Journal*, May 2, 2014, http://www.wsj.com/articles/SB10001424052702303678404579537603276498142.

21. Lanlan Liu, "The EU Required ZTE and Huawei to Increase Export Products' Prices by 29%," *BJNews*, January 31, 2013, http://epaper.bjnews.com.cn/html/2013-01/31/content_407518.htm?div=-1.

22. Jamie Doward, "Is Huawei a Friend or Foe in the Battle for 5G Dominance?," *The Guardian*, February 3, 2019, https://www.theguardian.com/technology/2019/feb/03/huawei-friend-or-foe-global-5g-dominance.

23. Ibid.

24. "Identification and Quantification of Key Socio-Economic Data to Support Strategic Planning for the Introduction of 5G in Europe," European Commission, Directorate-General of Communications Networks, Content & Technology, 2014, https://publications.europa.eu/en/publication-detail/-/publication/ee832bba-ed02-11e6-ad7c-01aa75ed71a1.

25. "Huawei's 30 5G Commercial Contract," *C114*, January 24, 2019, http://tech.huanqiu.com/comm/2019-01/14151251.html.

26. Schiller, *Digital Depression*, 153.

27. Kelly Motz and Jordan Richie, "Techno Two-Timing," *Wall Street Journal*, March 19, 2001, https://www.wsj.com/articles/SB984950042398710644.

28. Ibid.

29. "The Lawsuit between Cisco and Huawei," *Telecom World*, August 10, 2004.

30. Sunny Li Sun, "Internationalization Strategy of MNEs from Emerging Economies: The Case of Huawei," *Multinational Business Review* 17, no. 2 (2009).

31. Ibid.

32. Steve Stecklow, Farnaz Fassihi, and Loretta Chao, "Chinese Tech Giant Aids Iran," *Wall Street Journal*, October 27, 2011, https://www.wsj.com/articles/SB10001424052970204644504576651503577823210.

33. Zhengfei Ren, "To Achieve Win-Win Result by Focusing on Clients, Investment in Platform and Cooperation," speech at the 2010 PSST System Cadre Conference, Shenzhen, August 26, 2010, http://forum.huawei.com/portal.php?mod=view&aid=61.

34. Leo Panitch and Sam Gindin, *The Making of Global Capitalism* (London: Verso Books, 2012), 275.

35. "Investigative Report on the US National Security Issues Posed by Chinese Telecommunications Companies Huawei and ZTE," US House of Representative, 112th Congress, October 8, 2012, https://intelligence.house.gov/sites/intelligence.house.gov/files/documents/huawei-zte%20investigative%20report%20(final).pdf.

36. Heidi Marie Brush, "Cells, Nets, and the Security State: Transnational Political Organizations and the Governing of the Internet," in *New Frontiers in International Communication Theory*, ed. Mehdi Semati (Lanham, MD: Rowman & Littlefield, 2004), 232.

37. Schiller, *Digital Depression*.

38. Ellen Nakashima, "NSA Targeted Network of Chinese Tech Firm Huawei, Leaked Document Shows," *Washington Post*, March 22, 2014, https://www.washingtonpost.com/world/national-security/nsa-targeted-network-of-chinese-tech-firm-huawei-leaked-document-shows/2014/03/22/4b880788-b1fb-11e3-a49e-76adc9210f19_story.html.

39. Ping Guo, "The US Attacks on Huawei Betrays Its Fear of Being Left Behind," *Financial Times*, February 27, 2019, http://www.ftchinese.com/story/001081640/en.

40. Cecilia Kang and Alan Rappeport, "The New US-China Rivalry: A Technology Race," *New York Times*, March 6, 2018, https://www.nytimes.com/2018/03/06/business/us-china-trade-technology-deals.html.

41. Rob Taylor and Sara Germano, "At Gathering of Spy Chiefs, US, Allies Agreed to Contain Huawei," *Wall Street Journal*, December 14, 2018, https://www.wsj.com/articles/at-gathering-of-spy-chiefs-u-s-allies-agreed-to-contain-huawei-11544825652.

42. Dan Schiller, "Geopolitical-Economic Conflict and Network Infrastructures," *Chinese Journal of Communication* 4, no. 1 (2011): 98.

43. Jill Hills, *Telecommunications and Empire* (Urbana: University of Illinois Press, 2007), 5.

44. Parmy Olson, "Interview: Huawei's Cyber Security Chief Slams US 'Protectionism,'" *Forbes*, October 10, 2012, https://www.forbes.com/sites/parmyolson/2012/10/10/interview-huaweis-cyber-security-chief-decries-protectionism/#6702f46d5dc3.

45. Yu Hong, *Networking China: The Digital Transformation of the Chinese Economy* (Urbana: University of Illinois Press, 2017), 93.

46. Huawei, "21st Century Technology and Security—A Difficult Marriage," Huawei Cyber Security White Paper, September 2012, https://www.huawei.com/us/about-huawei/cyber-security/whitepaper/white-paper-2012.

47. Dara Kerr, "Huawei Reportedly Decides to Abandon the US Market," December 2, 2013, https://www.cnet.com/news/huawei-reportedly-decides-to-abandon-the-us-market.

48. Corazon Victorino, "Huawei Withdrawing from US Market after Surpassing Apple Global Smartphone Shipments," *International Business Times*, August 6, 2018, https://www.ibtimes.com/huawei-withdrawing-us-market-after-surpassing-apple-global-smartphone-shipments-2705974.

49. Peter Waldman, Sheridan Prasso, and Todd Shields, "Another Reason US Fears Huawei: Its Gear Works and It's Cheap," *Bloomberg*, January 24, 2019, https://www.bloomberg.com/news/articles/2019-01-24/huawei-stokes-u-s-fear-with-low-cost-networking-gear-that-works.

50. Zen Soo, "Trump's Huawei Ban Will Hit Rural US Carriers the Hardest as Replacing Equipment Will Cost 'Millions,'" *South China Morning Post*, March 4, 2019, https://www.scmp.com/tech/enterprises/article/2188422/trumps-huawei-ban-will-hit-rural-us-carriers-hardest-replacing.

51. Ren Zhengfei, interview with BBC, February 18, 2019, https://www.huawei.com/en/facts/voices-of-huawei/ren-zhengfei-interview-with-bbc.

52. Hong, *Networking China*; Schiller, *Digital Depression*, 236.

53. William I. Robinson, *Global Capitalism and the Crisis of Humanity* (New York: Cambridge University Press, 2014).

54. Schiller, *Digital Depression*, 236.

Chapter 4. From Path-Dependent to Pathbreaking? Huawei's Technological Capability Development

1. Evan A. Feigenbaum, *China's Techno-Warriors: National Security and Strategic Competition from the Nuclear to the Information Age* (Stanford, CA: Stanford University Press, 2003).

2. Yehzhi Zhao, "China's Pursuits of Indigenous Innovations in Information Technology Developments: Hopes, Follies, and Uncertainties," *Chinese Journal of Communication* 3, no. 3 (2010): 266–89.

3. Alex Inkeles and David H. Smith, *Becoming Modem: Individual Change in Six Developing Countries* (Cambridge, MA: Harvard University Press, 1974); Everett M. Rogers, *Diffusion of Innovations* (New York: Simon and Schuster, 2010); Wilbur Schramm, *Mass Media and National Development: The Role of Information in the Developing Countries* (Stanford, CA: Stanford University Press, 1964).

4. Andre Gunder Frank, *Capitalism and Underdevelopment in Latin America* (New York: NYU Press, 1967); Amartya Sen, *Development as Freedom* (New York: Oxford Paperbacks, 2001); Immanuel Maurice Wallerstein, *The Capitalist World-Economy: Essays* (Cambridge, UK: Cambridge University Press, 1979).

5. Samir Amin, *Imperialism and Unequal Development* (Hassocks, Sussex, UK: Harvester, 1977), 177.

6. Alice Hoffenberg Amsden, *Asia's Next Giant: South Korea and Late Industrialization* (New York: Oxford University Press on Demand, 1992).

7. Yu Zhou, *The Inside Story of China's High-Tech Industry: Making Silicon Valley in Beijing* (Lanham, MD: Rowman & Littlefield, 2007), 18.

8. Feigenbaum, *China's Techno-Warriors*.

9. Ibid., 29.

10. Ibid., 39.

11. Hongzhe Wang, "Machine for a Long Revolution: Computer as the Nexus of Technology and Class Politics in China 1955–1984," Chinese University of Hong Kong, 2014.

12. MEI, *Yearbook of Electronic Industry, 1986* (Beijing: Electronic Industry Press, 1986).

13. Ibid.

14. Xiaobai Shen, *The Chinese Road to High Technology: A Study of Telecommunications Switching Technology in the Economic Transition* (New York: St. Martin's Press, 1999), 147.

15. "China's Top100 Electronics Enterprises' R&D Spending Accounts for 3.9% of Sales Revenue," *Xinhua News Agency*, June 7, 2007, http://it.sohu.com/2007 0607/n250446798.shtml.

16. "Accelerate Technological Innovation with Prominent Innovation-Driven Effects," National Bureau of Statistics of the PRC, n.d., http://www.stats.gov.cn/tjsj%20/sjjd/201603/t20160309_1328568.html.

17. Xiaoling Wen, "The Exploration of Building Domestic Innovation-Driven Cities," People.com, February 10, 2006, http://theory.people.com.cn/GB/49154/49156/4092516.html.

18. "Shenzhen: The Making of 'China's Silicon Valley' during 40 Years of Reforming and Opening-Up," sznews.com, August 26, 2018, http://www.sznews.com/mb/content/2018-08/26/content_19955578.htm.

19. Dan Breznitz and Michael Murphree, *The Run of the Red Queen: Government, Innovation, Globalization, and Economic Growth in China* (New Haven, CT: Yale University Press, 2011).

20. Ibid., 187.

21. Xiaolan Fu, *China's Path to Innovation* (Cambridge, UK: Cambridge University Press, 2015), 5.

22. "Huawei 2015 Annual Report."

23. "The 2018 EU Industrial R&D Investment Scoreboard," EU Economics of Industrial Research and Innovation, 2018, http://iri.jrc.ec.europa.eu/scoreboard18.html.

24. Ibid.

25. Lihua Zhang, *Research and Development of Huawei* (Beijing: China Machine Press, 2014), 13.

26. Ibid., 35.

27. Shen, *Chinese Road to High Technology*, 135.

28. Ibid., 134.

29. Dieter Ernst and Barry Naughton, "China's Emerging Industrial Economy," in *China's Emergent Political Economy: Capitalism in the Dragon's Lair*, ed. McNally (London: Routledge, 2007), 53.

30. Shen, *Chinese Road to High Technology*, 132.

31. Zhao, "China's Pursuits of Indigenous Innovations."

32. "TD Alliance: China Owns More Than 50% of TD Patents with a Saving of RMB500 Billion Royalties," People.com, October 20, 2006, http://it.people.com.cn/GB/1068/42905/4938641.html.

33. Qilin Lin, "Is It Worth to Invest ¥200 Billion in TD?," *Beijing News*, December 25, 2014, http://epaper.bjnews.com.cn/html/2014-12/25/content_553852.htm?div=1.

34. China's Electronics Newspaper, *The Ten-Year Industrial Development of TD-SCDMA* (Beijing: Publishing House of Electronic Industry, 2008).

35. M. Hou, "Domestic 3G Standard Favored.," *China Daily*, October 31, 2002, http://german.china.org.cn/english/scitech/47266.htm.

36. "Huawei Independent R&D on TD," Sina Technology, October 1, 2006, http://tech.sina.com.cn/t/2006-12-01/01331265822.shtml.

37. Yu Hong, Francois Bar, and An Zheng, "Chinese Telecommunications on the Threshold of Convergence: Contexts, Possibilities, and Limitations of Forging a Domestic Demand-Based Growth Model," *Telecommunications Policy* 36, nos. 10–11 (2012): 914–28.

38. Phil Goldstein, "Report: Huawei, Ericsson Lead LTE Market amid Growing Deployments" *FierceWireless*, August 13, 2013, https://www.fiercewireless.com/wireless/report-huawei-ericsson-lead-lte-market-amid-growing-deployments.

39. "Huawei 5G Progress," Huawei.com, http://carrier.huawei.com/en/spotlight/5g.

40. Zhang Dong, "Exploring 5G NR Technology," August 5, 2016, https://www.huawei.com/cn/about-huawei/publications/communicate/75/5g-air-interface-technology-cn.

41. "Huawei's Founder Ren Zhengfei: Huawei Will Never Provide Government with Customer Information," January 15, 2019, https://www.huawei.com/en/facts/voices-of-huawei/interview-with-ren-zhengfei.

42. Hong, Bar, and Zheng, "Chinese Telecommunications."

43. "Ren Zhengfei's International Media Roundtable," https://www.huawei.com/mm/press-events/news/mm/2019/ren-zhengfei-international-media-roundtable.

44. Zehua Lu, "The Breakthrough of 'China's Chip' in the World," *People's Daily*, January 22, 2018, http://www.xinhuanet.com/world/2018-01/22/c_129795850.htm.

45. Zhengfei Ren, "Transcript of Ren Zhengfei's '2012 Lab Speech,'" Shenzhen, September 2012, http://tech.qq.com/a/20120911/000164.htm.

46. Xudong Gao and Jizhen Li, "Technological Capability in Complex Environments: The Case of the Chinese Telecom Equipment Industry," in *China's Evolving Industrial Policies and Economic Restructuring*, ed. Yongnian Zheng and Sarah Y. Tong (Abingdon, Oxon, UK: Routledge, 2014), 126.

47. Michael H. Siam-Heng, "Development of China's Semiconductor Industry: Prospects and Problems," in *China's Science and Technology Sector and the Forces of Globalization*, ed. Elspeth Thomson and Jon Sigurdson, 173–89 (London: World Scientific Publishing, 2008).

48. Zhang Chaohui, "The State Invests ¥120billion in the IC Industry Fund," *China Security Journal*, April 23, 2014, http://news.cnstock.com/industry,tt-201404-2996630.htm.

49. Ren, "Transcript of Ren Zhengfei's '2012 Lab Speech.'"

50. Tingbo He, "A Letter from HiSilicon CEO," 2019, https://world.huanqiu.com/article/9CaKrnKkxZ6.

51. Dan Schiller, *How to Think about Information* (Urbana: University of Illinois Press, 2007).

52. Peter Drahos and John Braithwaite, *Information Feudalism: Who Owns the Knowledge Economy?* (London: Earthscan, 2002), 171–73.

53. Ibid.

54. Don Clark and Maria Armental, "Qualcomm Profit Drops 46% on Antitrust Fine in China," *Wall Street Journal*, April 22, 2015, https://www.wsj.com/articles/qualcomm-sees-profit-decline-on-antitrust-fine-in-china-1429735814.

55. Liang Yan, "US Qualcomm's CDMA Chipsets Sales Is Expected to Increase," *Xinhua News Agency*, December 8, 2002, http://www.people.com.cn/GB/it/50/145/20021208/883475.html.

56. Paige Tanner, "Qualcomm: Its Challenges, Its Strategy, Its Future," Yahoo, March 23, 2016, http://marketrealist.com/2016/03/qualcomms-biggest-challenges-china.

57. Min Qin, "Chinese Smartphone Makers, Qualcomm in Battle Royale over Patent Payments," *Caixin Magazine*, March 24, 2014, https://www.caixinglobal.com/2014-03-24/chinese-smartphone-makers-qualcomm-in-battle-royale-over-patent-payments-101013476.html.

58. Drahos and Braithwaite, *Information Feudalism*.

59. Schiller, *How to Think about Information*, 46.

60. Chris Duckett, "Over $6b in IP Royalties Paid by Huawei, Nearly 80% to US Firms," *ZDNet*, June 27, 2019, https://www.zdnet.com/article/over-6b-in-ip-royalties-paid-by-huawei-nearly-80-to-us-firms.

61. Tao Tian and Chunbo Wu, *Will Huawei Be the Next to Fail?* (Beijing: CITIC Press, 2012).

62. Dengke Qiu, "Huawei: Seizing the Commanding Heights in the Era of Post-Cisco Lawsuit," *C114 Telecommunications*, July 15, 2008.

63. Yafang Sun, "Huawei Chairwoman Sun Yafang's Public Speech at the National Scientific Conference," Beijing, January 2006.

64. "Huawei Top Filer with European Patent Office in 2017," March 8, 2018, https://www.huawei.com/en/press-events/news/2018/3/Huawei-Top-Filer-European-Patent-Office.

65. Yan Huang and Linna Yi, "Huawei's WCDMA Patent Ownership Ranked Global Top 5," *Shenzhen Economic Daily*, June 27, 2005, http://tech.sina.com.cn/t/2005-06-27/0943646342.shtml; Kang Wang, "Huawei Owns 25% of 4G Patents," *China's Intellectual Property Newspaper*, January 22, 2015, http://ip.people.com.cn/n/2015/0122/c136655-26429874.html.

66. Tim Pohlmann, "Who Is Leading the 5G Patent Race?," *IPlytics GmbH*, December 12, 2018, https://www.iam-media.com/who-leading-5g-patent-race.

67. Zhao, "China's Pursuits of Indigenous Innovations."

68. Sun, "Huawei Chairwoman Sun Yafang's Public Speech."

69. Zhou, *Inside Story of China's High-Tech Industry*, 173.

Chapter 5. Ownership, Management, and Labor Discipline

1. Eli Friedman and Ching Kwan Lee, "Remaking the World of Chinese Labour: A 30-Year Retrospective," *British Journal of Industrial Relations* 48, no. 3 (2010): 507–33.

2. Barry Naughton, *The Chinese Economy: Transitions and Growth* (Cambridge: MIT Press, 2007), 298.

3. Lu Yun, *Ren Zhengfei Business Wisdom* (Beijing: Beijing United Publishing, 2014).

4. Dan Breznitz and Michael Murphree, *The Run of the Red Queen: Government, Innovation, Globalization, and Economic Growth in China* (New Haven, CT: Yale University Press, 2011), 178.

5. Naughton, *Chinese Economy*; Lutao Ning, *China's Rise in the World ICT Industry: Industrial Strategies and the Catch-Up Development Model* (New York: Routledge, 2009).

6. Ning, *China's Rise*, 60.

7. Ibid., 87.

8. Victor Nee and Sonja Opper, *Capitalism from Below: Markets and Institutional Change in China* (Cambridge, MA: Harvard University Press, 2012).

9. "Decisions of the CPC Central Committee on Some Issues Concerning the Establishment of a Socialist Market Economy System," Third Plenary Session of the CPC 14th National Congress, November 14, 1993.

10. Nee and Opper, *Capitalism from Below*, 115.

11. Shangquan Gao, "Gao Shangquan: Why Does the Huawei Model Succeed?," April 28, 2018, http://www.sohu.com/a/229785239_100160903.

12. Ibid.

13. "Reports on the CPC 15th National Congress," CPC, Beijing, September 12, 1997.

14. Christopher Balding and Donald C. Clark, "Who Owns Huawei?," April 17, 2019. Available at SSRN: https://ssrn.com/abstract=3372669 or http://dx.doi.org/10.2139/ssrn.3372669.

15. South China Morning Post (SCMP), "Transcript: Huawei Founder Ren Zhengfei's Responses to Media Questions at a Round Table This Week," January 16, 2019, https://www.scmp.com/tech/big-tech/article/2182367/transcript-huawei-founder-ren-zhengfeis-responses-media-questions.

16. Ibid.

17. "The Comparison of Employees' Wealth with Internet Companies' IPO," Xueqiu.com, October 9, 2014, https://xueqiu.com/9041141730/32056495.

18. SCMP, "Huawei's Founder Ren Zhengfei."

19. "China Rich List 2019 Ranking," *Forbes*, 2019, https://www.forbes.com/china-billionaires/list/#tab:overall.

20. Jerry Harris, *The Dialectics of Globalization: Economic and Political Conflict in a Transnational World* (Newcastle, UK: Cambridge Scholars Press, 2006), 28.

21. David De Cremer and Tao Tian, "Huawei: A Case Study of When Profit Sharing Works," *Harvard Business Review*, September 24, 2015, https://hbr.org/2015/09/huawei-a-case-study-of-when-profit-sharing-works.

22. William K. Carroll, *The Making of a Transnational Capitalist Class: Corporate Power in the Twenty-First Century* (London: Zed Books, 2010).

23. Christopher Williams, "Huawei Founder Ren Zhengfei Rejects 'Greedy' Public Markets," *The Telegraph*, May 2, 2014, http://www.telegraph.co.uk/finance/newsbysector/mediatechnologyandtelecoms/telecoms/108048.

24. Liu Fang Yuan, "The Virtual and Real Story Behind Huawei's IPO," *21st Century Business Herald*, October 20, 2012, http://finance.ifeng.com/news/tech/20121020/7176399.shtml.

25. John. H. Dunning, *Multinational Enterprises and the Global Economy* (New York: Addison Wesley, 1993); Rajneesh Narula and John H. Dunning, "Industrial Development, Globalization and Multinational Enterprises: New Realities for Developing Countries," *Oxford Development Studies* 28, no. 2 (2000): 141–67.

26. Richard D. Wolff, *Democracy at Work: A Cure for Capitalism* (Chicago: Haymarket Books, 2012), 87.

27. Demetri Sevastopulo, "Huawei Pulls Back the Curtain on Ownership Details," *Financial Times*, February 27, 2014, https://www.ft.com/content/469bde20-9eaf-11e3-8663-00144feab7de.

28. Yu Hong, *Labor, Class Formation, and China's Informationized Policy of Economic Development* (Lanham, MD: Lexington Books, 2011).

29. Shuo Qin, *Big Change: The Rising and Reform of Chinese Private Enterprises* (Guangzhou: Guangdong Tourism Press, 2002), 222.

30. Zhengfei Ren, "Dedication to Products and Customer Services: A Speech on Huawei Telecom R&D Engineers Meeting," August 15, 1998, https://www.sohu.com/a/133660113_205354.

31. Chunbo Wu, "Huawei Has No Secret: A Thought from 'The Angang Constitution,'" *Huawei People*, May 2, 1996.

32. Jing Wang, *Brand New China: Advertising, Media, and Commercial Culture* (Cambridge, MA: Harvard University Press, 2008).

33. Ibid., 160.

34. Li Ma, "Corporate Culture," in *Understanding Chinese Firms from Multiple Perspectives*, ed. Zhi-Xue Zhang and Jianjun Zhang (New York: Springer, 2014), 165.

35. Friedman and Lee, "Remaking the World of Chinese Labour," 509.

36. Yu Hong, *Labor, Class Formation, and China's Informationized Policy*.

37. Yuhang Wang, "Huawe's 30 Years," *Shangjie*, August 9, 2018, http://www.kanshangjie.com/article/153790-1.html.

38. Ibid.

39. Yongqing Ji, "Huawei's Ren Zhengfei Recruited Talents," Sina Technology, May 20, 2016, http://finance.sina.cn/chanjing/gsxw/2016-05-20/detail-ifxsktkr5787071.d.html?vt=4&pos=17.

40. Huawei, "Huawei 2015 Sustainability Report," 2015, http://www-file.huawei.com/~/media/CORPORATE/PDF/Press-Center/media-kit/2014Huaweisustainabilityreporten.pdf.

41. Ren Zhengfei, "The Responsibilities and Management of Huawei University," speech at Huawei University, Shenzhen, March 27, 2014.

42. Cyrus Lee, "Huawei Ups Pay for Entry-Level Staff," *ZDNet*, July 26, 2013, https://www.zdnet.com/article/huawei-ups-pay-for-entry-level-staff.

43. Huawei, "The Huawei Basic Law," Article 19 (April 6, 1998), https://wenku.baidu.com/view/c43e61eea417866fb84a8eab.html.

44. Chris Rowley and Fang Lee Cooke, *The Changing Face of Management in China* (New York: Routledge, 2014).

45. Jinjie Zhao, "Huawei Published 2017 Bonus Plan," *C114 Telecommunications*, February 6, 2018, http://www.c114.com.cn/news/126/a1042764.html.

46. Jichen Zhang, *Huawei's Human Resource Management* (Shenzhen: Haitian, 2012).

47. Christian Fuchs, *Digital Labour and Karl Marx* (New York: Routledge, 2014).

48. Baohua Dong, "Within and Beyond the Labor Contract Law," *China Employment Watch*, no. 13 (2009), http://www.cew.hk/web/cew/cn/article/?action=public-article&id=84&l=en.

49. Huawei Human Resource Department, "Building the Cutting-Edge 'Huawei Army,'" *Huawei Xinsheng Community*, February 14, 2019, http://xinsheng.huawei.com/cn/index.php?app=forum&mod=Detail&act=index&id=4176913.

50. Beverly J. Silver and Lu Zhang, "China as an Emerging Epicenter of World Labor Unrest," in *China and the Transformation of Global Capitalism*, ed. Ho-fung Hung (Baltimore: Johns Hopkins University Press, 2009), 176.

51. Enshi Zhou, "The Evolution of Huawei's Salary and Reward Systems," October 20, 2018, http://m.sohu.com/a/270230316_624053.

52. Celine Ge, "Housing Crisis in China's 'Silicon Valley': Huawei, Other Hi-Tech Giants Head for Cheaper Cities as Rising Costs Deter Talent," *South China Morning Post*, May 25, 2016, http://www.scmp.com/news/china/policies-politics/article/1952617/housing-crisis-chinas-silicon-valley-huawei-other-hi.

53. Huawei, "Connecting the Future: 2014 Sustainability Report," http://www-file.huawei.com/~/media/CORPORATE/PDF/Sustainability/2014%20Huawei%20sustainability%20report-final.pdf?la=en.

54. Zhengfei Ren, "Speech on Huawei's HR Meeting," June 24, 2014, http://www.cghuawei.com/archives/12190.

55. Chris Smith and Ngai Pun, "The Dormitory Labour Regime in China as a Site for Control and Resistance 1," *International Journal of Human Resource Management* 17, no. 8 (2006): 1456–70.

56. Lu Tang and Yonggang Tu, "Huawei's Overseas R&D Center Was Launched in India," *Xinhua News Agency*, February 6, 2015, http://www.xinhuanet.com//world/2015-02/06/c_1114277528.htm.

57. Ching Kwan Lee, "The Spectre of Global China," *New Left Review*, no. 89 (2014): 29–65.

58. Enricko Lukman, "Huawei Facing Second Labor Strike in Indonesia," *Tech in Asia*, March 4, 2013, https://www.techinasia.com/huawei-indonesia-protest.

59. Ho-fung Hung, "Introduction: The Three Transformations of Global Capitalism," in *China and the Transformation of Global Capitalism*, ed. Ho-fung Hung (Baltimore: Johns Hopkins University Press, 2009), 16.

Conclusion

1. Yu Hong, *Labor, Class Formation, and China's Informationized Policy of Economic Development* (Lanham, MD: Lexington Books, 2011).

2. Jerry Harris, "Outward Bound: Transnational Capitalism in China," *Race and Class* 54, no. 1 (2012): 13–32.

3. Lin Chun, "China: Changing the Rules of the Game," *Soundings*, no. 39 (2008): 13.

4. Alvin Y. So, "Rethinking the Chinese Developmental Miracle," in *China and the Transformation of Global Capitalism*, ed. Ho-fung Hung, 50–64 (Baltimore: Johns Hopkins University Press, 2009).

5. Xiaolan Fu, *China's Path to Innovation* (Cambridge, UK: Cambridge University Press).

6. Peter Nolan, *China and the Global Economy: National Champions, Industrial Policy and the Big Business Revolution* (Houndmills, Basingstoke, UK: Palgrave Macmillan, 2001), 176.

7. Yu Hong, *Networking China; Min Tang, Tencent: The Political Economy of China's Surging Internet Giant* (New York: Routledge, 2019).

8. Lutao Ning, *China's Rise in the World ICT Industry: Industrial Strategies and the Catch-Up Development Model* (New York: Routledge, 2009), 182.

9. Yuezhi Zhao, "China's Pursuits of Indigenous Innovations in Information Technology Developments: Hopes, Follies, and Uncertainties," *Chinese Journal of Communication* 3, no. 3 (2010): 266–89.

10. Fu, *China's Path to Innovation*, 385.

11. Jintao Hu, "Report at the 18th National Congress of the CPC," speech presented at CPPCC National Committee, November 27, 2012.

12. Lorand Laskai, "Civil-Military Fusion and the PLA's Pursuit of Dominance in Emerging Technologies," *RealClear Defense*, April 10, 2018, https://www.realcleardefense.com/articles/2018/04/10/plas_pursuit_of_dominance_in_emerging_technologies_113305.html.

13. Ibid.

14. Smart cities are proposed to use information and communication technologies to develop, deploy, and promote sustainable development practices in cities.

15. Zhengfei Ren, "Ren Zhengfei: China's Driverless Car Can Start with Tractor, Not Competing with the West on the Same Track," January 17, 2019, https://finance.ifeng.com/c/7jY2dAxGTvE.

16. So, "Rethinking the Chinese Developmental Miracle," 60.

17. Ibid., 58.

18. M. J. Meisner, *The Deng Xiaoping Era* (New York: Hill and Wang, 1996).

19. Ho-fung Hung, "America's Head Servant?: The PRC's Dilemma in the Global Crisis," *New Left Review* 60 (November/December 2009).

20. Ibid.

21. Nolan, *China and the Global Economy*, 203.

22. Ibid., 202.

23. Martin Hart-Landsberg, *Capitalist Globalization: Consequences, Resistance, and Alternatives* (New York: NYU Press, 2013), 47.

24. Yu Hong, Francois Bar, and An Zheng, "Chinese Telecommunications on the Threshold of Convergence: Contexts, Possibilities, and Limitations of Forging a Domestic Demand-Based Growth Model," *Telecommunications Policy* 36, nos. 10–11 (2012): 914–28.

25. Dan Schiller, "Geopolitical-Economic Conflict and Network Infrastructures," *Chinese Journal of Communication* 4, no. 1 (2011): 90–107; Dan Schiller, "Power under Pressure: Digital Capitalism in Crisis," *International Journal of Communication* 5 (2011): 933; Dan Schiller, *Digital Depression: Information Technology and Economic Crisis* (Urbana: University of Illinois Press, 2014).

26. Deborah Brautigam, *The Dragon's Gift: The Real Story of China in Africa* (Oxford: Oxford University Press, 2009), 307.

27. Yuezhi Zhao, "The Challenge of China: Contribution to a Transcultural Political Economy of Communication for the Twenty-First Century," in *The Handbook of Political Economy of Communications*, ed. Janet Wasko, Graham Murdock, and Helena Sousa, 558–82 (Malden, MA: Blackwell, 2011).

28. The term "Washington Consensus" was coined in 1989 and supported by prominent economists and international organizations such as the International Monetary Fund, the World Bank, and the US Treasury. The term refers to a set of neoliberal economic policies such as the ideas of liberalization, privatization, and deregulation. These principles were used as policy prescriptions for economic reforms of developing countries.

29. Ching Kwan Lee, "The Spectre of Global China," *New Left Review*, no. 89 (2014): 29–65.

30. Nadège Rolland, "Securing the Belt and Road: Prospects for Chinese Military Engagement Along the Silk Roads," National Bureau of Asian Research, September 3, 2019, https://www.nbr.org/publication/securing-the-belt-and-road-prospects-for-chinese-military-engagement-along-the-silk-roads/#_ftnref5.

31. Hung, *China Boom*, 140.

32. Hung, *China and the Transformation of Global Capitalism*.

33. Dan Schiller, "An Update on China in the Political Economy of Information and Communications," *Chinese Journal of Communication* 1, no. 1 (2008): 111.

34. "In Retreat: The Multinational Company Is in Trouble," *The Economist*, January 28, 2017, http://www.economist.com/news/leaders/21715660-global-firms-are-surprisingly-vulnerable-attack-multinational-company-trouble.

35. Nadège Rolland, "A Fiber-Optic Silk Road: China's Silk Road Initiative Has Profound Implications for Cyberspace, as Well as for Physical Infrastructure," *The Diplomat*, 2015, http://thediplomat.com/2015/04/a-fiber-optic-silk-road.

36. Yuezhi Zhao, "The BRICS Formation in Reshaping Global Communication: Possibilities and Challenges," in *Mapping BRICS Media*, ed. Kaarle Nordenstreng and Daya Kishan Thussu. (London: Routledge, 2015), 70.

37. Ibid.

38. Hui Wang, "On the Taiwan Issue from the Perspective of Contemporary Chinese History," *Wenhua Zongheng*, no. 1 (2015), http://old.21bcr.com/a/shiye/lishiguan/2015/0130/3550_4.html.

39. Lin Chun, *The Transformation of Chinese Socialism* (Durham, NC: Duke University Press, 2006), 244.

40. Armand Mattelart, *Transnationals and the Third World: The Struggle for Culture* (S. Hadley, MA: Bergin & Gravey, 1983), 25.

41. Huang Yue and Wang Zihui, "Xi Jinping Focused on These Issues in Northeast China," *Xinhua News Agency*, September 29, 2018, http://www.xinhuanet.com/politics/xxjxs/2018-09/29/c_1123505377.htm.

42. Daya Kishan Thussu and Kaarle Nordenstreng, "Introduction: Contextualizing the BRICS Media," in *Mapping BRICS Media*, ed. Kaarle Nordenstreng and Daya Kishan Thussu (London: Routledge, 2015), 7.

43. Hong Shen, "Across the Great (Fire) Wall: China and the Global Internet," unpublished dissertation, University of Illinois at Urbana-Champaign, 2017.

44. Ibid.

45. William I. Robinson, *Theory of Global Capitalism: Production, Class, and State in a Transnational World* (Baltimore: Johns Hopkins University Press, 2004).

46. Zhao, "China's Pursuits of Indigenous Innovations."

47. Chun, "China: Changing the Rules of the Game," 7; Chun, *China and Global Capitalism: Reflections on Marxism, History, and Contemporary Politics* (New York: Palgrave Macmillan, 2013).

48. Chun, "China: Changing the Rules of the Game," 19.

49. Andrea E. Goldstein, *Multinational Companies from Emerging Economies: Composition, Conceptualization and Direction in the Global Economy* (Basingstoke, UK: Palgrave Macmillan 2007), 151.

Index

1G (analog) standard, 126–27
2G standard, 126–27
21st Century Network (21CN), 95
3Com, 104–6
3GPP RAN1, 131
3G standard, 128–30
3Leaf, 106
3rd Generation Partnership Project (3GPP), 127
4G standard, 130
5G Infrastructure Public Private Partnership Program (5GPPP), 97
5G Promotion Group, 49, 131
5G standard, 130–32
863 Plan, 119
996 culture, 164, 168–69

Africa, 61–62, 68, 69, 70–76, 82–83, 85, 88–89, 170–72; Chinese military base in, 189; stereotypes about, 173
ALBA (Bolivarian Alliance for the Peoples of Our America) countries, 78
Alcatel, 90–92
Algeria, 74, 173
Alibaba: AI, 183; Ant Financial, 108; BAT, 62, 177; ownership, 150–51, 195; ranking, 7; in rural markets, 181

American Empire, 5
American Telegraph Company, 4
Amin, Samir, 116
analog mobile service, 126
Angang Constitution, 155
anticompetition, 134–35
anti-dumping, 100
anti-hacking, 105
anti-subsidy, 100
antiterrorism, 107
application specific integrated circuit, 133
ARM: architecture platform, 135; trade ban, 101
artificial intelligence (AI), 80, 183–84
Asian Development Bank, 33
Asian Tigers, 57
AT&T, 83, 106
attracting-in (economic policy), 30, 54–55, 58, 186; "trading market for technology," 33
Avago, 110

Baidu: BAT, 62, 177; ownership, 149–50; ranking, 7
Balong 5000, 134
Banverket Telenät, 94
Baseband, 130, 135

Basic Telecommunications Agreement, 6
BAT: Alibaba, 108, 150–51; Baidu, 149–50; Tencent, 149–50
Beijing Summit, 74
Beijing Wire Communication Plant, 21
Belt and Road Initiative (BRI): countries of, 205n72; geopolitical policy, 190–93; submarine cable projects of, 85
Beto Konzem, 68
BH01 switch, 122
Bolivarian Socialist, 78
Bolivia, 77, 78
Brazil, 61, 68, 77–78, 85, 192
BRICS (Brazil, Russia, India, China, and South Africa): alternative cable projects of, 192; counter-hegemonic alliance, 192
British empire, 4–5
broadband, 83, 92, 94–95, 77, 140
Broadcom, 108–10
BT Group: broadband development, 94–95; trade ban, 101
BTM, 34
bubble, economic: internet, 6, 47, 93, 94; real estate, 167

Cameroon-Brazil Cable System (CBCS), 85
C&C08 (digital switch): domestic market strategy, 37; internationalization, 67; R&D, 124
Cao Yian, 123
capitalist logic of accumulation, 9–10, 12, 138
Carrier Network: Huawei's business unit, 15; market strategy, 49
carriers. *See* telecommunications carriers
casual labor. *See* labor: casual and temporary
CDMA (code division multiple access): as 3G standard, 126–27; in China's market, 45; in foreign market, 72–74
Center for Information Technology (CIT), 123
Chen Jian, 72
Chen Yun, 25
China-Africa Development Fund (CADF), 74

China Development Bank (CDB): Chinese policy bank, 75; state-backed funding, 75, 79
China Huaxin, 62
China International Telecommunication Construction Corporation, 74
China National Electronics Import & Export Corporation (CEIE), 56
China Railway Construction Corporation, 81
China State Construction, 81
China Telecom, 45–47
China Unicom, 43–45, 85
Chinese model: as an alternative model, 188–89; debate, 11–16; of ICT development, 193–97
Chinese National Patents Development Strategy, 140
chipsets, 130, 142; core technologies, 50, 183; innovation strategies, 132–36, 181; markets, 137; multimode, 134
Chongqing Institute of Post and Telecommunications, 32
Cisco: innovation strategy of, 121; intellectual property, 138; lawsuit, 103–4; strategic partnership, 91
civil-military fusion, 182–83
co-branding, 96
co-development, 88
Cold War: anti-communist, 185; technology policy, 117
collaboration, inter-capitalist, 96, 103–4, 139
Colombia, 77
colonization, 3, 86, 188
Committee on Foreign Investment in the United States, 106
commodity chains, 5, 49–50, 95
Commonwealth of Independent States, 68
communication grids, 4
Communication Satellite Corporation, 5
communication services: fixed-line telecommunications, 36–37; mobile networks, 42; in rural telecommunications network, 41
communication technologies: digital switch, 36–37, 123–24; indigenous 3G, 127–28

communications: global, 9, 13; intracorporate, 6
communications industry: in Africa, 82–83; in Latin America, 76–77; market competition in China, 33–35; restructuring, 90–91
communications order: China's role, 83–85, 114, 198–99; historical evolution, 4–7
Communist Party of China, 23, 146; National Congresses, 26, 58, 146, 182
competition: inter-capitalist, 17, 90, 102–4, 109–10, 112–13, 126, 132, 181; inter-state, 9, 17, 88, 90, 109–10, 112, 132
Comsat, 5
Connecting Europe Facility, 98–99
convergence: of businesses, 6, 91 (*see also* restructuring); of networks, 95; of standards, 130
Coordinating Committee on Export Controls, 35
corporate model, American, 5
Corporation Law, 146
counterflow, 90
crossbar switch, 33
cyberattacks, 197
cybersecurity, 107, 110–11

Datang: in domestic market, 39; TD-SCDMA development, 127, 129, 130
deconvergence, of businesses, 91. *See also* restructuring
Democratic Republic of Congo, 71
Deng Xiaoping, 26
depression, economic, 2, 13–14, 69
Digital Agenda for Europe, 98–99
digital capitalism, 2, 6. *See also* economy, digital
Digital Equipment Corporation, 103
digital revolution: in China, 14, 27–28, 187; in the global South, 82–93; jumpstart practices, 29–30, 55, 195, 187; technocratic elites in, 26, 30
digital switching equipment, 33–37, 39, 67, 116, 122–25, 193–94; market, 41, 44
Dingqiao Telecommunications, 129

Djibouti, 189
dot-com (internet) bubble, 6, 47, 93, 94
DSLAM (digital subscriber line access multiplexer), 77, 95
dual-track development, 118, 179

East Asia: developmental model of, 12–13, 116–17; outsourcing centers in, 30
Eastern Telegraph Company, 3
EcoBank, 75
economic models. *See* attracting-in; Chinese model; East Asia: developmental model of; Foxconn: model; front shop and back factory model; going-out strategy
Economic Reform, Fifteen Measures of, 58
economy, digital: in China, 1, 13–15, 19, 178; in Europe, 101, 216n15; globalized, 56–57
Ecuador, 78
Edge Network, 44
e-government projects, 75
Ellis, R. Evan, 78
Emerson Network Power, 42
Emobile, 50
employee shareholding, 16, 18, 144–52, 162, 174, 195
Entel, 78
Ericsson, 91, 100, 122, 126; and African telecommunications market, 71–72; and Chinese telecommunications market, 34, 42–43, 126, 130; and European telecommunications market, 92, 94; as Huawei rival, 37, 66, 91, 130; labor procured from, 159; and Vodafone, 96
Ernst, Dieter, 125
Ethernet services, 94
Ethiopia, 74, 75, 76, 79, 80, 83
Ethiopian Telecommunications Corporation, 76
Europe: 5G in, 101–2, 190; Chinese investment in, 60, 71, 98–99, 190; companies based in, 66, 70–71, 90, 92, 93, 95–97, 100–101, 126 (*see also specific companies*); IP lawsuits, 139; links to other regions, 4, 83, 85, 192;

Europe (*continued*): markets in, 17, 57, 90–97, 101; R&D in, 92, 98, 190; standards backed by, 43, 48, 126–28; United States vs., 109; Western, 24, 92. *See also* European Union (EU); *and specific countries*
Europe 2020 strategy, 92–94, 216n15
European Research Institute, 98
European Union (EU), 100–101; 5G in, 97, 101; China overtakes, 2, 56; companies based in, 130; ICT R&D in, 94, 98–99; protectionism, 100. *See also* Europe; *and specific countries*
Export-Import Bank of China (Exim Bank), 75–76
exterritorial expansion, 85
extraterritorial network policy, 105

FDD-LTE (frequency division duplex long-term evolution), 48
Federal Communications Commission, US, 112, 126
Feigenbaum, Evan A., 117
fiber-optic technology, 179
Fifteen Measures of Economic Reform, 58
Five Eyes intelligence alliance, 108
Five-Year Plans, China's: 7th, 27; 9th, 39–41, 127; 10th, 58, 129; 13th, 49
fixed-line telecommunications, 35–37, 122–24
fixed-wage-and-benefit system, 148
"flying geese model," 62, 185
foreign cooperative JVs, 57
foreign direct investment (FDI): change to China's model, 60; domination of foreign companies, 34, 44–45; policy dependent on, 29
foreign-invested enterprises, 29–30, 57
Forum on China Africa Cooperation (FOCAC), 73–74
Four Modernizations, 25–26
Four Three Plan, 24–25
Foxconn: labor, 166–68; model, 14, 205n70
"front shop" and "back factory" model, 31
Fujitsu, 34

Future Internet, 94–95
FutureWay, 102
Fuzhou, 33–34

Gansu, 43
General Telephone and Electronic Corporation, 5
geoeconomics, 55, 109, 184–87
geopolitics: of global digital infrastructure, 4–7; in the global South, 82–85; of information, 25–26; in standardization, 125–26; theory, 9–10. *See also* Belt and Road Initiative (BRI)
geostrategy, 4, 78, 189
Ghana, 74, 75
GitHub, 168
Glassdoor, 173
global communications, 9, 13, 15, 18, 26, 54
Global Marine Systems, 83, 100
global North: global telecom equipment giants, 90–91; Huawei's entry mode in, 92–94; inter-state tensions, 100–102; localization, 110–13; R&D investment, 98–99; trade ban, 108–9
global South: geopolitics, 78, 82–83; going-out strategy, 58–60; state-backed funding, 74–76; telecommunications infrastructure, 83–85
Global System for Mobile Communications (GSM): in Chinese market, 43–45; standardization policy, 126–27
globalization, 10, 157; of accumulation, 186, 198; of capitalism, 9, 55, 102, 177, 185; of corporate China, 2–3, 8, 15, 55, 63–64, 73, 85–89, 157, 189; dialectics of, 19; and IP regulations, 137–38; multipolar, 11; of operations, 17; of production, 52, 62, 116, 169; of R&D, 121, 129–30. *See also* economy, digital; transnational capitalist class (TCC)
going-out strategy: geopolitical implication, 78, 82–83, 187–91; patterns, 60–63; policy, 58–59. *See also* Belt and Road Initiative (BRI)
Great Dragon Group, 35, 39
Greece, 97
GTE, 5

Guangdong Province, 41
Guangzhou, 43, 45
Guinea, 83
Guizhou Province, 22, 32, 45
Guo Ping, 107, 138

Haier, 29, 50
handsets: chipsets of, 134; manufacturers, 50–51
Harris, Jerry, 10, 19
Harvey, David, 10
HAX switch, 33
Heilongjiang Province, 37
Hengtong Optic-Electric Co., 85
Hewlett-Packard, 103–4
High Speed Packet Access networks, 97
high-value-added markets, 78, 191
HiSilicon, 133–35
HJD-04, 35, 123–24
HONET (network), 37
Hong, Yu, 13
Hong Kong, 56, 57, 66–67; companies based in, 32, 66; as financier, 31; subsidiary in, 105
HongmengOS, 135
HTC, 111
Hu Houkun, 106
Hu Qili, 56
Huawei Basic Law, 154–55
Huawei Marine Systems, 83–85
Huawei Technologies Co. Ltd., 1. *See also* entries for specific topics
Hung Nien Electronics, 32
Hungary, 61, 97
Hutchison Telecommunications, 66
hypergrowth in ICT industry, 39, 69

Iceland, 97
ICT (information and communications technology): in Africa, 72, 74–75, 82–85; enterprises, 27–28, 34, 39; in Europe, 94–95, 98–99; infrastructure, 6–7, 43–45, 82–83; labor, 10–11, 158–59, 169–74; in Latin America, 77–78; Maoist industrialization, 21–24; market-oriented industrial restructuring, 29–30; modernization, 26–27; opening-up policy, 29; in the United States, 109.

See also communications order; telecommunications development
import-substitution policy, 39, 52
IMT-2020 5G Promotion Group, 131
Indeed, 173
India, 4, 88, 122, 192; localization in, 171; TCC in, 10
Indonesia, 61, 173
industrialization, 12, 116, 129, 182–83, 193; and FDI, 17, 19; rural, 21; socialist, 20, 22–23, 27–28, 178, 185; urban, 24
Information Technology Agreement, 42
information technology research unit, 32
initial public offerings (IPOs), 62
Inner Mongolia, 43
integrated circuit (IC) technology, 23–34, 123, 130, 132, 133–34, 145
Intel, 77, 122
intellectual property practices, 107, 122, 184
intellectual property rights (IPR), 16, 31, 136–41; and fees, 127; infringements, 94, 104, 139
intelligence, artificial (AI), 80, 183–84
intelligence, political, 106, 108. *See also* surveillance
Intelsat, 5
inter-capitalist: collaboration, 96, 103–4, 139; competition, 17, 90, 102–4, 109–10, 112–13, 126, 132, 181; tensions, 15, 113, 185. *See also* capitalist logic of accumulation
intergovernment cooperative projects, 79
inter-imperialist rivalry, 4–5
international communications order. *See* communications order
International Monetary Fund, 70
International Telecommunication Union, 25, 88, 127
International Telephone and Telegraph, 4
International Wireless Standards Institute, 131
internet: bubble, 6, 47, 93, 94; companies, 7, 177–78; infrastructure, 7–8, 82–85; penetration rate, 83; policy, 182–83
Internet of Things, 49

Internet Protocol (IP), 95
interoperability, 37
inter-state relationships, 8–10, 67–69; conflicts and tensions, 15, 106, 109, 113, 136, 185. *See also* competition: inter-state
intracorporate communications, 6
intra-trading relationships, 57
Iran, 105

Japanese model, 12
JD.com, 7, 168, 180, 183
Jiang Zemin, 39, 58
Johannesburg Summit, 73
joint-stock companies, 3, 149
joint ventures (JVs), 29, 127, 129, 186; in Africa, 83; in Brazil, 77; in China, 34–35, 38, 42, 57; in Europe, 93, 100; in North America, 104; restructuring, 90–91; in Russia, 68
jump-start practices. *See under* digital revolution

Kenya, 70, 79, 80
Kirin series, 134
knowledge stocks, 62

labor: casual and temporary, 156, 166, 171, 173, 175; conditions, 149, 164–66, 169–71, 173, 189, 205n70; control, 18, 143–44, 152, 161–62, 163, 165–66, 168, 169, 171, 174; relations, 11, 16, 18, 143, 156, 166
LAN (local area network), 77
landlines, 83, 112
Laos, 68
Latin America, 61, 68, 70, 76–78; stereotypes about, 173. *See also specific countries*
LDPC (low-density parity check), 131
Leading Group for the Revitalization of the Electronics Industry, 27
Lee, Ching Kwan, 79, 86
Lenovo: asset-seeking motive, 62; collectively owned enterprises, 29; handset manufacturer, 50, 63; national champions, 58; R&D, 121–22
LG, 111
Li Ka-shing, 66

Li Peng, 27
Li Tieying, 56, 118, 180
Li Xiannian, 24
Liaoning, 45
Lin, Chun, 12, 179
loans: concessional, 75–76, 78, 80; vs. development fund, 74–75; for employee stock purchases, 147; from Ministry of Finance, 58, 100; offered to China, 33–34; from SOEs, 145; and tariffs, 33
Longgang District, 167
low-value-added goods, 185; in China, 47; in Europe, 96; in the United States, 110
Lucent, 34, 90
Luoyang Telephone Equipment Factory (LTEF), 124

M&A (mergers and acquisitions), 42, 62, 90–91, 134, 186
Made in China 2025 (MIC2025), 107, 182
mass campaign strategy, 21, 37–38
mass-line-style management, 24, 155
Mattelart, Armand, 5, 193–94
MEI, 28–29
Meng Wanzhou, 1, 91
mergers and acquisitions (M&A), 42, 62, 90–91, 134, 186
Mexico, 61
micro-level strategies, 55
Microsoft, 91, 136, 157
Middle East, 68, 69, 70, 85, 101; and communication networks, 4, 85; local staff in, 171
Millicom International Cellular, 71
Ministry of Commerce, 58
Ministry of Electronics Industry (MEI), 28–29
Ministry of Finance (MOF), 41, 59
Ministry of Foreign Trade and Economic Cooperation, 58
Ministry of Industry and Information Technology (MIIT), 63
Ministry of Information Industry (MII), 41
Ministry of Post and Telecommunications (MPT), 21, 123

mobile communications: in China, 20, 40, 41–42, 43–45, 50; in the global North, 109; standardization, 126–32
Mobile Telecommunications Company (MTC), 71
modernization, in China, 193; Four Modernizations strategy, 25–26; and imperialism, 4; MIC2025 plan, 182; military, 105; post-Mao, 26–27, 39; socialist, 20, 23–24; theories of, 116; and Western-style experience, 196
MoneyGram, 108
Motorola: 1G standard, 126; collaboration, 164; intellectual property infringement, 139; M&A, 62, 121
multilevel module networking, 37
multimode chipset, 134
multi-network interoperability, 37
multipolarity. *See* globalization
multisite operations. *See* operations
mythmaking, 150, 155, 196

Nanyou Corporation, 32
National Broadband Network, 108
national champions, Chinese: big business strategy, 180; going-out strategy, 54; state-owned enterprises, 198
National Conference on Technological Innovation, 119
National Congresses. *See under* Communist Party of China
National Electronics Industry Conference, 26
National Scientific Conference, 129, 139
National Telecommunications Corporations of Ecuador, 78
Naughton, Barry, 125
NEC (company), 34
neo-imperialism, 86, 116
neoliberalism, 6, 9, 68, 136, 138, 141, 189; and Chinese model, 11–12; and competition, 49; and development, 178, 197; and labor, 171; and liberalization, 27–29; and market policies, 179; and reform and restructuring, 39–42, 52. *See also* capitalist logic of accumulation; digital capitalism
network standards. *See specific standards*

networking systems, 5, 37, 95, 104, 111, 181; innovations in, 47; market for, 191; multilevel module, 37; optical, 92; software-defined, 49
New World Information and Communication Order, 5
Next Generation Networks, 77, 95
Nigeria, 72, 74, 75, 81
Ning, Lutao, 13
Ninth Five-Year Plan, 39–41, 127
Nokia: China's imported products, 43–44; M&A, 71
Nokia-Siemens Networks, 71
non-state-owned enterprises, 15; going-out activities of, 59; labor procurement, 157; liberalization, 28–29; state funding, 145;
non-state sector, 28, 157
Nortel Networks, 25, 34
NXP (company), 134–35

O2 Germany, 97
Office of the United States Trade Representative, 107
opening-up policy, 24–25, 29, 31, 55, 58, 118. *See also* attracting-in
operations: global and multisite, 17, 58, 95, 195; relocation of, 61. *See also specific companies*
OPPO, 51, 63
Orange (company), 71, 96
Orascom, 71
original-brand manufacturing (OBM), 116
original design manufacturer (ODM), 96
original equipment manufacturer (OEM), 50, 96, 103–4
outsourcing, 10, 30, 82, 171, 173, 175
outward foreign direct investment (OFDI): of China's ICT industry, 63; growth, 59–60; pattern, 60–62. *See also* going-out strategy
overtime work, 164–65, 168, 173

Pakistan, 62, 65, 85
Pakistan East Africa Cable Express (PEACE), 85
Patent Cooperation Treaty system, 140
patent law, 137. *See also* intellectual property rights

PCCW (company), 50
Pearl River Delta, 120
People's Liberation Army (PLA), 32, 35
polar codes, 131
political-economy: accumulation by dispossession, 136, 141; capitalist proprietary relationship, 137–38; class relations, 10–11; geopolitics, 82–85, 191–93; global reconstruction, 7, 85; imperialism, 9–10, 86; labor, 11, 156–74; neoliberal reform, 6–7, 40–42; ownership, 144–52; relationship between nation states and capital, 9–11. *See also* capitalist logic of accumulation; communications order; territorial logic
Portugal Telecom, 71
post and telecommunications bureaus (PTBs), 37–38, 43, 124
Post and Telecommunications Industry Corp (PTIC), 35
post and telecommunications sector, 32, 81
post-Mao: reforms, 26–30; technology policy, 118–20
PR (public relations), 39, 80, 164
Prague Summit, 190
pre-reform: industrialization, 22–23; management, 196
private equity, 74
private telephone branch exchange (PBX), 32
pro–foreign investment policy. *See* foreign direct investment (FDI)
pullback, 59, 105
Putian, 127–29

Qing China, 34
Qualcomm: acquisition, 108; anticompetition, 134–35; intellectual property, 110; semiconductor, 134; standard making, 45, 109, 126–27
Quidway, 93

R&D: firm-level activities, 122; in digital switching technology, 122–25; in semiconductor, 134–36; investment in Europe, 98–99; policy, 118–20; self-reliant mode of development, 121–22; standardization, 128–32
Radio Corporation of America, 4
Ranboss, 103
RCA, 4
realpolitik, 188
recession, economic, 67, 92–93, 97
red hat collectives, 144, 146
reforms, 18, 19–20, 40, 180; post-Mao, 26–30
Ren, Zhengfei: background of, 32, 144; management, 153–55, 157, 159–60, 165–66, 170, 174–75; market strategies in China, 36, 193; ownership, 148, 150–51; R&D strategies, 43, 131–33, 135, 141, 184; relationship with the government, 39; strategies of internationalization, 65–70, 96, 99, 111. *See also* transnational capitalist class (TCC)
research and development. *See* R&D
Robinson, William, 10, 81, 113, 195
Romania, 97
Rural Wireless Association (RWA), 111–12
Russia, 67–68, 92, 102, 122, 192
Russian Telecom, 68

S1240, 35
Samsung, 133–34
São Paulo, 77. *See also* Brazil
Sautman, Barry, 86
Schiller, Dan: commodity chain, 49–50, 95; digital depression, 2, 13–14; global political-economic order, 25; growth amid depression, 13; intellectual property, 138; two poles of growth, 1–2. *See also* digital capitalism; political economy
Section 301, Trade Act of 1974, 107–8
Segal, Adam, 13
semiconductors, 134–36
Seventh Five-Year period, 27
Shanghai Bell, 34–35, 42
Shanghai Electronics Components Factory, 24

Shanxi, 22
Shenzhen, 30–32, 119–21, 144, 166–68
Sichuan, 22, 43
Silk Road, fiber-optic. *See* Belt and Road Initiative
Singapore, 57, 108
Skycom Tech, 105
smartphone: Chinese market, 51; chipsets, 134; global markets, 15, 111; manufacturing, 134; vendors, 63
SMI, 134
Smythe, Dallas, 12
Snowden, Edward, 50, 107, 192, 210n104
socialism: and industrialization, 23–24; legacy of, 14; management, 153–54; mixed economy, 144, 146–47; modernization, 12, 20–21
soft loans, 34, 88
South Africa, 74, 192; companies based in, 71, 151
South America, 4, 85
South Korea, 57
Southeast Asia, 56, 61, 68, 69
southeastern China, 33
Southern Bloc, 192
South-South relations, 88, 188, 194. *See also* global South
Soviet Union, 21–22, 25, 155; collapse of, 67; and technology, 55. *See also* Russia
Spain, 97, 102
special economic zones (SEZs), 30–31
spin-off, technological, 117. *See also* trickle-down, of technology
Spreadtrum, 134
Sprint, 83, 106
standards, mobile network: 1G (analog) and 2G, 126–27; 3G, 128–30; 4G, 130; 5G, 130–32
standards-essential patents (SEP), 140
Starosielski, Nicole, 85
start-ups, 31, 144
State Council, 42, 58
State Development and Planning Council, 41
State Development and Reform Commission, 129

state-owned enterprises (SOEs): corporate restructuring, 157; reforms, 28–29, 145
stereotypes: about Chinese products, 65; racial and cultural, 173
sub-imperialism, 9–10
submarine cable, 83–85
subnational levels, 119–21
subnetworks, 97
Sudan, 74
Sun Microsystems, 103
Sun Yafang, 139–41
surveillance: in Iran, 105; in Kenya, 80; by United States, 106–7, 192
synchronous digital hierarchy (SDH), 37

TACS (Total Access Communication System), 126
Taiwan, 57, 67, 135
Taiwan Semiconductor Manufacturing Company (TSMC), 135
Tan, Zixiang, 42
Tanzania, 79
tariffs, 33, 107, 137
TCL (company), 29, 50, 63
TD-LTE (time division long-term evolution): in China's market, 48; standard-setting, 130
TD-SCDMA (time division synchronous code division multiple access): in China's market, 48; indigenous standard, 126–30
technocracy, 26, 30, 117; managerial, 16, 18
techno-globalism, 128–29
techno-nationalistic, 39, 115, 128, 179–80
telecommunication technologies: digital switching, 35–37, 122–24; mobile, 126–32; *See also* chipsets; ICT; semiconductors
Telecommunications Act (1996), 6
telecommunications carriers: in Africa, 70–71; in China and Europe, 94–97; in Latin America, 77; in the United States, 106
telecommunications development. *See* fixed-line telecommunications; mobile communications

telecommunications equipment: digital switch, 37 (*see also* digital switching equipment); GSM equipment, 43–45; handset, 50; of rural markets, 38
telecommunications infrastructure: 5G base stations, 131; CDMA networks, 45–46; in China's rural market, 41; GSM networks, 43–45; submarine cable, 83–85
telecommunications manufacturers, 39, 44, 50
Telefonica, 77
Telfort, 94
Telkom, 71
Tencent Holdings: BAT, 62, 177, 183; ownership, 149–51; ranking, 7
Tenth Five-Year Plan, 58, 129
territorialist logic, 3, 9–10
Thailand, 61, 62
Third Front Plan, 22–23
third world, 55–56, 87–88
Thirteenth Five-Year Plan, 49
Tiangang, 134
Tianjin, 45
Tianya, 168
tier-one operators, 37, 41, 95–97, 111
Time-Based Unit Plan (TUP), 172
Toffler, Alvin, 26–27
Torch Plan, 119
township and village enterprise (TVE), 29
Trade Act of 1974, 107
trade-related intellectual property rights (TRIPS), 128–29
trading, 3; export-oriented, 56; intra-, 57; "market for technology," 33, 39, 178, 193 (*see also* Chinese model); partners, 137
transnational capitalist class (TCC), 10–11, 169; blocs and fractions, 70, 81, 100, 113, 142; identity, 195; nationalist, 70, 80, 188; network, 68, 151
transnational corporation (TNC): Chinese capital, 79–81; multinational-led communication order, 4–7; outward investment, 61–64; relationship with the state, 8–9; western companies, 90–91. *See also* capitalist logic of accumulation
trickle-down, of technology, 117, 124, 183
Tunisia, 74
Turbo2.0, 131

UN Security Council, 24
Upadhya, Carol, 10
US Commerce Department, 108
US Defense Department, 105
US House Intelligence Committee, 106
US National Security Agency (NSA), 107

Venezuela, 77, 78
Verizon, 83, 106
Vietnam, 61
Vivo, 51, 63
Vodacom, 71, 83
Vodafone, 70–71, 96–97

Wang, Hongzhe, 12
Wang Hui, 192
Washington Consensus, 188, 227n28
WCDMA (wideband code division multiple access), 94, 127–28, 140
Wen Minsheng, 26
West Africa, 83
Western China, 22, 192–93
Western Europe. *See under* Europe
Western Union, 4
wholly foreign-owned enterprises (WFOEs), 57
"win-win" development model, 85–86, 189
World Bank, 33–34, 70–71, 227n28
World Intellectual Property Organization (WIPO), 140
World Trade Organization (WTO), 6, 42, 137
Wu Bangguo, 73
Wu Yi, 68

Xi Jinping, 100, 112, 194
Xiaomi, 51, 63, 150
Xinsheng Community, 154

Xinwei Telecommunications, 127

Yan Hairong, 86
Yemen, 68
Yiwu, 37
Yuanhua Smuggling Case, 44

Zhang, Guobao, 129
Zhao, Yuezhi, 12, 35–36, 192
Zhejiang Geely, 99
Zhejiang Province, 37

Zhengzhou Institute of Information Engineering, 123
Zhenhua Electronics Corporation, 28
Zhou Enlai, 24
Zou Jiahua, 65
ZTE Corporation: in China, 39, 45, 48; internationalization, 63, 65, 74–75, 78; ownership, 29; R&D, 129–30, 140; in the United States, 100, 108–9, 111, 119–20; varieties of Chinese capital, 79–82

YUN WEN is a senior economist at an economic policy research firm in Vancouver, Canada.

THE GEOPOLITICS OF INFORMATION

Digital Depression: Information Technology and Economic Crisis   *Dan Schiller*
Signal Traffic: Critical Studies of Media Infrastructures   *Edited by Lisa Parks and Nicole Starosielski*
Media in New Turkey: The Origins of an Authoritarian Neoliberal State   *Bilge Yesil*
Goodbye iSlave: A Manifesto for Digital Abolition   *Jack Linchuan Qiu*
Networking China: The Digital Transformation of the Chinese Economy   *Yu Hong*
The Media Commons: Globalization and Environmental Discourses   *Patrick D. Murphy*
Media, Geopolitics, and Power: A View from the Global South   *Herman Wasserman*
The Huawei Model: The Rise of China's Technology Giant   *Yun Wen*

The University of Illinois Press
is a founding member of the
Association of University Presses.

University of Illinois Press
1325 South Oak Street
Champaign, IL 61820-6903
www.press.uillinois.edu